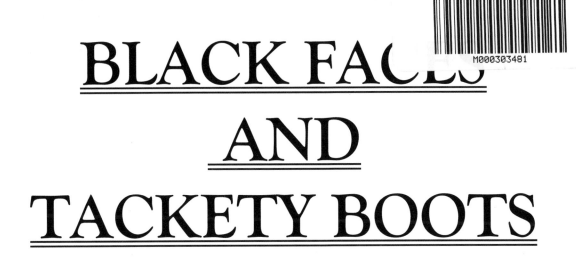

# BLACK FACES AND AND TACKETY BOOTS

## By

## WILMA S. BOLTON

Printed by the J.R. Reid Print & Media Group Blantyre
Published by Wilma S. Bolton
This second edition with minor revisions © 2007 by Wilma S. Bolton

www.wilmabolton.com

ISBN 0-9552998-0-2

# THE END OF A LONG HARD SHIFT

*Photograph courtesy of Hamilton Town House Reference Library.*

A scene common in any coal mining town was the sight of miners returning home at the end of their shift, covered from head to toe, in the black powdery coal dust which would eventually put them into an early grave.

The above photograph has frozen in time, the sight of four such miners walking up Quarry Street, Hamilton, approximately 100 years ago.

Just visible below the knees of their trousers, are tied the pieces of string generally referred to as "nicky tams" which were used by the miners to stop the bottom of their trousers getting covered in mud and the rats from running up their legs.

# EXHAUSTED

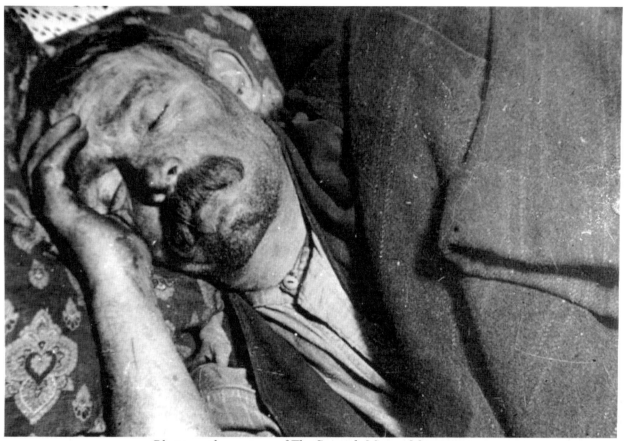

*Photograph courtesy of The Scottish Mining Museum.*

And when I'm exhausted and feelin' sae din,
'Tis then that I wish I'd ma day's tae begin,
I'd learn up ma lessons, each nicht I wid sit,
For I vow I wid never look near haun' a pit.

\*    \*    \*

*"Some Thochts Frae the Mine"*
*By J.D. (Douglas Water) circa 1933,*
*Page 40*

# BLACK FACES
## AND
# TACKETY BOOTS

## BY WILMA S. BOLTON

### PREFACE

*40 Selkirk Street Hamilton -- May 1937*

Having been brought up in a community where many of the men worked in the coal mines, my earliest childhood memories reflect this environment. I can still vividly recall the sound of tackety boots echoing in the still, early morning air as the miners left for the pit and the colour of my father when he came home from his work as a brusher in Bothwell Castle Colliery. He was, quite simply, coal black and more often than not, soaked to the skin, from working in appalling conditions.

Long before he walked through the door of our single end home at 40 Selkirk Street, my mother would have the water heating in pots for his bath.

*The street echoed with the sound of tackety boots.*

On his return from work, the big portable zinc bath would be placed in front of the fire, the water added and then, in a ritual which was being repeated in thousands of miners' homes throughout the county, my father would begin to wash away the coal dust which covered him from top to toe. I have vivid recollections of helping to wash his back and I would look on in childish wonder, at what appeared to me to be snakes moving down his back from his hair line to his waist. It was of course, the water running through the black coal dust.

My mother would then scrape and brush the dirt off the soaking wet moleskin trousers, hang them over the winterdykes and place them in front of the fire to dry.

My father's boots would be put beside the hearth and later, after they had dried out, the boots would be scraped, brushed clean, Dubbin applied to make them waterproof and then left out, ready for the next morning. *Wilma S. Bolton.*

THIS BOOK IS DEDICATED
TO THE MEMORY OF MY LATE FATHER
JIMMY RUSSELL
A COAL MINER
AT
EARNOCK, AUCHINRAITH
AND BOTHWELL CASTLE COLLIERIES

1908-1960
ALSO
TO THE MEMORY OF EVERY MAN, WOMAN AND
CHILD WHO WORKED IN THE COAL MINES OF
LANARKSHIRE

# INTRODUCTION

The countless millions of pounds of profit made from the coal fields of Lanarkshire, found its way into the bank accounts of a small select group of already wealthy and influential people. The coal miner received but a pittance for a wage and this was reduced even further, as the coalmasters, with a greed which is hard to comprehend, bled them dry, in the form of off takes, the truck system and fines.

When coal was difficult to sell, miners' wages were cut, never to be increased when the market improved. With this happening almost every year, the miners' wages were gradually reduced to starvation levels, while the coal masters and their families lived a life of luxury.

The suffering inflicted on the mining community by the men of wealth and power was incalculable. In the obscene race for money and power, humanity and compassion for their fellow men were pushed aside and the miners and their families were treated with contempt, by the very men who became extremely rich from their labours.

Health and safety at work was unheard of and thousands of Lanarkshire men died in pit accidents. In Hamilton parish alone I have managed to document the names of approximately 1200 men, boys and girls who were killed while employed both at the surface and underground. Countless thousands of others were permanently maimed by accidents and a great many more, including my own father, died prematurely, their health and lives destroyed by the appalling working conditions.

This book contains an eye witness account by Hugh Brown, survivor and explorer of the 1877 Blantyre disaster; an account of the 1878 overwinding accident and 1879 Blantyre disaster; the tragic story of the Dykehead/Summerlee disaster; the Greenfield Colliery boiler explosion with it's child victims; the Udston Colliery disaster and the names of 200 miners who were in the rescue teams; the eviction of 750 men women and children from Eddlewood Rows, Hamilton and many more true stories from the mines and miners' rows of Lanarkshire.

Also included, are the names of approximately 2000 Lanarkshire miners. Many of these names are instantly recognisable; men with the same names still live in the local towns and villages. These men are the descendents of the old time coal miners and their names have been passed on down through their families, from generation to generation.

Included in the book is a selection of "pit poems" which were written by local coal miners and published in local newspapers. The talent displayed by these men, is to say the least, impressive. The eloquence of their words is indicative of their high intelligence, as they graphically describe the lives of the Lanarkshire miners through their poetry.

Today, people still say with pride that they belonged to *Allanton, Cadzow, Eddlewood, Earnock, Dixon's, Ferniegair, Murray's, Merryton and Summerlee Rows etc*. The feeling of belonging is still as strong as ever, although almost all trace of the colliery rows have gone.

In essence, the book tells the story of the lives of these wonderful, hard working people and of how they lived, loved and died, in an era when there was very little they could do to control their destiny.

This collection of true stories and pit poetry enables us to look back through the mists of time into the past and feel a warm glow of pride for our mining ancestors, who lived and worked, in an extremely hostile environment.   *Wilma S. Bolton*

# CONTENTS

# FOREWORD

In a lifetime spent involved with coal mining, from being born and brought up in a mining village to my present interest in the Scottish Mining Museum, I can honestly say that Wilma Bolton comes into a fairly select group of most remarkable people I have encountered.

Our contact has been largely by letter and telephone, but I never cease to be amazed at her enthusiasm and dedication to her research of a subject which, without I hope being considered chauvinistic, is not one normally associated with our ladies.

In this book, I think Wilma has captured beautifully the essence of mining life in Lanarkshire in the period when it was the power house of Scotland's Industrial Revolution. She quite rightly pulls no punches with her views on the ruthlessness and greed of certain landowners and coalmasters of the times. She balances this, however, by giving credit where it is due to those among them whose contribution and conduct was more reasonable.

She has considerably enhanced her book by the introduction of many fascinating poems.

I have said it often at the Museum - and I repeat it again here - I wish we had a Wilma Bolton in every Scottish mining district.

George Archibald
Volunteer- Scottish Mining Museum
Ex-Chief Surveyor and Minerals Manager for the National Coal Board,
Scotland.

\*　　　\*　　　\*　　　\*

With the passage of time, it becomes increasingly more difficult for the Scottish Mining Museum to obtain material relating to the coal mines of Lanarkshire, yet, hidden away in attics, drawers and boxes, there must remain many important documents, photographs, etc which would help to record the lives of our local coal miners.

These items can be found in the most unexpected of places, as the discovery in the summer of 2004, at Arden Road, Hamilton, of a substantial number of payslips from a Blantyre colliery demonstrates. The payslips were found hidden beneath the linoleum on a bedroom floor during renovation and had been put there by John McGuire, father of the owner of the house, in a successful attempt to prevent his wife from discovering how much he earned.

It was sixty years before they were discovered and were a very welcome addition to the library of the Scottish Mining Museum.

The Museum would welcome any photographs or documents etc, relating to mining. All photographs and documents can be copied and the originals returned to owners if requested. *Wilma S. Bolton.*

# ACKNOWLEDGEMENTS

The publication of this collection of mining stories and poems would not have been possible had it not been for the assistance and good will of a number of people and to them, I offer my sincere thanks.

Pearl Murphy, David Young and Angela Logan of Hamilton Reference Library, whose advice and help made it possible for me to write this book. A special thanks to Pearl Murphy for proof reading some of my articles, for suggesting and providing, sources of information and for her encouragement when I needed it.

A special thanks also to George Archibald volunteer at the library of the Scottish Mining Museum, Newtongrange, for all his invaluable help, advice and assistance over a number of years, for proof reading the finished document for which I shall always be grateful and for selecting and providing suitable photographs, also Campbell Drysdale at the library of the Scottish Mining Museum for all his help.

Jim Wallace, Burnbank and George Hay, Blantyre, two men who have a great love of local history and who generously shared their private research and extensive knowledge with me. Grateful thanks also for the illustrations drawn by Jim and the photographs provided by both George and Jim.

Don Boyle Hamilton, for his excellent reminisces of Earnock Rows, his poetry and his drawings, which bring to life again, this unique little pit village. To Thomas Edgar, formerly of Hill Street, Udston, Burnbank and now in Australia; for his memories of his *own piece of real estate* Earnock bing, in a poem never to be forgotten and dedicated to Nancy Wright, nee Newlands and who with her husband Jim, were lifelong friends of Tom; sadly Nancy died last year. Many thanks also to Jim Prentice, for allowing me to include his father's wonderful poem "Childhood," which takes us back to the Earnock Rows of many years ago.

Helen Moir and Ann Rankin of Larkhall Heritage Group for providing photographs of local collieries and valuable advice.

The people of Lanarkshire who have kindly allowed me to use their precious family photographs and for sharing with me equally precious family memories.

The identified and unidentified poets of the evocative pit poetry included in my book. This wonderful poetry, most of which appears to be written by local miners, documents a vanished way of life. It is a legacy which should be proudly cherished by the people of Lanarkshire.

Special thanks also to my grandsons, Dylan Farnan (10) and Andrew Seeds (9) for giving me instruction in computer skills, which, up until their intervention, were almost non-existent. Special thanks also to my daughter Lesley Farnan, for her patience as she escorted me round old colliery sites and for her photographic skills which supplied records of places now gone.

A special thanks also to The Mining Institute of Scotland Trust for their assistance.

Several anonymously published pictures, poems and articles appear in this book and I would be pleased to include acknowledgements in these cases for future editions.

# THE PRICE OF COAL

Deep down in the bowels of this beautiful
      earth,
On his dark throne sits King Coal
He calls for his revenue every day,
Caring neither for body nor soul.
When to the grim monarch the miner
      descends,
He remembers the saying divine;
Not one of us knows what a day may bring
      forth,
So true of the lads in the mine.

Deep down in the bowels of this beautiful
      earth,
Death lurks unseen, unheard;
Till with a roar, or a blinding flash,
On the lives of men he has fared
'Tis then that spirit the men display,
When faith and valour combine,
In deeds that are known but to God and
      themselves---
So true of the lads in the mine.

Deep down in the bowels of this beautiful
      earth
We sat, my mate and I,
To plan our work; yet little we thought
 In a moment one would die.
O God, 'twas a cry I shall never forget
As my mate paid his price at the shrine;
A price that is sought by the monarch of
      coal
From the lads who toil in the mine.

Deep down in the bowels of this beautiful
      earth,
 Down in that dark domain;
Men grovel and toil for the treasure it holds
 Their bodies oft aching with pain.
As you sit by your fireside in comfort and
      warmth
 And watch the firelight twine;
Give a thought to the price that's paid for
      in lives
Of our lads who work in the mine.

*MATTHEW BROWN, circa 1936*

# THE COLLIER SLAVE

Up until the seventeenth century, wood and peat were the chief fuels used for domestic purposes and there was little need for coal. However, there were some small coal mines scattered around the country supplying the small domestic and industrial markets. Because of the very nature of the work, colliers and their families lived isolated from society and they were, to all intents and purposes, *"a breed apart."* With the coming of the industrial revolution, great quantities of coal were needed to fire the steam engines which turned the wheels of industry and as the demand for coal increased dramatically, the demand for colliers also increased.

In 1606 the Scottish Parliament passed an act which effectively made Scottish colliers serfs or slaves. Part of the Act stipulated *"That no person within this realm (Scotland) shall hire or induce any colliers or coal bearers without sufficient testimonial of their masters whom they last served, and the said colliers and coal bearers are to be held as thieves and punished in their bodies for stealing themselves from their masters."* During this period when a coal mine was being sold, the miners and their families were included in the price and sold with the colliery.

Men who broke the law could also be sentenced to work in the coal mines and in effect he was sentenced to a life of working underground. Not only was the man sentenced to work in the coal mine for the rest of his life, his children were born into slavery. At the baptism of a collier's child, the coalmaster would be present and the minister would be witness at the *"arling"* ceremony, when coins were given by the coalmaster to the father, in respect of the child's future labour. This effectively bound the child, for the rest of his life, to be a *"slave"* to the coalmaster. It wasn't until 1799 that an Act of Parliament freed colliers from slavery.

In 1842, a collier from Musselburgh gave evidence before the Scottish Mining Commission, that he had wrought as a slave and he, his father and his grandfather had been born slaves.

In 1878, an old Larkhall collier called *Jamie McGhie* speaking about the young taking up work as colliers, remarked that *"there's a great future afore the minin' trade o' Britain. Up tae noo it has maistly been followed by unfortunates an' their families wha, like my great-grandfather, had the audacity tae defy the lairds o' the laun'. Or commit some ither equally unpardonable sin, an; sae forfeit, no only their ain freedom, but their children's children for a' future generations."* By making this statement, *Jamie McGhie* had given the history of how his forefathers became miners and slaves, condemned to a life working at the coal face.

Even when the collier received the right to leave his place of employment, there were still laws controlling him. Up until 1876 men could be and were imprisoned, for leaving their work without the consent of their employer. The act which allowed this was called the Master and Servant Act, where workers were not treated as equal before the law. They were subject to this act which reflected the Common Law conception, of the master's absolute authority over the servant. It was a criminal offence to disobey the master, leave work without permission or fail to attend work, or commit any other misconduct or misdemeanour.

On 13th "April 1866, two men *Walter* or *George Scott* and *Charles McDonald*, appeared at Hamilton Justice of the Peace court charged with "*deserting their service*" (terminating their employment without notice) as miners at the Braidwood Colliery owned by Mr *Dixon* of Calder. The prisoners pleaded not guilty, but *John Meek* Esq. who was on the bench that day, thought otherwise and sentenced both men to be imprisoned in Hamilton prison, for a period of fourteen days with hard labour. After the verdict, the agent for Braidwood Colliery stated that "*the case had been brought to show the workmen at the colliery, that they were not entitled to set aside the published rules for their pleasure and that if the prisoners and their two neighbour workmen would agree to return to service, they would be at once liberated from prison.*"

A second example of the absolute power the coalmasters wielded over their workmen took place at Hamilton Justice of the Peace court, on 11th January, 1875, when *John Menzies,* a collier from Swinhill, Dalserf appeared on a charge of having left the employment of Miller & Rodger, coalmasters, without just or lawful excuse. The court was told that when he went to lift his "*graith,*" he was told by the manager to go on with his work and to fulfil his fortnights warning. John Menzies refused to do this and his fate was sealed before he stepped into the dock. The justices on the bench that day were *Captains, Stevenson, Hamilton and McNeil-Hamilton* and *Alexander Grant* and *Thomas Paterson.* He was fined £2 with £5 3s of expenses a total of £7. 3s, more than he got for two months work. He was given the alternative of one months' imprisonment.

Despite the fact that a collier could go to jail for leaving his employment, the coalmaster could discharge him without notice and evict him and his family on to the street, without fault or explanation.

In court, the collier stood little chance. The law of the land was weighted heavily in favour of the masters, who were the industrialists and land owning gentry, with large estates, coalmines and other industries. Many of these men were Members of Parliament and because of this, it was inevitable that they were going to pass laws which would be of benefit to them and increase their wealth.

The working man's rights were few and far between, due primarily, to his lack of representation in Parliament and the road leading to justice and working class Members of Parliament, proved to be a long and weary road.

# THE EARLY SCOTTISH MINERS
## (1833)
# TRANSCRIBED FROM AN ARTICLE PUBLISHED IN THE HAMILTON HERALD, 1892

In connection with the miners' eight hours movement perhaps a few notes on the development of Scottish mining and mining customs during nearly the last 60 years by one who has been an onlooker may not be amiss.

In 1833 I was at a small land sale colliery; there were two pits drawing coals and one pit sinking. One of the former was 10 fathoms deep. It worked a coal four feet thick, which was principally for burning lime. Ten colliers worked in the pit and each was assisted by his wife and one or more of his children.

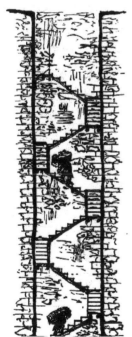

The coal was flat, rising about 1 in 12 and dry and it was worked by stoop and room—rooms 9 feet wide, stoops 9 feet square, the collier rigidly taking care to get his "cut coal." In the pit was a circular wooden stair; the steps were five inches deep. The women and boys and girls carried the coals in "creels" from the face of the working up the stair to the surface and laid them down on the collier's own particular bing. There were thus 10 bings of coal on the pithead, one belonging to each collier. One of the colliers had "the sale" at a time until his bing was cleared off. It took sometimes three or four months before his bing was cleared away; but in the meantime, until this was done, a man and his bearer were paid about 20s to account weekly and when the balance was ascertained he got it.

*Carrying coal weighing 1- 1 ½ cwts up the circular stairs to the pithead.*

I recollect very well there was no stated oversman or roadsman in the pit, but if there was any deficiency, the overman would go down and see it. The collier kept his own road and contributed any repairs to the main road, but it required very little.

There was no clerk at the pit; the collier who had the "sale" gave a note of the sales to the manager at night. There was no weighing machine. The buyer filled his cart a certain size, but the collier saw that he did not put on more than he ought to do. He had a direct interest in seeing that the buyer did not take too much on the cart.

The collier went down to his work about four o'clock in the morning, his "bearer" came about seven bringing his "parritch" and they worked away till four o'clock in the afternoon. The collier would make about 2s 9d or 3s a day, his "bearer" 1s 2d and the children in proportion. They had free house and coals, the woman carrying home a lump of coal on her back. This system had worked for more than fifty years and there was never a hitch.

In some neighbouring collieries there were "stores," where the men were expected to take their provisions. Indeed, before the passing of the Truck Act the men were paid with copper counters, which, if they spent at other than the store, the owner took a penny or twopence on the shilling in exchanging; but at this time, in the particular pit in question, there was no store and every man was paid in cash and did what he liked with it.

In the other pit, which was about 14 fathoms deep, there was a gin, and about 12 men worked in it. The seam of coal was from 28 to 30 inches thick. It was worked by stoop and room—rooms 5 yards, stoops 5 yards square; and, as before, the collier was particularly careful to get the advantage of a "cut coal."

The roof was good, but it had to be cut down to make a road 3 ½ feet high. The working was not so dry as the other, but the water got away to another colliery which was at a lower level. There was good natural ventilation. The coals were drawn from the face in round tubs holding 2 ½ to 3 cwt. These tubs were fastened on to trams, which ran on iron rails, 10lb to the yard. When the tubs reached the pit bottom they were drawn up the pit by the gin and emptied on the pithead to be filled into carts. Only the round coals were drawn; the dross was all left in the pit. There was one horse in the gin, the driver, a boy and one banksman.

*A horse gin used for raising coal*

The tubs were drawn by women. Each collier had his wife or daughter or someone else for a drawer and he was paid so much per tub of coal landed at the pit bottom. Each drawer hung on his or her own tub; there was no bottomer.

The collier came to his work at four o'clock in the morning and slid the rope to the pit-bottom carrying his picks stuck down the back of his coat neck. The women came about seven and if the gin horse was not there, they too slid the rope, but generally they brought the colliers breakfast. The gin drew coals for about eight or nine hours and drawing up the workers finished the day's work.

The only "oncost" was the man who blasted down the roof for the roads; he was paid so much per fathom and one woman, who kept the road; she had 1s 2d a day. The oversman was engaged at the sinking pit, but at the week end, or before pay-day he went through the pit, measured the stone-work and bargained for any deficient work. The colliers were paid 3d a "lade" in the summer time and 4d a "lade" in winter, when the price of coal was 7s 6d and 8s 4d a ton respectively. This had been the rate for 50 years, but there was a sliding scale in this way. In order to make the coals turn out, the collier allowed the masters two to the score. This was called "tinsel," and was a recognised reduction. Sometimes in the summer season, when the sale was bad and not equal to two or three days work in the week, the men used to complain and the master would agree to bing to give them constant work, on the condition of the men giving him an extra tub of "tinsel" temporarily was as high as four to the score, or even six to the score, but the price of per tub was always the same.

In like manner, the selling price was generally the same, 7s 6d per ton in summer and 8s 4d in winter. Good customers got a reduction, but it was generally in the form of getting better weight. There was no weighing machine, the buyer got as much as the banksman would give him. He generally wanted seven load (14 cwt.) but would not get less than 18 cwt.

A curious custom was the giving of "maggs" or a discount, to carters who came for coals. The "maggs" were 3d a cart and farm-servants coming for coals, although their masters got coals on credit, got maggs, which we fear, was spent on whisky, which, by the way, was then only 6d a half mutchkin, or a penny per glass, sometimes called a "penny-wheep."

In this pit, the colliers went down about four o'clock to get the coals ready for the drawers, who came about seven and they worked on till four. The men were a contented and respectable lot of people, seldom shifted; only young men for whom a place could not be found had to go a-field. They lived in the "maister's hooses" in the village and enjoyed themselves. Most men had a nickname---"Hatty," "The Hare," "The Jake" and so on, by which he was better known than his own. These men might make 2s 9d to 3s a day—perhaps 14 to 15 shillings a week, one week with another; women 1s 2d a day. An oversman had 16s a week; banksmen. 11s. It must be kept in mind that at that time, the ordinary wages for masons were 14s a week in winter and 18s in summer; joiners, 14s; blacksmiths 14s; and ordinary labourers, 9s and 10s a week.

While this was the state of matters at the colliery referred to, on other collieries there were powerful engines at work pumping water and for raising coal, but the output from each pit would be from 80 to 100 tons a day, but the wages were about as stated.

In 1836, things were improving. Horses were introduced into advanced pits to shorten the distances hauled by men and women and the homely fashion of sending down the men's breakfast was abandoned.

In 1842 Lord Ashley's Act prohibiting the employment of women underground was passed. No doubt it was hardship to some poor people at first, but it has done good upon the whole

*An early water wheel*

In 1841 cages had not been introduced into the Lanarkshire pits. The coals were drawn from the coal face in hurlies or hutches made of wood or basket-work. These "hurlies" held about 6 cwt. When they reached the bottom they were emptied into a round corf, or basket, which held just one hutchful and raised to the surface, where they were landed on a tram and run out to the carts or to the waggon screens. About 1842 cages came into general use in Lanarkshire and the West of Scotland and four or five years after that time there was not a pit without them. Wages were about 3s 6d a day. In 1845 and 1846 they were 5s a day, but such was the influx of Irish workmen that while the collier had 5s a day, roadsmen and underground labourers had not more than 14s or 15s a week and labourers on the surface 11s and 12s a week. (R.) Ref. Hamilton Herald. 1892.

*Waterwheel with chain and buckets used for taking water up the shaft*

# THE COLLIER'S RAGGED WEAN

He's up at early morning, howe'er the win' may blaw,
Lang before the sun comes roun' to chase the stars awa';
And 'mang a thoosan' dangers, unkent in sweet daylight,
He'll toil until the stars again, keek through the chilly night.
See the puir wee callan' 'neath the cauld clear moon!
His knees oot through his troosers and his taes oot through
  his shoon,
Wading through the freezing snaw and thinking ower again,
How happy every wean maun be that's no a colliers' wean.


His cheeks are blae wi' cauld and the chittering winna cease
To gie the hungry callan' time to eat his morning piece;
His lamp is burning on his heid, wi' a feeble, flickering ray,
And in his heart the lamp of Hope is burning feeble tae.
Nae wonner that the callan's sweert to face his daily toil,
Nae wonner he sae seldom greets the morning wi' a smile,
For he kens he's growing up to face the cauld disdain
That lang the world has measured oot to every collier's wean.


The puir wee hirpling laddie! how mournfully he's gaun,
Aye dichting aff the ither tear wi''s wee hard, hackit haun'!
Sair, sair, he's temptit' mang the snaw to toom his flask o' oil,
But, ah! ae flash o' faither's ire were waur than weeks o' toil.
In vain the stars look on the youth wi' merry twinkling een,
Through clouds o' care sae dense as his, their glory is nae seen;
He thinks 'twad been a better plan if coal had 'boonmost lain,
And wonders why his faither made a collier o' his wean.


Oh" ye that row in Fortune's lap, his waefu' story hear,
Aft sorrows no sae deep as his, ha'e won a pitying tear,
And lichter wrangs than he endures, your sympathy ha'e won---
Although he is a collier's mind he's still a Briton's son.
And ye wha mak' and mend oor laws, tak' pity on the bairn;
Oh! bring him sooner frae the pit, and gie him time to learn;
Sae shall ye lift him frae the mire 'mang which he lang has lain,
And win a blessing frae the heart' o' every collier's wean.


*David Wingate.*
*Circa 1860*

# THE EMPLOYMENT OF
# WOMEN AND CHILDREN
# IN
# LOCAL PITS

*Illustration Courtesy of Jim Wallace*

Prior to the 1842 Coal Mines Act, it was common for women and children to work both underground and at the pithead. What is less well known is that in Lanarkshire, women also worked as coal hewers. Larkhall miner, poet and writer, *Thomas Stewart*, writing in 1878 about the lives Larkhall miners, records women working at the coal face in the small local coal pits.

He spoke of the amusement of the younger fraternity including himself, as they listened to an elderly miner recalling the employment of these "*underground amazons.*" Describing one female collier, the old man said, "*She was the bonniest picksman ever I saw.*" *Stewart* also describes the flooding of "*Harleyhowe*" (*Hareleeshill)* Coal Pit when a "*half-witted*" woman called *Jenny Dang* is among the entombed miners. Jenny worked underground with her half brother *Jock Blyth*. The men and *Jenny* were eventually able make their escape after the flood water was removed.

Children were known to have been employed in the early coal mines of Lanarkshire. The 1841 census records the *Hume* family living at Laigh Quarter near Hamilton. *James,* a coal miner and his wife *Ann Hume* had three children and the occupation of their eldest child also called *James,* aged 9, is listed as a coal miner

In July 1838, Queen Victoria ordered a public inquiry after 26 children were drowned in Huskar Colliery, Silkstone, West Yorkshire, when the mine flooded during a violent storm. Eleven of the victims were girls aged 8 to 17; the other fifteen victims were boys aged 7 to 16 years. Of the twenty-six victims 19 were twelve or under.

Prompted by these deaths, *Lord Ashley* persuaded parliament to set up a royal commission to look into the employment of children in mines. The publication of statements given to the commission by the women and children interviewed horrified the nation.

In June 1842 *Lord Ashley introduced* a Bill in Parliament designed to prevent the employment of female labour underground and to exclude children under thirteen years from work in the pits. Three weeks later, influential coal-owners mounted powerful opposition against it and fought its introduction at every stage. The Bill became law on August 10th 1842, but it was much changed from the original Bill, due to the powerful and influential opposition from the men who were making vast amounts of money from the labours of women and children. The new Act prohibited female labour, but the proposal to outlaw the employment underground of boys under the age of thirteen, had been altered to boys less than ten years of age; wages were not to be paid at or near a public house; also mine inspectors who would visit and inspect mines and collieries were to be appointed by the Home Secretary.

The human cost to women and children working down the pit is incalculable. The very nature of the work and the heavy loads carried, caused the women to frequently miscarry or give birth to premature or stillborn babies and maternal death was common. When women were banned from working underground, some of them obtained employment at the pithead, usually at the "picking tables" sorting the waste from the coal.

In 1903, at a meeting of the Scottish Miners' Federation, it was proposed that the employment of female labour be abolished. The question asked was asked *"why did the pit-owners employ female labour?* Not because they did better work; it was because the labour was cheaper. Girls got the "handsome" wage of 1s 3d per day." In 1903 there was a large increase in the employment of women at pit-heads due to the fact that many collieries had been turned into limited liability companies and had shareholders to please. Women were cheaper to employ, therefore profits were increased. It was said that *"limited companies had no conscience"* and the increase in the employment of women appears to reinforce this statement.

Children were killed working in the mines and in 1898 *Thomas Stewart* graphically described a scene he witnessed in a coal mine in his home village of Larkhall. He wrote of an old woman who would frequently turn up at the pit-head. She would *"gaze wistfully at the pit mouth as if she anxiously expected some one from among the miners who were occasionally coming up on the cage." Standing back at first she would draw nearer and nearer as each group of men were brought up. The men obviously felt uncomfortable at her appearance and were anxious to avoid her. The foreman would warn them "watch an' no' let her doon the pit na,'" and eventually he would reluctantly order her to go home. "Is he no up yet?" she would say, gazing yearningly at the black hole. In her mind she thought the search for her missing boy was still going on and her visits to the pit and her mournful interrogation of the miners, as she asked again and again " is he no up yet," never failed to touch the hearts of all who witnessed her vigil.*
*It had been forty years since she had lost her "first-born boy" and as she spoke to the foreman, if was as if it had happened the previous day. The boy had left his father's side in the mine for a few moments and was never seen again despite everything being done that could be done to find him."*

There is no doubt that this incident happened just as *Thomas Stewart* described it. His stories were read by the miners of Larkhall who would soon have made it known had he strayed from the truth. The youngest underground coal mining deaths documented in Hamilton parish are of the following two ten year old boys who were killed while working in the coal mines of Quarter.

# THE WEE BOY BROUNLIE
## AGE 10
## AVONBANKS MINE

The first of the two ten year olds to die was (--------) *Brounlie* who was killed in an explosion on 16th March 1841, while he was employed in the Duke of Hamilton's Avonbanks Mine. The coal from this mine was obtained from an opening cut into the rich seams of coal which outcropped or reached the surface on the steep banks of the Avon Gorge at Hamilton. These mines were known as drift mines, or ingaun e'e's and Avonbanks had two entrances, one at the Avon Gorge and the other much nearer the small village of Quarter. The *Brounlie* boy was one of eleven victims who lost their lives that morning. We know very little about him because only the briefest of details were recorded. He was the only child underground on the day of the explosion and he was working with his father *William Brounlie* and five other men who also died in the blast. His Christian name was not recorded.

The day prior to the disaster, a miner had been burnt in a fire-damp explosion. Despite this, the colliers appeared to have found no cause for alarm, turning up for work as usual the following morning. The explosion happened at eight a.m. and was thought to have been caused by the sudden release of gas from a fissure connected by a rise in the headings. The mine had been thoroughly examined by two oversmen and reported to be free of danger before the men started work.

After the sound of the explosion was heard, seven men working at the mouth of the mine entered the workings to see if they could help those underground, but almost immediately, they were overcome by afterdamp. The one man left on the surface became concerned for their safety when they did not reappear and he went in to help. Inside the mine he found the men lying on the floor of workings and managed to drag them all out. Four of the men were dead and the three who were alive survived. Of the three who recovered only two names have survived the passage of time, *Ord Adams* manager of the mine and *Michael Forrest* coal miner. It was not until the following day that the mine was declared safe enough to enter and the badly mutilated bodies of the seven victims of the blast were recovered.

The explosion at Avonbanks mine was the first major mining disaster in the Hamilton area and the town was reported to be in a state of shock at the news. Seven of the victims were married and between them they left 60 dependants. The Duke of Hamilton paid all the expenses of their funerals and Duffie's wife was recorded years later in the Duke of Hamilton's records, as receiving a pension.

### THE VICTIMS OF THE DISASTER

| | | |
|---|---|---|
| *William Brounlie* | | *Hugh McLean* |
| *--------- Brounlie* | | *John Smith* |
| *James Duffie* | | *William Wotherspoon* |
| *John Duffie* | | *James Fleming* |
| *George Pate* | *James Fyfe* | *James Fisher* |

# WILLIAM BLACK
## AGE 10
## QUARTER COLLIERY

The second ten year old to be killed was *William Black,* who was born at Barriedale in Old Monklands Western District, on the 19th April 1860, to *Hugh Black* and *Agnes Teesdale*. Sometime after his birth, the family settled in the Quarter area, where his father obtained employment as a coal miner. On the 18th of February 1871, William was crushed to death by a roof fall while removing stoops in the Splint seam of Quarter No. 1 Pit.

As a result of his death, the owners of Quarter Collieries, Messrs Colin Dunlop and Co., were charged *"that they did employ William Black and did allow him to work in Quarter No. 1 Pit, although he was under the age of twelve and without having obtained a "certificate" from a competent schoolmaster, that such boy was able to read and write or without a certificate that such boy had attended a school for not less than three hours a day for two days, in each week, in every subsequent lunar month, during which the said boy was so employed."* The charge was denied and went to trial at Hamilton Sheriff Court.

Witnesses were produced for the defence to prove that the boy had been working in other collieries in the district and had been receiving half a "ben" or half a man's wage; the rule in the district being that between the years of ten and twelve boys had to be quarter "ben" and those above twelve half a "ben." It was stated in court that when *Hugh Black* was seeking employment for his son, he told the oversman Mr *Frew* that *"he did not require to be certified as he had been working half "ben" at other collieries,"* which led the oversman to believe he was above twelve years."

The defence produced the registration book and schoolmasters' certificates of other boys employed in the company's collieries and stated that they were very exact in regard to the employment of boys. In his summing up, Sheriff Spens said, that while the boy's father did not directly misrepresent his age, he had so acted and conducted himself towards his employer, as to lead to the 'bona fide' impression and belief on the part of the manager that the boy was not under the specified age. The complaint was dismissed.

This prosecution was the first of its kind to take place in Hamilton. Newspaper reports covering the death of this little boy at no time actually mentioned that he was ten years old. In one report he was said to be eleven years old and the article covering the trial of Messrs Colin Dunlop Ltd., although it gives his date of birth states that he is under the age of twelve. It would appear that the public, although not being lied to, were not being told the exact truth about his age.

# CATHERINE NUGENT
## 1892

# ELIZABETH FINLAY
## 1895

# SARAH McDOWELL CUNNINGHAM
## 1928

It was not just underground that colliery workers were killed. Working at the pit head where the unguarded machinery could kill the unwary was just as dangerous. The deaths of the following three women involved screening machinery.

*1. Catherine Nugent* (16) worked at the screening tables sorting coal at Haughhead Colliery. On the 4th June 1892 she died from strangulation and multiple injuries after her dress became entangled in a belt attached to the rapidly revolving shaft of the travelling screen engine. Catherine was carried round at least twenty times before the engine could be stopped. She was dead when she was untangled from the machinery.

*2. Elizabeth Findlay* (33) worked as a stone picker at the sorting tables at Hamilton Palace Colliery. On the 14th October 1895, joiners had been repairing the floor and had removed two planks leaving a hole. As Elizabeth stepped over the hole her petticoats were caught in the revolving shaft beneath the floor and she was pulled down into the machinery. She died soon after from a broken back and head injuries.

*3. Sarah McDowell Cunningham* (14) was killed on the 3rd October 1928 at No. 1 Pit, Hamilton Palace Colliery on her first day working at the picking tables. Sarah had sat down on the iron plate at the top of the chute leading to the stone conveyer, when the floor lifted and she overbalanced and fell into the chute which was only 18 inches wide at the foot. She was caught by the conveyer and carried along for a distance of 24 feet where she was crushed between the top of the floor and the conveyer.

*Women and girls who worked at the picking tables at Hamilton Palace Colliery
Bothwellhaugh, circa 1925*

*Bothwellhaugh, photograph courtesy of the Scottish Mining Museum*

*Girls at their work at the picking tables, better clothed but the work was still dirty,*
*cold and dangerous*
*Photograph courtesy of the Scottish Mining Museum*

# A MINER'S FIRST DAY

*Photograph courtesy of the Scottish Mining Museum*

At six in the morning he's out of his bed,
And at seven he's near the dark pit-head;
The cage comes up and he steps in,
The shrill bell rings, the cage drops with a din,
With an awestricken gasp he clasps the side,
At last! thank heaven, 'tis the end of the ride.
And out he steps to a lamp-lit space,
Where the water drips from the roof to his face,
His companions call him and forward he goes,
Now he is thankful for his sodden old clothes,
His life as a miner has just begun.
He arrives at an office, and the manager's son
Takes his name and hands him a lamp and tools.
He's now a miner—not a job for fools,
He sets off along a railroad track,
A shout—and into a manhole they quickly pack,
A string of hutches rumbles slowly past.
On he goes and his seam, he reaches at last,
All day long with shovel and with pick
He works, 'mid the dust laden air so thick.
At last, soon after the hour of five,
With a thankful heart that they're still alive,
The miners wait for the cage so fast,
That will take them to sunlight and air at last.
And so at the end of a day's weary toil
He's free at last from the smoke and oil.
To return to his warm and cheery fireside,
Where naught but peace and happiness bide.

*J.T.F. Jnr. Circa 1924.*

# SUFFER THE LITTLE CHILDREN

The following names are of children up to the age of 16 years known to have been killed while working at the surface, or underground, in the coal mines of Hamilton Parish. In all probability there were many others whose names have not been documented.

| Date. | Name. | Age | Colliery | Cause of death |
|-------|-------|-----|----------|----------------|
| 16.03.1841 | ------ Brounlie | 10 | Avonbank | Explosion |
| 07.08.1861 | Alex, Hamilton | 16 | Dykehead | Fire in shaft |
| " | Hugh Craig | 15 | Dykehead | Fire in shaft |
| 04.03.1872 | Wm. B. Small | 14 | Quarter | Roof fall |
| 17.05.1866 | John Lang | 15 | Haughhead | Explosion |
| " | William Barrie | 15 | Haughhead | Explosion |
| 21.03.1867 | Robert Wilson | 14 | Dykehead | Crushed by hutches |
| 15.12.1867 | Richard Williams | 16 | Dykehead | Crushed by cage |
| 18.02.1871 | William Black | 10 | Quarter | Roof fall |
| 11.04.1871 | Francis Jackson | 15 | Quarter | Fell down shaft |
| 07.05.1871 | Robert Pheely | 13 | Ferniegair | Explosion |
| 08.08.1872 | James McGinnes | 14 | Ferniegair | Roof fall |
| 09.04.1874 | John Hailes* | 5 | Greenfield | Boiler explosion |
| " | Robert Maxwell* | 8 | Greenfield | Boiler explosion |
| " | Jeannie Moffat* | 7 | Greenfield | Boiler explosion |
| 09.05.1875 | John Stewart | 13 | Greenfield | Internal injuries |
| 15.05.1877 | John Wilson | 14 | Greenfield | Caught in machinery |
| 01.01.1879 | Dennis Hasson | 13 | Haughhead | Roof fall |
| 14.06.1879 | William Kerr | 14 | Barncluith | Run down by wagons |
| 31.12.1879 | John Anderson | 12 | Quarter | Roof fall |
| 29.12.1880 | Thomas Wyper | 14 | Greenfield | Roof fall |
| 03.04.1880 | Patrick Curran | 15 | Ferniegair | Explosion |
| 15.04.1882 | George Shaw | 11 | Merryton | Killed by hutches |
| 15.03.1882 | Wm. Morrison | 13 | Udston | Explosion |
| 18.05.1882 | James Cowan | 13 | Home Farm | Jammed in haulage wheel |
| 24.04.1883 | Thomas Steel | 16 | Bent | Killed by hutches |
| 26.04.1883 | Thomas Gibson | 16 | Haughhead | Internal injuries |
| 28.09.1883 | John Wright | 15 | Ferniegair | Roof fall |
| 22.03.1884 | Charles Barnes | 15 | Bog | Roof fall |
| 12.09.1884 | John Neilson | 12 | Home Farm | Run down by hutches |
| 13.10.1884 | Thomas Bulloch | 12 | Bog | Head injuries |
| 05.08.1885 | David Dunn | 15 | Bent | Fall of coal |
| 18.01.1887 | Robert Richardson | 13 | Greenfield | Fell 840 feet down shaft |
| 28.05.1887 | James McCulloch | 14 | Udston | Explosion |
| " | David Shanks | 13 | Udston | Explosion |
| " | James Kain | 14 | Udston | Explosion |
| " | James Gaw | 13 | Udston | Explosion |
| " | John McGinnes | 16 | Udston | Explosion |
| " | Daniel Robertson | 15 | Udston | Explosion |
| " | John Dodds | 13 | Udston | Explosion |
| " | Andrew Lawson | 16 | Udston | Explosion |

| | | | | |
|---|---|---|---|---|
| 28.05.1887 | Edward Jones | 15 | Udston | Explosion |
| " | Gavin R. Malcolm | 15 | Udston | Explosion |
| " | James Nelson | 16 | Udston | Explosion |
| " | John Nelson | 14 | Udston | Explosion |
| 26.12.1888 | John McNamara | 15 | Eddlewood | Run down by hutches |
| 12.05.1889 | Constantine Kelly | 13 | Clyde | Roof fall |
| 20.02.1890 | Robert Gregory | 14 | Hamilton Palace | Roof fall |
| 26.03.1890 | Wm. C. Davidson | 13 | Bog | Caught in flywheel of haulage engine |
| 08.08.1890 | William Graham | 15 | Eddlewood | Run down by pug engine |
| 27.02.1891 | John Brown | 15 | Eddlewood | Crushed by hutches |
| 27.03.1891 | James Rogerson | 15 | Allanton | No details, fractured ribs |
| 28.05.1891 | John McDonald | 13 | Clyde | Roof fall |
| 31.08.1891 | Alex. Browning | 15 | Earnock | Roof fall |
| 22.08.1892 | Robert Todd | 14 | Merryton | Run down by hutch |
| 07.02.1894 | Andrew Frame | 15 | Bog | Jammed between two hutches |
| 14.01.1895 | Patrick Kells | 16 | Fairhill | Fractured spine |
| 16.02.1895 | David Woods | 15 | Bog | Run down by hutches |
| 12.11.1895 | William Allan | 15 | Clyde | Kicked in face by pony |
| 22.01.1896 | Walter Johnson | 13 | Earnock | Roof fall |
| 25.09.1896 | Wm. Crawford | 13 | Bent | Crushed between wagon and buffers |
| 19.03.1897 | James Wyper | 13 | Earnock | Roof fall, compound fractures right leg |
| 16.10.1897 | James Smith | 15 | Merryton | Roof fall |
| 03.01.1898. | George Somerville. | 14 | Earnock. | Roof fall |
| 05.01.1898 | James Wyper | 13 | Earnock | Multiple fractures |
| 15.02.1898 | Wm. Henderson | 13 | Ross | Roof fall |
| 22.04.1898 | Archd. Scott | 16 | Allanton | Internal injuries |
| 09.04.1899 | Alex. Taylor | 16 | Ferniegair | Fell down shaft |
| 13.07.1899 | Jas. McCawley | 14 | Earnock | Crushed by hutches |
| 10.10.1890 | Wm. Armour | 14 | Hamilton Palace | Explosion |
| 12.06.1900 | William Renwick | 16 | Cadzow | Overturned cart |
| 05.12.1903 | George Boyd | 16 | Udston | Roof fall |
| 07.02.1904 | James Brown | 15 | Greenfield | Crushed by hutches |
| 10.07.1905 | John Paterson | 16 | Wellhall | Dragged down shaft by cage |
| 30.09.1907 | William Martin | 14 | Allanton | Roof fall |
| 14.09.1909 | Francis Slaven | 16 | ---------- | Fall of stones at coal face |
| 17.01.1910 | Duncan Wilkie | 13 | Neilsland | Fell 1200 feet down shaft |
| 27.01.1910 | Wm. B. Johnston | 14 | Ferniegair | Fall of stone at coal face |
| 15.06.1915 | John Ramage | 16 | ---------- | Fractured skull |
| 12.11.1915 | Michael Fleming | 16 | Quarter | Fractured skull |
| 09.07.1916 | John Craw | 14 | Dykehead | Caught in machinery |
| 06.06.1917 | Isaac Callison | 16 | Clyde | Run down by Hutches |

| | | | | |
|---|---|---|---|---|
| 21.08.1918 | Wm. Inglis | 15 ½ | Clyde | Fractured ribs |
| 29.01.1920 | Wm. Stannage | 14 | Greenfield | Caught in machinery |
| -.02.1923 | Robert Ballantyne | 16 | Homefarm | Fractured skull |
| 30.12.1923 | James Fulston | 16 | ----------- | Sepsis following injury |
| 10.02.1924 | Alex. Anderson | 14 | Allanton | Run down by hutches |
| 03.10.1928 | Sarah Cunningham | 14 | Hamilton Palace | Crushed to death at screening tables |
| 31.03.1928 | Anthony Strain | 16 | Hamilton Palace | Fractured skull |
| 20.02.1933 | James Tannock | 14 | Ferniegair | Crushed between buffers and a rake of wagons |

*John Hailes, *Jeannie Moffat* and *Robert Maxwell* were killed when a pithead boiler exploded at Greenfield Colliery. Because this was a colliery accident, these children have been included in the figures.

*Women and children drawing a hutch full of coal*

# INJURIES TO CHILDREN WORKING IN COAL MINES

The accident rate among children working in the mines was appalling. For every child killed, there were many more who were seriously injured. Children were maimed for life as they worked among the machinery at the picking tables and also from injuries received from the numerous types of accidents which took place on an almost daily basis, both on the surface, and underground. The following examples, give an indication of the type of injuries inflicted on the children of the mines.

In March 1893, at Auchinraith Colliery, Blantyre, Edward Liddell aged 13 years was only a few hours into the first shift of his working life, when his left foot became caught amongst the pulleys at the picking tables. His foot was wrenched off. Ref. The Lanarkshire, 10.03.1893, page 3

Two months later at the Bent Colliery Hamilton, Henry Morrison jun., age 14 years, had his arm severed at the shoulder while he was trying to disentangle his clothes which had become caught up in the machinery at the picking tables. Ref. The Lanarkshire, 12.05.1893, page 4.

# HIS LAST SUNRISE

A summer morn: the mists lift slow,
As through the haze the sun's red glow
Breaks with a slow, majestic sway,
A vision of grandeur, coming day;
White, shifting mists in valley lie,
And, overhead, hilltops look nigh;
Receding night, incoming morn,
Another day in splendour born.

A miner leaves his lowly home,
And climbs the valley side; there's some
Who ne'er can know a miner's thought
At leaving light of day; they never wrought
Down 'neath the rocks, 'midst mud and clay;
Oh, those so placed can realise
The beauty of a glad sunrise.

The lad, for but a lad is Hugh,
Ascends the hill, then turns to view
The glory of the breaking morn,
The wreathing mists, the glinting corn;
He views the bonnie, babbling brook:
Ah, how he knows it, every nook
He has explored it in boyhood days:
He loves its noisy, prattling ways.

His eye across the vale is cast,
Where mother watches to the last;
Both wave, he turns, and steps from view:
That was the last she saw of Hugh:
A fatal shot, in darkest gloom,
No chance had he to avert doom;
A lightening flash of blinding light,
A rending crash—then all is night.

Another added to the roll
Of lives, that is the worker's toll;
A widow stricken to the dust,
She can't believe, yet still she must—
The others, sisters, brothers dear,
Sit silent, hushed; the dripping tear
Bedew their cheeks; in mother's eye
No trace or sign of tear is nigh:
She sits in mute and stony grief,
Too great for tears to give relief.          *Unknown. Circa 1929.*

# THE COLLIERS
## OF
## LAIGH (LOW) QUARTER
### 1841

*Laigh Quarter, built 1681*

| NAME | AGE. | OCCUPATION | PLACE OF BIRTH |
|---|---|---|---|
| James Webster | 35 | Blacksmith | Scotland |
| Robert Hart | 45 | Coal Miner | Lanarkshire |
| William Scott | 20 | Coal Miner | Lanarkshire |
| Neil McMillan | 36 | Coal Miner | Scotland |
| James Hume | 30 | Coal Miner | Scotland |
| James Hume | 9 *(1) | Coal Miner | Scotland |
| Robert North | 30 | Coal Miner | England |
| Robert Scott | 30 | Coal Miner | England |
| John Gardiner | 35 | Coal Miner | Lanarkshire |
| Gavin Brownlie | 15 | Coal Miner | Lanarkshire |
| Robert Hamilton | 50 | Coal Miner | Lanarkshire |
| Jas. Cunningham | 85 | Coal Miner | Lanarkshire |
| John Ballantyne | 25 | Coal Miner | Lanarkshire |
| Donald Livingston | 35 | Coal Miner | Scotland |
| John Harper | 20 | Coal Miner | Ireland |
| James Harper | 15 | Coal Miner | Ireland |
| Thomas Harper | 25 | Coal Miner | Ireland |
| Wm. Johnston | 14 | Coal Miner | Lanarkshire |
| James Hamilton | 45 | Enginekeeper | Lanarkshire |
| James Meikle | 25 | Coal miner | Lanarkshire |

| | | | |
|---|---|---|---|
| John Fleming | 30 | Coal Miner | Lanarkshire |
| Alex. Fleming | 13 | Coal Miner | Lanarkshire |
| Wm. Fleming | 12 | Coal Miner | Lanarkshire |
| Peter Duffie | 14 *(2) | Coal Miner | Ireland |
| John Bolton | 40 | Coal Miner | Lanarkshire |
| John Bolton | 20 | Coal Miner | Lanarkshire |
| James Wilson | 30 | Coal Miner | Lanarkshire |
| Michael Forrest | 30*(3) | Coal Miner | Lanarkshire |
| John Meikle | 45 | Coal Miner | Lanarkshire |
| John Meikle | 20 | Coal Miner | Lanarkshire |
| John Gray | 20 | Coal Miner | Lanarkshire |
| Michael Fleming | 15 | Coal Miner | Lanarkshire |
| Robert Marshall | 30 | Coal Miner | Lanarkshire |
| James Morrison | 20 | Coal Miner | Lanarkshire |
| James Rowan | 20 | Coal Miner | Lanarkshire |
| Thomas Hamilton | 30 | Wright | Lanarkshire |
| John Wilson | 55 | Coal Miner | Lanarkshire |
| John Wilson | 55 | Blacksmith | Lanarkshire |
| Alex. Fleming | 35 | Farrier | Lanarkshire |
| John Wilson | 15 | Coal Miner | Lanarkshire |
| James Hodge | 20 | Coal Miner | Lanarkshire |
| John Bolton | 15 | Coal Miner | Lanarkshire |
| John Wotherspoon | 10* (4) | Coal Miner | Lanarkshire |
| John Forrest | 65 | Coal Miner | Lanarkshire |
| Douglas McPhail | 10 | Coal Miner | Lanarkshire |
| Wm. Young | 20 | Coal Miner | Lanarkshire |
| Wm. Wilson | 60 | Engineworker | Lanarkshire |
| Archibald Wilson | 15 | Engineworker | Lanarkshire |

(1) James Hume is listed as working as a coal miner at the tender age of 9 years.

* * *

This list contains surnames known to have been among the dead and the survivors from the Avonbank disaster two months prior to the census.

(2) Peter Duffie comes from a family of eight children including a baby of 2 months. There is no mention of his father, but in the 1851 census, his mother is listed as a widow. Two Duffie men were among the victims of the Avonbanks disaster. Many years later Mrs Duffie/Duffy was still living in Quarter and the Hamilton and Kinneil estate papers record her as receiving a pension from the Duke of Hamilton.

(3) Michael Forrest was one of the men from the rescue party who survived.

(4) A William Wotherspoon was also killed in the explosion and John Wotherspoon aged 10 is listed as living with two young women with the same surname. He appears to be the breadwinner at the age of 10 years.

# THE COLLIER'S
## OF
## QUARTER
### 1851

\*     \*     \*

## LAIGH QUARTER

| NAME | AGE | OCCUPATION | PLACE OF BIRTH |
| --- | --- | --- | --- |
| John Gardiner | 49 | Pitheadman | Lanarkshire/Hamilton |
| Alex. Gardiner | 17 | Coal Miner | Lanarkshire/Hamilton |
| Robert North | 40 | Coal Miner | England |
| Thomas North | 16 | Coal Miner | Lanarkshire/Hamilton |
| Andrew North | 11 | Coal Miner | Lanarkshire/Hamilton |
| James Hodge | 29 | Coal Miner | Lanarkshire/Hamilton |
| James Hodge | 10 | Coal Miner | Lanarkshire/Hamilton |
| John Inglis | 34 | Coal Miner | Stirling/Falkirk |
| Neil McMillan | 50 | Coal Miner | Argyle/Kilchoman |
| Wm. McMillan | 15 | Coal Miner | Lanarkshire/Hamilton |
| Neil McMillan | 13 | Coal Miner | Lanarkshire/Hamilton |
| James Webster | 48 | Blacksmith | Stirling/Larbert |
| Robert Bolton | 23 | Coal Miner | Lanarkshire/Hamilton |
| Robert Hart | 58 | Coal Miner | " Old Monklands |
| John Brownlie | 18 | Coal Miner | Lanarkshire/Hamilton |
| James Brownlie | 15 | Coal Miner | Lanarkshire/Hamilton |
| Thomas Harper | 28 | Coal Miner | Ireland |
| Jas. Cunningham* | 94 | Retired Coal Miner | Renfrew/Eaglesham |
| Gavin Brownlie | - | Coal Miner | Lanarkshire/Hamilton |
| Peter Duffie | - | Coal Miner | Ireland |
| John Duffie | 21 | Coal Miner | Lanarkshire/Hamilton |
| John Meikle | 31 | Coal Miner | Lanarkshire/Hamilton |
| Michael Fleming | 28 | Coal Miner | Lanarkshire Hamilton |
| Thomas Fleming | 22 | Coal Miner | Lanarkshire/Hamilton |
| John Harper | 32 | Coal Miner | Ireland |
| John Harper | 12 | Coal Miner | Lanarkshire/Hamilton |
| Robert Harper | 10 | Coal Miner | Lanarkshire/Hamilton |
| John Bolton | 52 | Coal Miner | Lanarkshire/Hamilton |
| John Bolton | 30 | Coal Miner | Lanarkshire/Hamilton |
| John Bolton | 12 | Coal Miner | Lanarkshire/Hamilton |
| James Shearer | 35 | Coal Miner | Lanarkshire/Glassford |
| William Wilson | 33 | Coal Miner | Lanarkshire/Hamilton |
| James Scott | 28 | Coal Miner | Lanarkshire/Stonehouse |
| Michael Forrest | 43 | Coal Miner | Lanarkshire/Hamilton |
| John Forrest | 12 | Coal Miner | Lanarkshire/Hamilton |
| James Meikle | 35 | Coal Miner | Lanarkshire/Hamilton |
| Wm. Johnstone | 23 | Coal Miner/Oversman | Lanarkshire/Hamilton |
| Matthew Reid | 32 | Engineworker | Ayrshire/Fenwick |
| Hugh Wilson | 32 | Engineworker | Lanarkshire/Hamilton |

| | | | |
|---|---|---|---|
| Wm. Fleming | 21 | Coal Miner | Lanarkshire/Hamilton |
| John Fleming | 43 | Coal Miner | Lanarkshire/Hamilton |
| James Cathcart | 26 | Coal Miner | Lanarkshire/Hamilton |
| John Meikle | 56 | Coal Miner | Lanarkshire/Dalserf |
| Matthew Meikle | 23 | Coal Miner | Lanarkshire/Hamilton |
| William Meikle | 17 | Coal Miner | Lanarkshire/Hamilton |
| Henry Taylor | 21 | Coal Miner | Lanarkshire/Hamilton |
| Archd. Wilson | 28 | Coal Miner/Oversman | Lanarkshire/Hamilton |

*James Cunningham is listed as having a pension from the Duke of Hamilton

## COLLIERY, QUARTER

| | | | |
|---|---|---|---|
| Matthew Walker | 52 | Coal Manager | Linlithgow/Bathgate |
| Thomas Walker | 18 | Weigher | Lanarkshire/Hamilton |

## HIGH QUARTER

| | | | |
|---|---|---|---|
| John Wilson | 64 | Coal Miner | Lanarkshire/Hamilton |
| Wm. Scott | 30 | Pitheadman | Lanarkshire/Stonehouse |
| Wm. Gilchrist | 46 | Pitheadman | Lanarkshire/Hamilton |
| John Findlay | 20 | Coal Miner | Lanarkshire/Hamilton |
| Thomas Forrest | 31 | Coal Miner | Lanarkshire/Hamilton |
| Wm. Wilson | 73 | Retired coal miner | Lanarkshire/Hamilton |
| Wm. Wilson | 61 | Blacksmith | Lanarkshire/Hamilton |
| Duncan Wilson | 20 | Coal Miner | Lanarkshire/Hamilton |
| John Wilson | 25 | Coal Miner | Lanarkshire/Hamilton |

## QUARTERGATE

| | | | |
|---|---|---|---|
| Adam Hamilton | 20 | Coal Miner | Lanarkshire/Hamilton |
| Adam Murray | 14 | Coal Miner | Lanarkshire/Hamilton |

## CASTLEHILL

| | | | |
|---|---|---|---|
| Donald Livingston | 47 | Coal Miner and farmer of 20 acres | |
| | | | Argyle/Kildalton |
| Donald Livingston | 21 | Coal Miner | Lanarkshire/Hamilton |
| James Livingston | 14 | Coal Miner | Lanarkshire/Hamilton |

## AVONBANK

| | | | |
|---|---|---|---|
| James Hamilton | 55 | Engineworker | Ayrshire/Cumnock |
| James Hamilton | 26 | Engineworker | Lanarkshire/Hamilton |
| John Hamilton | 18 | Coal Miner | Lanarkshire/Hamilton |
| Thomas Hamilton | -- | Apprentice Engineworker | |
| | | | Lanarkshire/Hamilton |
| John Hamilton | 38 | Enginekeeper | Lanarkshire/Hamilton |

| James Wilson | 44 | Coal Miner/Oversman | Lanarkshire/Hamilton |
| James Wilson | 20 | Coal Miner | Lanarkshire/Hamilton |
| Arthur Wilson | 17 | Coal Miner | Lanarkshire/Hamilton |
| John Wilson | 16 | Coal Miner | Lanarkshire/Hamilton |
| Robert Wilson | 14 | Coal Miner | Lanarkshire/Hamilton |

## SUNNYSIDE ORCHARD

| William Wilson | 47 | Coal Miner | Lanarkshire/Hamilton |
| William Wilson | 15 | Coal Miner | Lanarkshire/Hamilton |
| Andrew Wilson | 11 | Coal Miner | Lanarkshire/Hamilton |

## PLOTCOCK

| Wm. Marshall | 20 | Coal Miner | Lanarkshire/Muirkirk |

*Quarter No. 7 Pit, photograph courtesy of the Scottish Mining Museum.*

# QUARTER NEWS
## 1856-1860

Up until the 1850's, the village of Quarter had been a quiet, sleepy little backwater, where nothing ever changed and the locals got on with the serious business of putting food on the table and surviving the winter. However, with the development of the rich seams of coal and iron-stone under the surrounding countryside, this way of life was soon to vanish for ever.

By 1856, blast furnaces were being built and coal and ironstone pits were already being worked. A railway line which would eventually terminate at Strathaven was in the process of being constructed, making access to Quarter much easier  This new line branched off from the main Hamilton Railway, halfway between Hamilton and Blantyre Stations and from there it proceeded to the village of High Blantyre. Convenient for the limestone fields of Crossbasket Park, the line travelled on through the lands of Udston and Townhill Farms to the iron-stone fields of Earnockmuir, where ironstone pits were already in operation. The next farms to play host to the railway were Neilsland, then Chapel and on till Quarter was reached.
For approximately £50,000 the railway was then extended to Strathaven, travelling through the lands of Broomtod, Laigh Airybog, Brownmuir, Righead and Whiteshawgate.

The first furnace was set in full blow on Tuesday, 3rd March, 1857 and the second one followed two weeks later. There was now a chronic housing shortage due to the large influx of workers for the blast furnaces.

Colliers' wages which had been previously good were now being reduced and people were beginning to feel the pinch. Up until then, as surviving Hamilton Estate Papers for the year 1835-1836 indicate, the old Laigh Quarter mining families such as the *Boltons, Brownlies, Flemings, Gilchrists, Hamiltons, Harpers, Harts, Inglis, Maxwells, Meikles, Scotts* and *Wilsons* had all made a reasonable living from Avonbanks and Quarter mines. The accounts also show that two miners, *John Bolton* and *John Meikle* were consistently among the highest paid hewers at Quarter.

With the increase in residents, there was also an increase in drunkenness on a Saturday pay night, when miners could be seen "*wending*" their way home "*o'er a' the ills o' life victorious,*" with their wives by their side, carrying on their backs a week's provisions wrapped in a large bundle. However, a few gentlemen among the miners willingly divided the burden with their better-half, but some of the women were just left to stagger on under the weight, until they reached home.

The work of Hamilton Sheriff and Justice of Peace Courts also increased. Quarter residents now started to appear before the bench on a variety of charges and the women were not exempt from this trend. *Ann Manning* or *Shearer,* wife of *James Shearer,* (drawer) was fined 10s or 7 days imprisonment in February 1858, for assaulting Mrs *Agnes Miller or Smallwoods,* wife of a miner, by "*striking her with her fists and a bread-roller to the effusion of her blood and injury to her person and for maliciously breaking a door.*" She paid the fine. Drunkenness accounted for many of the sorry sights before the bench. Typical of this was *James Wilson,* a Quarter miner who had been arrested for being drunk and disorderly in Cadzow Street and Duke Street, Hamilton in August, 1858, and had forfeited a pledge of 5s (25p).

The winter was always a particularly hard time, with work being scarce for many folk and during the early months of 1858, the Kirk Session distributed coal to the needy.

By summer 1858, things were looking up, the two blast furnaces were employing a good many hands and the character of the village had changed for ever. Previously quiet and peaceful, it was now a bustling village, with new faces being seen almost every day. The quiet of the country had been replaced with the roar of the furnace, the shrill whistle of the locomotive and the puff of the winding engine.

In the mid 1850's, a local minister had remarked that Quarter was 200 years behind the age. How quickly times could change! Quarter, as a letter to the Hamilton Advertiser stated, was by then *"considerably elevated above our friends in Hamilton; and no one can deny that we are the most enlightened people in the neighbourhood for we have no scant of light by night or by day—summer and winter"* and he was right. In Quarter it was always light, darkness never fell for the light from the blast furnaces lit up the whole village, as if it were day.

*Colin Dunlop & Co.* built a new Chapel in which the first service was preached at 12 o'clock on Sunday, 2nd September, 1858, by the *Rev. Dr Keith* and at 6 p.m. by the *Rev. Mr McPhail.*

In March, 1859, complaints were being voiced about the deplorable state of the busy road from Millheugh to West-Quarter by Sunnyside, where the depth of the mud was estimated to be ten inches deep. Among the travellers who used this road daily were upwards of 50 colliers and miners going to and from their work. The proprietors of Sunnyside Farm and Quarter Works were appealed to, in the hope that they would take pity on the poor travellers and improve the state of the road.

On the 13th July, 1859, the Quarter Colliery Friendly Society held their annual procession which started at 12 o'clock when the Newarthill Brass Band Society started parading through the miners *"Rows,"* led by the gallant Captain of the Society, who with a sword in his hand, looked rather formidable. After giving every villager a call and receiving a good supply of *"the crater (1)* from the guidwives at Quarter, they departed home, no doubt hoping to be called back next year.

Following the bands departure, the games started and there were the traditional stands with *"rowley powleys," nut barrows* and *"sweety stauns."* This was followed by a barn dance in *Mr S. Hamilton's* barn where they danced the night away till it was *"broad daylight in the morning."* The whole affair passed off quite well, with no fighting or quarrelling to speak of, but this was possibly due to the number of police present. The *"Fair"* was seen as an opportunity for the locals to meet a future husband or bride.

> *"There were storemen quite lively, and colliers fu' gay,*
> *Miners and drawers and men that make hay,*
> *Milkmen and drainers and carters were there,*
> *All resolved to have their matches at the Quarter Fair."*

(1) Whisky.

August was a bad month for the local feathered pets. An adventurous and swaggering cockerel long resident at Divitty, took it into its head to visit a neighbour's pig hoping to obtain a meal from the side of the pig's trough. The pig however wasn't receiving visitors that day and resenting the intrusion, ate the bird, feathers and all. All that was left of a much loved pet was a portion of one of his legs….and the weans wept!

On Friday, 5<sup>th</sup> August, 1859, the pit bottomer at No. 1 Pit was surprised to hear a dull thud at the bottom of the pit. When he went to look at the shaft he was amazed to find a peacock in the "*last agonies of life.*" The bird, property of local man *Mr Walker,* was taken to the surface, where it soon expired and was duly buried in his owner's garden. Such was the interest in this incident the following poem was published in the Hamilton Advertiser.

> *"Nae mair will eager weans assail,*
> *The treasures of his gorgeous tail;*
> *And wi' the plunder, wives and lassies*
> *Nae mair will deck their looking glasses.*
> *The glories he was proud tae wave*
> *Are crushed and humbled in the grave;*
> *And this sad lesson reads to all*
> *From pride to carrion's but a fall."*

In January, 1859, a scandal rocked the village. One of the local miners, *James Hodge or Black,* aged 38 years, "*24 of which he had worked at Quarter Pit,*" vanished in the middle of the night from his one roomed home in Laigh Quarter, abandoning his wife who had borne him twelve children. Eight hours later, the 48 years old widow and mother of twelve next door also vanished, leaving behind her offspring.

The following week *James Naismith*, Inspector of Poor for the parish advertised in local newspapers the reward of 1 guinea, for information leading to *Hodge's* apprehension. The burden of keeping his wife and most of the children from the two families had now fallen upon the parish. *James Hodge* the runaway husband, was described as 6 ft. tall, with fair complexion and ruddy red whiskers. He was also said to be wearing a blue polka jacket, dark moleskin trousers and striped cravat when he left home. The pair were spotted at Maybole in Ayrshire several days after absconding and it appears that they got clean away, for there is no record of him appearing in court.

On the 9th August 1860, approximately 120 Sunday school children and 20 teachers followed behind the Larkhall Brass Band, waving banners and singing at the top of their voices as they made their way down to Fairholm House, where the Hamiltons had allowed them the use of their grounds.

A good time was had by all the children present, but there was a darker side, some of the village boys who had previously gone on day trips were not present; there were to be no more Sunday school picnics for them. At the tender age of ten years, many of the village boys of Quarter had to put their happy carefree days behind them, to work beside their fathers. Each boy knew that on his first morning down the pit he left his childhood behind to become a collier, a man among men. ….A WORKING MAN .

*A YOUNG QUARTER MINER*
*Photograph courtesy of John Carrigan*

# SOME THOCHTS FRAE THE MINE

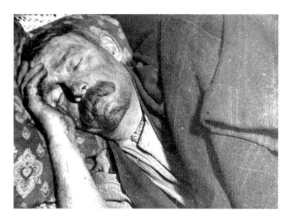

Sometimes when I'm workin' deep doon in the pit,
No' feelin' quite able—in fact, haur'ly fit---
Some strange thochts come tae me, I feel ma heart burn,
When I think on the days that will never return.

I look away, years back, when I wis a boy,
Ah, yes, these were days I did fairly enjoy,
When I wis sae happy attending the school,
Ne'er dreaming that some day I'd be sic a fool.

I regret, noo, the day I neglected tae learn,
When I went tae the pit, there ma leevin' tae earn,
I ken years ago that I made a mistake,
I wish I'd kept learning, jist for ma ain sake.

And also for those that I work tae sustain,
That's assumin' ma effort had not been in vain,
But I think wi' a try, I can quite safely state,
That a different job wid, at least, been ma fate.

I then look at nature frae mony a source,
When ma energy's taxed tae its utmost, of course,
Ma legs and ma arms are beginning tae tire,
And I feel jist like some yin aboot tae expire.

And when I'm exhausted and feelin' sae din,
'Tis then that I wish I'd ma day's tae begin,
I'd learn up ma lessons, each nicht I wid sit,
For I vow I wid never look near haun' a pit.

I've been employed there for thirty-four years,
When I think o' that time I could almost shed tears,
 I've laboured and slaved on, frae mornin' tae nicht,
And mony a day I ha'e ne'er seen daylicht.

Hooever, it seemed that the pit wis ma lot,
A lesson I learned that I've never forgot,
So I trust a' young boys will tak' ma advice,
Ere they start doon a pit, they'll consider it twice.

*J. D. Douglas Water, circa 1933*

# KNOWN DEATHS AT QUARTER COLLIERIES

| DATE | NAME | AGE. | CAUSE OF DEATH |
|---|---|---|---|
| 16.03.1841 | WM. BROUNLIE | -- | EXPLOSION OF FIREDAMP |
| " | (CHILD) BROUNLIE | 10 | EXPLOSION OF FIREDAMP |
| " | JAMES DUFFIE | -- | EXPLOSION OF FIREDAMP |
| " | JOHN DUFFIE | -- | EXPLOSION OF FIREDAMP |
| " | HUGH McLEAN | -- | EXPLOSION OF FIREDAMP |
| " | JOHN SMITH | -- | EXPLOSION OF FIREDAMP |
| " | WM. WOTHERSPOON | -- | EXPLOSION OF FIREDAMP |
| " | JAMES FLEMING | -- | AFTERDAMP |
| " | GEORGE PATE | -- | AFTERDAMP |
| " | JAMES FISHER | -- | AFTERDAMP |
| " | JAMES FYFE | -- | AFTERDAMP |
| 09.02.1857 | JAMES WILSON | 27 | ROOF FALL |
| 23.04.1857 | THOMAS NORTH | 21 | ROOF FALL |
| 08.12.1857 | THOMAS McNEISH | 30 | TRAPPED BY MACHINERY |
| 13.12.1858 | FRANCIS McLANACHAN | -- | ROOF FALL (Stone 9 ft long) |
| 25.12.1858 | MATTHEW LAW | 61 | FRACTURED SPINE |
| 04.03.1862 | WM. BURNSIDE SMALL | 14 | ROOF FALL |
| 03.11.1865 | JOHN SWANBRICK | 45 | ROOF FALL |
| 20.09.1869 | WM. FLEMING | 42 | HEAD INJURED IN SHAFT |
| 14.07.1870 | JOHN WATSON | 22 | EXPLOSION OF FIREDAMP |
| " | GAVIN WILLIAMSON | 21 | EXPLOSION OF FIREDAMP |
| " | JAMES WARD | 35 | EXPLOSION OF FIREDAMP |
| " | WILLIAM MORE | 22 | EXPLOSION OF FIREDAMP |
| 18.02.1871 | WILLIAM BLACK | 10 | ROOF FALL |
| 11.04.1871 | FRANCIS JACKSON | 15 | FELL DOWN SHAFT (360ft) |
| 15.12.1871 | JOHN SEMPLE | 17 | RUN DOWN BY HUTCHES |
| 14.10.1875 | GEORGE CAMPBELL | 55 | HIT HIS HEAD OFF BEAM |
| 30.12.1879 | DONALD McDONALD | 35 | CRUSHED ON SURFACE |
| 31.12.1879 | JOHN ANDERSON | 12 | ROOF FALL |
| 03.08.1880 | DAVID WHITE | 19 | ROOF FALL (3 tons) |
| 14.12.1881 | JAMES PRENTICE | 38 | FELL DOWN SHAFT (534ft) |
| 08.11.1884 | JOHN F. KEITH | 36 | TRAPPED UNDER MANURE |
| 07.11.1885 | EDWARD McCANN | 55 | ROOF FALL (Fractured ribs) |
| 29.05.1890 | SAMUEL REID | 21 | CRUSHED BY CAGE |
| 02.03.1896 | JOHN WILSON | 34 | MULTIPLE INJURIES |
| 17.08.1896 | JOHN GEMMELL | 30 | ROOF FALL (1 cwt) |
| 18.05.1898 | HARRY L. SMITH | 72 | SHOCK, RESULT OF INJURY |
| 17.07.1903 | JOHN G. CROSSLEY | 32 | ROOF FALL |
| 29.02.1904 | HUGH KYLE | 45 | CAUGHT IN HAULAGE ENGINE. |
| 11.05.1904 | JAMES SMITH | 35 | ROOF FALL (Trapped 2 hours) |
| 23.05.1904 | WILLIAM COYLE | 20 | RUN DOWN BY HUTCHES |
| 24.09.1904 | WILLIAM RAMAGE | 41 | FELL DOWN SHAFT (520ft) |
| 30.09.1904 | JOHN ROBSON | 45 | ROOF FALL (Fractures of skull and spine) |
| 24.11.1904 | JOHN BAIRD | 41 | STRUCK BY STONE |

| | | | |
|---|---|---|---|
| 29.12.1904 | WILLIAM PIRRIE | 20 | NO DETAILS (Internal injuries) |
| 12.11.1905 | JOHN McLEAN | 58 | MULTIPLE CRUSHING INJURIES |
| 21.12.1906 | ROBERT GARDINER | 49 | COLLAPSE OF SHAFT |
| " | ANDREW MAXWELL | 60 | COLLAPSE OF SHAFT |
| " | JAMES McGINTY | 39 | COLLAPSE OF SHAFT |
| 29.03.1907 | JAMES BELL | 44 | FALL OF COAL |
| 10.07.1907 | JOHN HERON | 62 | CRUSHED BY HUTCH |
| 09.08.1910 | EDWARD THOMAS | 64 | ROOF FALL |
| 10.10.1913 | JOHN McERLAIN | 30 | ROOF FALL |
| 12.11.1915 | MICHAEL FLEMING | 16 | NO DETAILS (Fractured skull) |
| 05.12.1916 | JAMES S. PRINGLE | 48 | NO DETAILS (Multiple injuries to head and limbs |
| 10.02.1917 | JOHN HAMILTON | 61 | MULTIPLE CHEST INJURIES |
| 18.12.1919 | ALEXANDER CLELLAND | 37 | FRACTURED SKULL |
| 02.01.1920 | ANDREW D. PROSSER | 31 | NO DETAILS (Fractured spine) |
| 16.04.1920 | ROBERT PARKER | 25 | LEGS AMPUTATED BY COAL CUTTING MACHINE |
| 05.07.1922 | JAMES LENNOX | 55 | NO DETAILS (Chest injuries) |
| 13.10.1924 | ALEXANDER DUNN | 46 | CRUSHED BY HUTCH (Pelvic injuries and shock) |
| 20.03.1934 | JAMES HAMILTON | 41 | ROOF FALL (30-40 tons trapped 2 hours) |
| 07.02.1942 | WILLIAM CROOKS | 69 | NO DETAILS (Internal crushing injuries) |
| 08.01.1947 | JAMES RITCHIE | 58 | GASSED |
| " | ALEXANDER KERR | 67 | GASSED |

*Quarter miners playing "bools" during the 1926 strike.*

# THE DYKEHEAD/SUMMERLEE COLLIERY DISASTER
## 1861

Dotted along the road between Hamilton and Larkhall, were a chain of coal mines, one of which was the Dykehead /Summerlee Colliery. Developed on the lands of Dykehead Farm and situated approximately three miles from Hamilton, the colliery, at 40 fathoms, or 240 feet, was not particularly deep. A medium size pit, it employed up to 300 miners and surface workers, with most of them living at either the Dykehead colliery cottages, or in Larkhall.

At half past four, on the morning of Wednesday the 7th of August, 1861, 50 men and boys descended the collieries only shaft to begin their shift. It was just an ordinary working day for the miners and all appeared to go well until one o'clock in the afternoon, when, to the horror of the surface workers, large volumes of smoke were seen pouring from the mouth of the shaft. Within five minutes the pit was a raging inferno, with the flames rolling up the bratticing and setting fire to the framework and headgear at the pithead.

On the surface, workers, stunned at the nightmare unfolding before them, were quick to organise chains of men to fight the fire with pails of water and a rider was dispatched to Hamilton to summon the town fire engine.  Before the horse reached Ferniegair, the burning headgear and framework had collapsed into a heap of ashes, leaving nothing, but debris and a gaping hole in the ground. The flames roaring from the mouth of the shaft burned with such ferocity, that they rose to the height of a two storey building and could be seen in Motherwell, two miles away.

At the pit head, there was pandemonium, relatives of the trapped men flocked to the site. Hysterical women were screaming for someone to help their men, while shocked ashen faced children clung to their mother's skirts, their eyes reflecting the horror they were witnessing.

From other local collieries, miners and officials were arriving at the scene to offer help and advice and within a short time; more than 1600 people were crowded into the area surrounding the burning pit.

Mr *W.G. Simpson* of Dundas, Simpson and Co, whose colliery bordered on Dykehead Colliery, instructed his miners to start driving a 30 foot roadway through into the waste of the Dykehead workings. His rationale was that if all else failed, they may just be able to break through and save some of the entombed colliers.

The Hamilton fire engine arrived at two o'clock, followed at four o'clock, by the fire engine from Hamilton Palace. Working flat out, the firemen aimed water from two hoses on to the burning mass. By five o'clock the flames had visibly reduced and there were signs that they were winning the battle. Before long, the fire which had been raging in the shaft's wooden lining was almost extinguished.

Trapped underground, the 50 miners, choking and fighting for breath, had to retreat back into the mine, as the smoke rolling through the roadways like swirling black thunderclouds, threatened to engulf and destroy them.  The noise of debris falling down the shaft and echoing through the workings, brought home to the men the possibility that their only means of escape and oxygen might be blocked off and several of them went back to have a look

The miners' fears proved a reality; the burning timber was threatening to completely block the shaft and entomb them, so with their bare hands, they started frantically pulling at the large pile of red hot wood which was raining down from the walls of the shaft. The conditions underground were indescribable, with the miners choking from the smoke and fumes, and struggling for every breath. As the men removing the debris collapsed from exhaustion, their places were taken by others, who came from further back in the roadway.

When the fire was finally brought under control, several of the entombed miners started to climb up the shaft by holding on to the hot cast iron pipes normally used to pump water up the pit. The fathers went first, with their sons following behind them and as the older men became exhausted, they stood on the shoulders of their sons to rest. Inch by inch they climbed the shaft, desperately trying to escape from the hell of the burning coal mine. Resting when too tired to go on, some of the men eventually reached the surface. Several of the miners who were unable to maintain their grip, plunged to bottom of the shaft.

When it became obvious that only a few men were going to escape by climbing up the shaft, a rope was lowered down and one of the trapped miners succeeded in tying it round his body, allowing the men on the surface to pull him up. More men were saved by this method, but it was far too slow and with the condition of the miners deteriorating by the minute, they were soon too weak to tie a knot. The rescuers knew that that time was rapidly run out and the entombed men would be lost if they didn't devise a faster and safer method of bringing them up.

A pair of temporary pulleys were quickly constructed above the shaft and with a rope attached to a makeshift hutch; there was now a way of transporting the seriously ill and unconscious men from the pit bottom.

The problem of the smoke which was still pouring from the pit was partially solved by Mr *Austine,* one on the local coal-masters, who suggested a means of redirecting the smoke from the fire to one side of the shaft, by installing a temporary vent, made up from poles thrown across the mouth of the mine. Tarred cloths attached to the poles were then lowered down into the mine, creating a vent, giving the rescuers a better chance of reaching the trapped men.

*Walter Nelson* a partner in the firm who owned the colliery was frantically looking for volunteers to descend the pit and offering all sorts of rewards. The miners present were understandably reluctant to allow themselves to be lowered 240 feet down into the burning pit, in a hutch tied to a rope which was being lowered and raised by the brute strength of the rescuers working on the surface.

One incredibly brave man, an ironstone miner called *Andrew Hunter,* stepped forward and volunteered to be the first man to go down into the underground inferno. In an attempt to filter out the smoke and fumes, he tied a rag across his mouth and nose and climbing into the hutch, was lowered down into the unknown.

Arriving at the bottom of the shaft, he found that his carbide light was unable to penetrate the smoke and gloom. Groping about in the darkness, in the indescribable conditions of a burning pit, Andrew soon found that he was making very little headway. Deciding to return to the surface, he sent up a signal indicating that he wanted to be drawn up.

When he arrived at the pit bank, he reported on the condition of the shaft and underground workings. He told of how it was almost impossible to see anything in the smoke filled mine and that alone and without a light, he could do nothing, but with decent lamps and assistance, he would be willing to go back down and give it another try.

At this point, another man called *Fleming,* who had been standing among the crowd listening to his story, stepped forward and volunteered to accompany Hunter down the shaft. Slowly and steadily, they were lowered down into the smoke filled pit. On reaching the pit bottom, the two men got out of the hutch and with their hastily issued safety lamps barely penetrating the gloom, they started their search of the workings. Inch by inch, they crawled on their hands and knees, looking for the men they knew were there and at last, not far from the shaft, they found a group of unconscious men and started dragging them one at a time back to the hutch, to be hauled to the surface.

A number of men were brought up this way, but because of the appalling underground conditions, the two rescuers were soon overcome by the smoke. With their lungs feeling as if they were on fire and finding it almost impossible to breathe, the men desperately signalled the surface to lower down the hutch. Crawling into it, they were found collapsed in a heap and unconscious from smoke inhalation when the hutch was drawn up to the surface. Immediately their places were taken by other volunteers and the slow unbelievably dangerous process of bringing men out of the burning pit continued.

As the stretchers were carried from the pithead, shrieks of relief and joy could be heard as survivors were recognised by their relatives. For some of the miners help had arrived too late and as stretcher after stretcher was carried across the yard in pouring rain, the wails and sobs which echoed round the colliery, confirmed to the silent waiting crowd, that another man or boy had lost his life.

Miners' cottages at the pit took on the appearance of a hospital. Every room was prepared to receive the suffering, the dead and the dying, as one by one, the men were brought up the pit. Here in this makeshift casualty clearing station, miners' mothers, wives, sisters and daughters fought a desperate battle with death, as side by side they worked flat out with five local doctors, in a desperate attempt to save the unconscious men.

By 9 o'clock, 28 men had been rescued and harrowing eyewitness accounts from the rescues parties, told of how the men who remained trapped underground, were "*lying huddled together, like lifeless corpses and all insensible.*" Two young brothers had been found dead, lying locked together inside a hutch where they had gone after becoming exhausted trying to clear the shaft.

At half past nine, *Claude Neilson* (40) was brought to the surface, but died soon afterwards; despite desperate efforts to revive him. He left a wife and six children, one of whom was only a baby.

The superhuman efforts of the rescue parties continued, but the rescuers themselves were getting into difficulty because of the thick smoke and choke damp. Within minutes of going down the shaft, they too were on the verge of collapsing. The rescue took twelve hours from the start of the fire, until the last man was brought up. Most of the men who had been brought out alive were unconscious and very seriously ill.

Late on Wednesday evening and during the early hours of Thursday morning, the bodies of the men and boys who had died were taken home by cart, with their sobbing relatives walking behind them.

One of the rescued men, *Neil Thomson,* died the following day and *David Maxwell* died eleven day's later. In all, a total of thirteen men and boys lost their lives. Among the dead were three pairs of brothers; the *Hamiltons*, the *Potters* and the *Craigs*. For one young man *Thomas Currie*, it was his first and last day at the pit. He had started as a driver only that morning.

The cause of the fire was the cube or ventilation furnace at the pit bottom setting fire to the sooty deposit on the wood lining the shaft. Once ignited, the burning soot set fire to the wood within an unbelievably short time. Only five minutes prior to the smoke issuing from the shaft, three men had travelled up it and had seen nothing unusual.

The underground fire was eventually extinguished after the shaft was sealed with a wood and clay cap to cut off the oxygen supply. Once it was safe to do so, the cap was removed, major repairs carried out, and the colliery reopened.

It was months before some of the rescued miners recovered from their ordeal and even then, it was doubted if they would ever be fit enough to work in the pits again. Only the generosity of the public and local colliers stopped the bereaved and injured from starving.

The disaster fund set up to help the people affected meant that financial assistance was paid on a weekly basis for some months after the accident. However, the spectre of the four dead miners' widows living off of the pittance they received from the Parish Poor Relief, haunted many who witnessed it. The same poverty awaited the families of the men unable to work because their lungs were irreversibly damaged by smoke and fumes.

The roadway from the neighbouring pit was never finished, as it became apparent during the course of the rescue, it was not going to be required.

Five months after the Dykehead disaster, in an accident at New Hartley Colliery, Northumberland, 204 men and boys were entombed when the giant beam of the pumping engine snapped in two and 21 tons of cast iron and debris cascaded down the colliery's only pit. It was almost a week before the rescue parties managed to gain access to the workings and when they did, they found all 204 miners dead from gas poisoning.

Following this tragedy, a bill was passed making it compulsory as from January 1865, for all coal mines to have at least two shafts, ensuring that in the event of an accident, trapped miners would have a second escape route. Prior to the passing of this law, many hundreds of miners died entombed in coal mines, with no means of escape. Many of the men and boys died a slow, lingering, horrendous death from starvation.

The incredible bravery displayed by the rescuers at Dykehead Colliery was rewarded by the paltry sum of less than three pounds each, given to them by Wilson & Co., the colliery owners. This company had spent only £139 on the expenses involved in the rescue and the burying of the dead.

At least fourteen miners volunteered and were lowered down the shaft into conditions that were indescribable; two of the men are known to have gone down at least twice to rescue the trapped miners. Most of the names of these brave men are lost in the mists of time; with five exceptions, *Andrew Hunter* ironstone miner, *Robert Hutchison* collier and *James Harris* fireman, all employed by *Mr Nisbet,* coal-master at Ferniegair Colliery and *James Graham* and *Fleming,* the first miner to volunteer..

The names of the rescued are also lost, except for two*, James Muir* and *Daniel Faulds*. In 1879 the Hamilton Advertiser reported on the death of oversman *Daniel Faulds*, who it said was one of the Dykehead survivors. The obituary told of how he had made a remarkable escape from the burning pit by climbing up the shaft and then went on to describe how he met his death on 2nd October, 1879, when he was crushed to death by a roof fall in Dykehead colliery. --------THE PIT HAD FINALLY CLAIMED HIM.

## THE VICTIMS

| | |
|---|---|
| ALEXANDER HAMILTON | 16 |
| DAVID HAMILTON | 21 |
| JOHN POTTER | 34 |
| THOMAS POTTER | 19 |
| JOHN CRAIG | 18 |
| HUGH CRAIG | 15 |
| FRANCIS CASEY | 19 |
| CLAUDE NEILSON | 40 |
| THOMAS MILLER | 23 |
| McLETCHIE BAXTER | 25 |
| NEIL THOMSON | 25 |
| DAVID MAXWELL | 19 |
| THOMAS CURRIE | 18 |

*Dykehead Rows, the miners' cottages which were used to treat the survivors.*
*Photograph courtesy of Larkhall Heritage Group*

*Photograph courtesy of Larkhall Heritage Group.*

# KNOWN DYKEHEAD/SUMMERLEE COLLIERY DEATHS

| DATE | NAME | AGE | CAUSE OF DEATH |
|------|------|-----|----------------|
| 07.08.1861 | McLETCHIE BAXTER | 25 | FIRE IN SHAFT |
| " | FRANCIS CASEY | 19 | FIRE IN SHAFT |
| " | JOHN CRAIG | 18 | FIRE IN SHAFT |
| " | HUGH CRAIG | 15 | FIRE IN SHAFT |
| " | THOMAS CURRIE | 18 | FIRE IN SHAFT |
| " | ALEX. HAMILTON | 16 | FIRE IN SHAFT |
| " | DAVID HAMILTON | 21 | FIRE IN SHAFT |
| " | DAVID MAXWELL | 19 | FIRE IN SHAFT |
| " | THOMAS MILLER | 23 | FIRE IN SHAFT |
| " | CLAUDE NEILSON | 40 | FIRE IS SHAFT |
| " | JOHN POTTER | 24 | FIRE IN SHAFT |
| " | THOMAS POTTER | 19 | FIRE IN SHAFT |
| 07.08.1861 | NEIL THOMSON | 25 | FIRE IN SHAFT |
| 21.03.1867 | ROBERT WILSON | 14 | CRUSHED BY HUTCHES. |
| 15.12.1867 | RICHARD WILLIAMS | 16 | CRUSHED BETWEEN CAGE AND DOORHEAD |
| 27.02.1873 | GARDINER BELL | 38 | ROOF FALL |
| 12.12.1876 | JAMES SWEENY | 24 | ROOF FALL (30 Cwts) |
| 17.02.1877 | WILLIAM MITCHELL | 22 | ROOF FALL (10 Cwts) |
| 19.03.1878 | JOHN CHAPPEL | 23 | CRUSHED UNDER CAGE |
| 02.10.1879 | DANIEL FAULDS | 40 | ROOF FALL (Multiple injuries) |
| 29.11.1886. | GEORGE MAIR | 42 | ROOF FALL |
| 20.01.1894 | JOHN BARNES | 58 | ROOF FALL |
| 29.06.1899 | ROBERT SCOTT | 53 | ROOF FALL (5 Cwts. Multiple injuries) |
| 11.01.1908 | JAMES McGHIE | 68 | FALL OF COAL |
| 09.06.1907 | GEORGE FRAME | 23 | NO DETAILS (Fractured skull) |
| 07.10.1908 | ROBERT McQUEEN | 50 | FEACTURED PELVIS INTERNAL INJURIES |
| 14.06.1912 | DAVID PHILLIPS | 52 | FALL OF COAL FROM FACE (one ton) |
| 25.04.1916 | ARCHIBALD BANKS | 57 | ROOF FALL |
| " | ARCHIBALD BANKS Jnr | 18 | ROOF FALL |
| " | THOMAS RUSSELL | 18 | ROOF FALL |
| 09.07.1916 | JOHN CRAW | 14 | CAUGHT IN THE CREEPER CHAIN |
| 21.11.1917 | WILLIAM HAMILTON | 35 | ROOF FALL (2 ½ ton stone) |
| 26.03.1919 | WILLIAM D. CAIRNS | 27 | CRUSHED BY HUTCH. |
| 02.03.1922 | JAMES S. CLARK | 23 | SEVERE HEAD INJURIES |
| 19.10.1929 | ANDREW MUIR | 27 | ROOF FALL (Compression of chest and face) |
| 31.08.1937 | ROBERT FARRELL | 35 | NO DETAILS |
| 23.04.1937 | JOHN McCUTCHEON | 22 | ROOF FALL (Stone -- 4ft X 3ft.) |
| 09.05.1939 | ALEX. STEWART | 36 | FELL DOWN SHAFT (360 ft) |

# THE
# GREENFIELD BOILER EXPLOSION
## 9/4/1874

On Thursday, 18th May 1859, Hamilton's Provost *Nisbet,* with much ceremony, cut the first sod of his new colliery which lay on the lands of Greenfield farm Burnbank.

*Ord Adams* coal master had recently sunk bores on the grounds of Greenfield at a cost of £300 and had found coal in seams seven feet thick but for some reason had given up the enterprise. Provost *James Nisbet,* a coalmaster who had already sunk and developed Ferniegair Colliery, had then leased this land from owner *Lewis Potter* Esquire, Udston and he was hoping to increase his fortune by harvesting this great mineral wealth lying 700 feet underground.

However, the sinking of the shafts was plagued by problems, among them severe flooding which was so bad, that specially designed and exceptionally powerful steam pumps and engines had to be built to cope with removing the huge amounts of water. Six enormous egg ended boilers 30 feet long, 5 ½ feet in diameter with plates 3/8th of an inch thick and working at a pressure of 40 to 50 lbs per square inch were required to power the engine. The boilers were installed three on either side of the high chimney.

The extra expenditure required to develop Greenfield Colliery bankrupted Provost *Nisbe*t who, after spending £14,000 on the project, came to the end of his money and his credit and found himself in Glasgow Bankruptcy Court on 29th Sep. 1863. The colliery was then acquired by the Hamilton Coal Co.

Built close to the colliery were the colliery houses which were rented to the miners. Known as Greenfield Rows there were 100 houses, 22 single ends, 76 room and kitchens, 1 two room and kitchen for the oversman and a 5 roomed house for the manager. For the children of the "Rows" there was a school which was also used for various social occasions.

On the evening of Thursday 16th April, 1874, a prayer meeting was being held in the school and the preacher, *Charles Edgar* of Chapel Street U.P. Church was being assisted by a young Californian student. Quite a number of people had come from Glasgow to Greenfield for the meeting, but many of the village's male population had retreated to Hamilton, leaving to the women and children to go themselves.

Up at the pit several children were hanging about; brothers *John* and *William Hailes* were standing at the furnace room door heating themselves and another two youngsters were sitting near the top of the boiler seat.

Standing at the door of the engine-house were two engineers, *John Miller* and *James Morgan* who were deeply engrossed in conversation when suddenly, without any warning, one of boilers exploded, split into three pieces and shot over the heads of the terrified children. Both engineers were burned by boiling water and seriously injured by the debris as pieces of shattered boiler hurled in opposite directions. One part travelled eastwards for three hundred feet destroying everything in its path including railway lines, wagons and telegraph wires.

Another part, 20 feet in length, headed for the miners' rows and struck a house at the north east corner then, continuing on its path of destruction, shot at high speed along the street, tearing off roofs, demolishing walls and finally, reaching the schoolhouse seconds after the preacher had announced the first hymn. The boiler crashed through the roof almost destroying the southern gable wall and stopped only 3 inches from the floor, with its massive weight supported by the cross beam of the roof.

The people seated at the north side of the school-house escaped with shock and minor injuries, but those at the south side where the boiler had come to rest, were buried under tons of wood, slate, stone, red hot water and metal from the boiler.

The sound of the explosion was heard for miles around and brought in hundreds of men from the surrounding district to assist with the rescue of victims trapped at the pithead, their homes and in the schoolhouse.

The men urged on by the terrified screams of the trapped victims, laboured as if possessed, tearing at the debris with their bare hands, but it was some hours before many of them could be rescued.

At the schoolhouse, the boiler was lying in a slanting position from the South East to the North West, with one end suspended above the floor and the other end resting on a surviving part of the south wall. Trapped underneath, were many of the worshipers, whose precarious hold on life, depended on the strength of the roof joists which were already straining and groaning under the boiler's massive weight.

Before the injured could be set free, the boiler had to be secured and this was achieved by the rescuers levering it up three or four inches with planks of wood and then holding it in that position until a dumb screw (screw jack) was put in place. With the aid of the screw, the boiler was raised further still and then secured, allowing the rescuers access to the trapped congregation.

Among the people who were trapped were the *Maxwell* family. Mrs *Maxwell* was only slightly injured as was the four months old baby she had been holding in her arms. Their eight years old son *Robert* was not so fortunate. Crushed by the boiler he was dead when rescuers reached him. *Robert* it was said had not been at all keen to go to the meeting, but had been coaxed at the last minute into attending.

*George Moffat* and his wife had been sitting at the south wall with their daughter *Jeannie* age 7, when the boiler hit the building. Trapped under the weight of the boiler, *George* was lucky to survive. His wife was seriously injured, but *Jeannie,* pinned to the ground by debris, suffocated before she could be released.
*William Davis* and his wife *Helen* were injured when debris fell round about them. *William* escaped with an injured leg but *Helen,* heavily pregnant, was severely bruised about the body.

Up at the furnace room, twelve years old *William Hailes* was being dug out and his pleading cries of *"Oh save my wee brother"* tore at the hearts of the rescuers. When asked where his brother was he replied, *"He is standing ahint me;"* but there was no trace of him. When his wee brother *John Hailes,* aged 5, was eventually found, he was dead.

The engineman *John Millar,* a married man and father of three children, died from his injuries at his High Blantyre home the following day, bringing the total of dead to four, with twenty eight men women and children seriously injured.

Many people had narrow escapes; of the two children who had been sitting on the boiler seat at the time of the explosion, only one of them received slight injuries. Another twelve children who had been playing rounders in the street at Greenfield Rows when the boiler flew through the village miraculously escaped with only minor injuries.

Part of a large valve landed 150 feet away, smashing through the roof of a house where a miner was sitting at the fire with a child on his knee. Both were uninjured.

One old lady who lived in the house next to the school, escaped uninjured when part of her roof was lifted off and debris rained round about her as she lay in bed. In another house three friends who had been sitting having a cup of tea, also escaped with only minor injuries when a shower of bricks, timber and slate fell down on top of them.

Many of the colliery houses were seriously damaged, debris lay everywhere and it was almost impossible to walk along the street. The houses tenanted by miners *Cochrane, Mason, Sim, Struthers* and *McGregor* were left without roofs. In these devastated homes, pictures hung askew on walls and furniture covered by debris stood waiting for the houses being made safe enough to enter.

That night, the darkness of the "Rows" was broken by a solitary miner's lamp hanging outside a door and the occasional gentle glow from an oil lamp shining through a window. Inside the damaged houses, women were nursing the injured and laying out the dead.

The day of the explosion had been a fast day and the railway between Hamilton and Glasgow had been exceptionally busy, with almost 3,000 passengers using the trains. Had the explosion been five minutes later, the boiler would have cut through a crowded train. As it was, the quick thinking of pointsman *George Wilson* averted a rail disaster, when, on hearing the noise of the explosion, he immediately put on the block signals and prevented the train reaching the damaged railway lines.

Two days later, the funerals of the dead children took place. *Robert Maxwell* was buried in Rutherglen, *John Hailes* was interred in Hamilton Cemetery and *Jeannie Moffat* in Old Monkland Churchyard. The following Tuesday engineman *John Millar* was buried in Blantyre.

*Ralph Moore* H.M. Inspector of Mines, reporting on the cause of the explosion, said that although he could find no evidence that the boiler had been short of water, there was evidence of substantial corrosion and water leakage about the water line. He reported that the boilers had been thoroughly worn out and on his suggestion they were replaced by six double flued boilers, which had were capable of working safely at 50 to 60lbs to the square inch.

Considering the scale of the explosion and the size of the area involved, it was a miracle that the death toll was only four. Another miracle took place three days later, when injured miner's wife, *Helen Davis,* who had suffered severe abdominal bruising, gave birth to a healthy baby girl whom they named *Jessie.* It was eight days before her father was fit to register the birth.

Despite the explosion and the colliery's close proximity, the Davis family continued to live at Greenfield Rows. Twenty-five years later, on the last day of a century which had seen Hamilton transformed by industry into the largest and most important town in Lanarkshire, William and *Helen Davis* celebrated the marriage of their miracle child Jessie to coal miner *William Wilson* and watched as she left her Greenfield home to start a new life, with a new husband, in a new home…..IN A NEW CENTURY.

# KILLED

| JOHN MILLER | 34 | Engineman |
| JOHN HAILES | 5 | Miner's son |
| ROBERT MAXWELL | 8 | Underground manager's son |
| JEANIE MOFFAT | 7 | Miner's daughter |

# THE INJURED

*JAMES MORGAN.* (28) Engine-Keeper. Severely injured, cut and burned about face, hands, arms and legs.

*GEORGE MOFFAT,* miner Mrs MOFFAT and two sons. Mr and Mrs Moffat severely injured. Two children were only slightly injured.
(Less than two years later on 25th January 1876 *George Moffat* lost his foot and ankle in an accident in the same colliery.)

*JANET KERR or RENNIE,* wife of *Alexander Rennie,* fireman. Cut severely on head and bruised on body, seriously injured.

*WILLIAM HAILES,* (12) son of *Joseph Hailes,* miner.

*ROBERT MAXWELL.* Sen. Mrs MAXWELL and child four months old both injured but not severely.

*ELIZABETH RENNIE,* wife of *Wilson Rennie,* (fireman,) right leg injured

GEORGE ROBERTSON. (14) Son of *Archibald Robertson*, miner, leg injury. He had been playing at ball with a number of his companions near the scene of the accident and their safety was ascribed to the fact that they were sheltered by the stalk or chimney which stood at the west end of the pit engine-house.

WILLIAM DAVIS, (miner,) and his wife HELEN DAVIS. William injured about leg and his wife (who was in a delicate state of health) bruised about body.

MARGARET MARSHALL, wife of *Gabriel Marshall* miner was bruised about the shoulder by a joist. ---She had four of her children with her, two hurt and two were slightly injured.

MARY MARSHALL, (9) daughter of above bruised about head and body.
*Alex. Marshall.* (15) brother of *Mary,* slightly injured about head.

HELEN HASTIE, (16) JOHN HASTIE (1), JANET HASTIE. (9), WILLIAM HASTIE *(5)* children of the pit manager were all slightly injured.

CHARLES EDGAR, missionary. Cut and bruised about head and back and severe shock to nervous system.

HENRY WILSON, (12) son of *Robert Wilson,* roadman was slightly injured on head and right leg.

JAMES STRUTHERS, (18) son of *Thomas Struthers*, collier was severely injured about head and bruised about back.

DAVID WILSON, (7) son of Thomas Wilson, miner, received severe cuts to head and face.

MARTHA SEATON, (14) an orphan residing with *George Johnstone*, miner received cuts to back of head.

JANET MAXWELL *or MUIR*, wife of *Robert Muir* fireman was severely bruised on left limb and all over body.

ANDREW FOYE *or FOYER,* (10) son of *William Foye* received cuts to head, leg bruises and slight burns to head and face.

\* \* \*

## KNOWN GREENFIELD COLLIERY DEATHS

| DATE | NAME | AGE | CAUSE OF DEATH |
|---|---|---|---|
| 10.02.1866 | WM. DOCHARTY | 70 | DROWNED IN PIT |
| 31.01.1867 | DAVID BLACK | 27 | EXPLOSION |
| " | ALEX MILLER | 38 | EXPLOSION |
| 02.03.1868 | WM. McGINNES | 22 | ROOF FALL ( 5 tons) |
| 13.01.1871 | ROBERT BROWN | 22 | ROOF FALL |

**Greenfield Colliery deaths continued.**

| DATE | NAME | AGE | CAUSE OF DEATH |
|---|---|---|---|
| 16.10.1872 | WM. CARRICK | 52 | FELL DOWN SHAFT (780 ft) |
| " | ANDREW CARRICK | 17 | FELL DOWN SHAFT |
| " | THOS. DOCHERTY | 30 | FELL DOWN SHAFT |
| 03.01.1874 | OWEN O'HARE | 44 | BOTH LEGS FRACTURED |
| 09.04.1874 | JOHN MILLER | 34 | BOILER EXPLOSION |
| " | JOHN HAILES | 5 | BOILER EXPLOSION |
| " | RBT. MAXWELL | 8 | BOILER EXPLOSION |
| " | JEANIE MOFFAT | 7 | BOILER EXPLOSION |
| 09.05.1875 | JOHN STEWART | 13 | RUN DOWN BY HUTCHES |
| 12.05.1876 | JOHN STEVENSON | 40 | FALL OF COAL AT FACE (4 tons) |
| 09.01.1877 | THOS. DOCHERTY | 20 | ROOF FALL (4 tons) |
| 15.05.1877 | JOHN WILSON | 14 | CAUGHT IN HAULAGE MACHINERY |
| 30.08.1878 | JOHN GREENHORN | 18 | RUN OVER BY HUTCH |
| 02.02,1879 | JAS. JOHNSTON | 27 | ROOF FALL (13 cwt) |
| 25.11.1880 | THOS WYPER | 15 | ROOF FALL (Head and chest injuries) |
| 01.02.1882 | DAVID LEES | 31 | ROOF FALL |
| 09.04.1884 | PETER DOWNIE | 24 | ROOF FALL (Amputation of right arm) |
| 03.10.1884 | ALEX. JENKINS | 22 | ROOF FALL |
| 24.07.1885 | DAVID DUNN | 57 | COMPOUND FRACTURE OF LEG |
| 24.09.1886 | JAS. BULLOCH | 53 | BURSTING OF STEAM PIPE |
| 18.01.1887 | RBT. RICHARDSON | 13 | FELL DOWN SHAFT (840 Feet) |
| 02.04.1891 | JAMES GRAY | 59 | NO DETAILS (Multiple injuries) |
| 15.06.1892 | WILLIAM BOYD | 18 | ROOF FALL (18 tons) |
| 30.11.1897 | JOSEPH CHAPMAN | 46 | ROOF FALL (Back broken) |
| 25.09.1901 | JAMES MURDOCH | 26 | FALL OF COAL (Internal injuries) |
| 07.02.1904 | JAMES BROWN | 15 | HEAD CRUSHED BY HUTCHES |
| 13.12.1904 | GEORGE GLEN | 36 | RUN DOWN BY HUTCHES |
| 23.01.1908 | JOHN WILSON | 41 | FELL DOWN SHAFT (780 feet) |
| 04.06.1909 | AUDLEY McKEOWN | 62 | ROOF FALL (Multiple fractures) |
| 14.09.1909 | FRANCIS SLAVEN | 16 | ROOF FALL (Fractured skull) |
| 10.11.1909 | EDWARD LUSK | 43 | ROOF FALL (Fractured skull) |
| 11.10.1911 | JAS. McDOWALL | 55 | RUN DOWN BY WAGONS |
| 30.08.1915 | JAMES HUNTER | 41 | ROOF FALL |
| 25.09.1917 | DAVID McBETH | 49 | ROOF FALL (Fractured skull) |
| 12.12.1917 | DAVID SMITH | 57 | ROOF FALL (Multiple fractures) |
| 30.05.1918 | JOSEPH VICKERS | 52 | ACCIDENT AT COAL FACE |
| 27.08.1919 | JOSEPH ROBB | 49 | COMPOUND FRACTURE OF THIGH |
| 29.01.1920 | WM. STANNAGE | 14 | CAUGHT IN MACHINERY (Multiple injuries) |
| 21.02.1920 | JOHN McFARLANE | 64 | HEAD INJURIES |
| 04.04.1922 | WM. BOLE | 67 | CRUSHED BETWEEN ROOF AND BOGGIE |
| 01.08.1922 | ADAM CASEMENT | 34 | ROOF FALL |
| 07.02.1924 | ISAAC CALLISON | 42 | SHOT FIRING ACCIDENT |
| 10.11.1926 | JAMES JAAP | 51 | ROOF FALL (Traumatic asphyxia) |
| 23.01.1929 | HUGH C. MURRAY | 70 | FELL DOWN SHAFT |
| 19.11.1929 | THOS. FINEGAN | 27 | CRUSHED BETWEEN WALL AND HUTCH |
| 08.11.1931 | ARCHD. ARCHIBALD | 42 | ROOF FALL |

# THE HERO

There is praise for the hero of air, land and sea,
For those who have worthily won the V.C.,
But what of the hero who works down the mine,
Who risks unseen dangers all the time,
No medals for him, no honour, 'tis true,
Down he must go, his toil to pursue,
'Midst poisonous gases, foul air and grime—
The hero who works down the mine.

At the break of day he trudges along,
Off to his work, with the lilt of a song,
Down the mine—it's no terrors for him,
Though many a time things are sordid and grim
No sunshine to guide him—only a tiny red peep,
And to his work he has often to creep,
So let us give honour at some little time
To the hero who works down the mine.

Alas! What is that? A deafening sound—
Something has happened; soon the news
    will go round,
An explosion, 'tis true, God help those below,
As wives, sweethearts, brothers, to the pithead
    they go,
Volunteers are called for to face life or death
To help save their comrades trapped underneath,
And who are they who assist at this time?—
Brother heroes who work down the mine.

As the rescuers descend to the mine below,
With dauntless courage, onward they go,
Searching their way through debris and stone,
All that's to guide them is a sigh or a moan,
As another poor mortal breathes his last,
Gone from this world, his troubles all past,
Thy duty done, the honour be thine—
The hero who works down the mine.

As the watchers wait at the pithead gate,
Anxious as to their beloved one's fate,
Again they hear the clang of the bell—
Alas! 'tis the note of a funeral knell;
The women shed tears, men bow the head,
As the rescuers slowly and softly tread,
So let us honour his name and enshrine
The hero who works down the mine.

*Robert Cameron,*
*Burnbank*
*Circa 1935*

56

# THE WIDOW'S WAIL

Oh! Let me see them ance again,
    My dear dear deid bring hame!
I ken they're gane—oh God abune!
    Yon fearfu' blast o' flame!
Awa' fause Hope—I ken ye're fause;
    But let, oh let me see,
The dear, dear forms jist ance again—
    Oh, bring them hame tae me!

Hoo could I be sae blythe yestreen?
    An' was it then the last
O' a' oor sacred e'enin' walks,
    ( O pleasures ever past)
Amang oor bairns on Calder banks?
    Ah! whaur's my bravest three?
An' Johnnie, oh! My love, my life!
    Thou kin' guid man tae me.

They ca'd him rude—puir narrow sauls—
    They ca'd him rude and low;
'Cause whiles he spak the scaithin' truth,
    Was falsehood's open foe;
But honest worth could licht the lowe,
    O' love, in yon blue e'e,
An' warm the heart, an' wake the tongue,
    That sang sae sweet tae me.

I ken it's useless yaumerin'—
    'Twill ne'er restore the past;
But oh! It's unco sair tae thol
    this bitter, bitter blast!
Oh! Could I but hae pressed their broos,
    Hae seen my dear anes dee;
But ah! They faucht sae far below
    Withouten help frae me.

Ay, open wide yer purses, frien's,
    I wat fu' weel ye may,
For Britain's treasure dear we pay—
    Its proof—this direfu' day;
But, oh, it's sweet—yer sympathy,
    It soothes me sae tae see,
Ye'll fend my puir wee bairnies left,
    Noo doubly dear tae me.

*Thomas Stewart.*
*Circa. 1877.*

# THE BLANTYRE EXPLOSION

## 22/10/1877

A great many words have been written about Scotland's worst pit disaster which took place on 22nd October, 1877 and I have no intention of adding to them.

It is suffice to say that approximately 216 men and boys lost their lives in a series of explosions caused by the ignition of fire-damp and coal dust.

Some families lost four members and how the women left behind coped with the loss is beyond our understanding.

*Hugh Brown* was not only a survivor of the explosion, he was also a member of one of the first rescue teams to attempt to clear the debris from and gain entry to No. 3 shaft.

In 1927, fifty years after the disaster, this obviously highly intelligent man had the story of his experiences of the disaster published in the Hamilton Advertiser.

Nothing anyone could write would describe the scene half as well as *Hugh Brown's* account of the disaster, for he was there and only someone in his situation could tell the true story of the disaster as he has.

It is to his memory and to the memory of all the men and boys who lost their lives, the rescue teams who displayed incredible bravery and the men, women and children left without husbands, fathers, sons, brothers and grandsons, that I include his account of the disaster.------ *Wilma S. Bolton.*

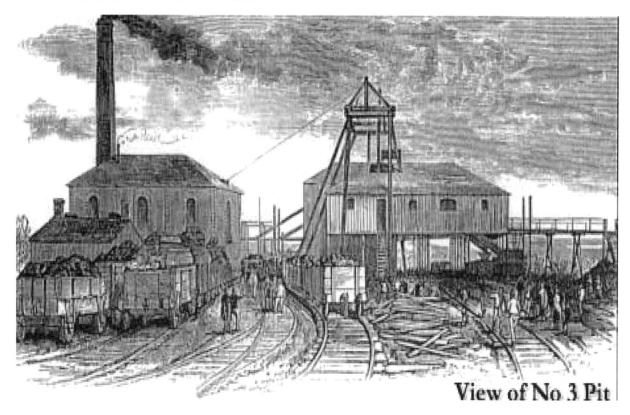

**View of No. 3 Pit**

# A TRUE STORY OF THE BLANTYRE COLLIERY EXPLOSION
## October 22nd 1877
## BY ONE OF THE EXPLORERS

*Calling for volunteers to go underground*

For many years I have had a strong desire to put on record my experiences as an explorer in that great colliery disaster, but hitherto I have not had sufficient time at my disposal. Now, having a little leisure, I shall try to give some of my experiences in as clear and truthful a manner as I can.

In the first place, I may state that I had been employed in Blantyre Colliery for about two years prior to the disaster. I had worked for a short time in No. 3 pit and in several places in No.2. At the time of the explosion however, I was working in the north side of No. 2 pit and was double shifting with *Andrew Clark* and his neighbour (a boy). We were driving the main dook leading to No. 4 pit as a communication. There was a companion dook in which *John Nelson* and *Andrew Forrest* wrought on the one shift and *Gilbert Harper* and his neighbour on the other, whilst *George Watt* and his neighbour were employed driving places through at certain intervals to connect the two dooks. This was for the purpose of carrying the ventilation. This place that *George Watt* and his neighbour worked was only single shifted, *Samuel Nelson* and I worked together as neighbours and it was our day-shift that week. *John Nelson,* Samuel's brother and *Andrew Forrest* worked together on the same shift in the back dook.

At the time of the explosion I was engaged in steming a hole for the purpose of blasting down the coal, when suddenly my hands were stayed by a strange sensation which I could not describe very well. The whole place shook as if an earthquake had taken place. All sound was gone. I felt as you would feel if you were to put your fingers into your ears. This was due to the fact that the air was cut off. This continued only for a short time and then to our great relief the air came back.

When things had returned to their normal, I said to my neighbour; "*Some poor soul has caught it this morning,*" meaning by this that some one of our fellow workers had been burned, because we knew that an explosion had taken place somewhere.

Samuel only answered by saying: "*I doot it*" meaning that he was afraid someone had been burned by an explosion of gas. We had no idea that the explosion was so great and that so many lives had been lost. While Samuel and I were discussing with each other as to the locality of the explosion his brother John called us to hurry up and get on our clothing, because we were only partially dressed. I answered saying that we would fire our shot first but he said "Never mind the shot, come away quickly." So we went away and left the shot unfired.

We joined *George Watt, Andrew Forrest, and John Nelson* in a consultation as to where the explosion was likely to have been. *George Watt*, a man of large experience said he thought it was likely to be in the long wall section, about 100 yards further up the dook.

When we got to the entrance into that section he suggested that we should wait there until he returned to us. After he had gone away I suggested to the others that we might have our breakfast. They agreed to my proposal, so we sat down and had our breakfast.

After a short time *George Watt* returned and along with him were all the men who had wrought in that section. No explosion had taken place there, so we wondered where it could have been. All at once we were startled by cry of the pony driver, *Willie Welsh*, who told us that all the men in the pit had been killed and that his father had been killed too. We then began to realise the gravity of the situation. We all joined the pony driver and made our way towards the pit bottom. On our way towards the pit bottom we found that the air was very much mixed with black-damp, so *George Watt* told us to put our scarfs over our mouths, which we did.

On reaching the pit bottom, we were horrified at the spectacle which met out gaze, men dead and dying all around us. The groans of those who were alive were pitiful to hear and we discovered that the shaft was wrecked and we had no idea as to when it would be repaired.

We were face to face with that great monster called Death, because the black damp was coming over from the south side of the pit, making it difficult for us to breathe; and with no prospects of getting up the shaft, we resigned ourselves to our fate. Even then we did not realise the narrow escape which we had by the air being cut off, nor did we realise the full extent of the explosion. It was only when we got up the pit and learned that No. 3 pit had blasted as well as No. 2.

Both pits were involved in the explosion. I should explain here how this came about. Well the explanation is this: - They were both downcast shafts with the return at No. 5 burning for the purpose of increasing the ventilation. The air coming down No. 2 Pit split at the bottom, one half going to the north side and the other to the south, both returning to the upcast shaft at No. 5 but No. 3 was also a downcast shaft.

The air, after coming down No. 3 shaft, travelled through the places in No. 3 pit and then joined the air coming from the south side of No. 2 pit. Both travelled together and aired the places to the rise in No. 2 pit south side and thence to the upcast shaft at No. 5. It must have been in this locality that the gas was kindled, because as every miner knows, the flame always goes against the air until the air gets too strong for the flame, hence an explosion. In this case, after the gas was kindled, the flame would travel against the air until it would come to the place where the two airs joined each other, the gas would divide itself into two halves, the one half travelling towards No. 3 pit bottom, so that there must have been two explosions at the same time. The air was cut off from us in the north side of No. 2 Pit, because it was a flame of fire that was going up the shaft.

Had No. 2 shaft been wrecked in the same way as No. 3 there would have been no one alive to tell the tale, for No. 3 shaft was completely closed. It took the workmen fully two hours to repair the shaft at No. 2. It was a great relief to those who were waiting at the pit bottom when the workmen came down and said that the shaft was now in a safe condition for them to ascend. There was a great scramble as to who should get on the first cage. It was a case of" the weakest to the wall."

During the time we were waiting at the pit bottom, *John Nelson* and I went over to the south side and lifted up a man who was still alive but was terribly burned and was groaning with pain. We could not recognise him because his face was as black as a piece of coal. We carried him across the pit bottom to the north side where the air was purer. We decided to take him up the shaft with us as he was able to stand on his feet and this made the task comparatively easy. When we got to the pit bank his relatives were waiting to receive him. We were told that the man's name was *Thomas Black* and that the two men who had taken him away were his two brothers.

While we were in conversation with the people who were assembled on the pit bank another cage came up and we were horrified to see his brother *Samuel* lying on the bottom of the cage quite unconscious. He had been overcome by the damp. After having him removed from the cage and put in a place of safety, his brother John said to me that I might go for *Robert Muir* to come and attend to him. This *Robert Muir* was a great friend of ours and he acted as our medical adviser. He lived in the village of High Blantyre, so I set off to run, but only got a few yards when I stumbled and fell. I got up again and began to run, with the same result. I believe I fell twenty times before I reached High Blantyre; my legs were so feeble that they could not bear the weight of my body. This was the effect of the black damp which I had swallowed. When I arrived at *Mr Muir's* place and told him how I felt and what had happened to Samuel he said I was to stay there while he attended to *Samuel.* On his return he gave me some medicine which made me all right again.

I then proceeded to go home to Barnhill where I had a wife and a baby boy. The same evening I went back to the colliery to find that the rescuing party had got up all the

61

dead bodies, which were scattered all over the pit bottom in No. 2 and had laid them out in order in a stable near the colliery offices. They were laid out in order for the purpose of identification and the general public were invited to come in and inspect them.

*Neil Douglas.*

This arrangement was under the charge of *Mr Neil Douglas* the cashier. Mr *Douglas* observed that on the body of one of the dead was a silver watch and some time afterwards he saw a suspicious looking person extracting the watch from the pocket of the dead man, so he laid hold of him and handed him over to the police. The crowd wanted to lynch him, but the police would not allow them to interfere with their prisoner. It was certainly a mean and contemptible form of theft, but some men are mean enough for anything.

Later in the evening there was an urgent appeal made by those in authority for volunteers to go down No. 2 pit, so I expressed my willingness to go down there and then. After a band of volunteers had been selected we went down to bottom of the pit, but were not allowed to leave the bottom without permission from those in authority. I might state here that *Mr Dickenson*, the Chief Inspector of Mines, was in charge of the arrangements. Of course he had three or four assistants with him, including Mr *Ralph Moore.* He had also with him about ten or twelve colliery managers from neighbouring collieries. The manager of Blantyre Colliery was not present because he was severely burnt on the pit-head at No. 3 pit by flames coming up the shaft. He was confined to his bed for months.

The arrangements made by this board of management included, among other things, a line of communication between the two pits. This was formed by placing men at a distance of about twenty yards apart, No's, 1, 2, and 3 right along the line. Each man was supplied with a Scotch gauze lamp. No. 1 had to cry at the pitch of his voice "all's well." And No. 2 had to cry the same and so on all along the line until No. 3 pit bottom was reached and then the cry "all's well," came again to No. 2 pit bottom.

This was to be kept up all night. I formed part of that line for a time. I was No. 15, but I was relieved later on by someone taking my place so that I was allowed to go into the interior of the workings. On reaching No. 3 pit bottom we discovered that the shaft was on fire and the burning wood was falling down the shaft, so it was decided to suspend further operations until the fire was extinguished because there was the danger of a second explosion, so we began to retrace our steps back towards No. 2 pit bottom, but on our way back we met *Dr William Grant* with a band of fresh men. He insisted upon going into some of the working places in a certain section of the pit called *Martin's* level, so we accompanied him into that section and found two men and one boy alive, but terribly burned all over the face and body. I don't remember their names, although I remember the incident quite distinctly. Under the directions of *Dr. Grant* they were carried on stretchers to the pit bottom and thence to the pit bank. They were taken into the engine-house where they were washed and dressed by *Dr. Grant,* but they died shortly afterwards. *Dr. Grant* did all he could do to save their lives, but they were too far gone to bring them round for in addition to their burns they had swallowed a considerable amount of black damp. This I will say of *Dr. Grant,* he proved himself to be a hero of the very first magnitude.

After this the officials concluded that it would be useless looking for any more men alive in either of the two pits and in view of the dangerous condition of the mine, it was agreed to suspend operations in No. 2 pit and to apply our energies to the extinguishing of the fire in No. 3 shaft and so the line of communication was no longer required.

The first step at No. 3 pit was to pump water down the shaft. After the officials had decided that the fire was out they appointed a band of men to go down the shaft to clear away the debris and to make a passage for the air to go down into the workings below. This was extremely dangerous work and it was very dirty too, so the men were supplied with suitable clothes and they were also supplied with food and refreshments. It was arranged that the men should work only four hours at a time. This work of clearing the shaft was under the charge of *Mr William Gilchrist.* There was a scarcity of men for that kind of work and in view of the fact that there were no restrictions in the supply of refreshments many of the men indulged too freely, with the result that they were not able to turn out to their work, so that the others had to do a double shift very often.

There were two men working there who lived beside me at Barnhill, viz., *Thomas Cook* and *John Bowie* and they asked me to go with them to work on the shaft, but I said that I never was used to that kind of work. They replied, "Never mind, we will show you what to do." I went along with them and did not return home for a whole week. I had a little sleep in the engine-house at the pit. It was arranged that three men would be sufficient to go down the shaft at one time, so *Thomas Cook, John Bowie* and myself got on to the kettle and were lowered down the shaft very slowly.

We had not gone far down when we met with the obstruction. We began by filling the kettle with stone and broken sticks and sending it up again to the pit bank. It took a considerable time before a hole was made through the debris to allow the kettle to go down through it. When this was accomplished we decided to go right down to the bottom which we did, with the result that we plunged into the water at the bottom to the depth of four feet and this water extended for a long distance both east and west of the bottom. After we recovered from our immersion we were horrified to see about twenty or thirty dead bodies floating on the surface of the water. The clothes had been burnt off of them by the fire.

*Taking timber down the shaft in the kettle during the recovery of the bodies*

We had to come up to the pit bank again and bring down timber to erect a platform in the pit bottom. We made a platform large enough to hold six bodies and went into the water up to our waist and brought out one of these dead bodies and wrapped it in a white cotton sheet and laid it upon this platform. We then went back for another and did the same with it and so on until we had the six collected together and then we began to make arrangements to have them taken up the pit. It was agreed that the best way to do this was to put one of the dead bodies into the kettle standing straight up and that my two comrades should stand one on the one side and one on the opposite side.

These two men had to guide the kettle up the shaft and it required very careful handling to guide the kettle through that narrow hole which was in the middle of the shaft; but these two men, *Bowie* and *Cook,* were experts at that kind of work. They got on to the side of the kettle and gave the signal for the engineman to raise them up, but I was left alone in the company of the other five dead bodies to await their return. I did not believe in ghosts but I must say I felt very unhappy during their absence. When they did come back we got another dead body into the inside of the kettle and they mounted on the sides of the kettle and gave the engineman the signal to hoist up and so I was left alone again. This was continued until all the dead bodies were taken up to the pit bank and then we started to wade through the water and fetch out more dead bodies and arrange them on the platform as before. This work was carried on for a considerable time until we got all the dead bodies out of the water. That finished my work in the shaft at No. 3 pit. *Bowie* and *Cook* continued at work repairing the shaft at No. 3 pit but I was sent back to work in No. 2. Pit under *Mr John Pickering.*

This was very great work, because the ventilation was completely destroyed by the explosion. We had stoppings to put in where they had been blown out and we had falls of roof to clear and timber to put up and we had canvas cloth to lead from room to room. Perhaps I should explain here that these two pits were worked on the stoop and room system. There was gas in nearly all of these rooms and this had to be cleared away before we could get to the dead bodies. When we got to the dead bodies we rolled them up in white sheets and putting them on stretchers carried them to the pit bottom and thence to the pit bank. This ended our part of the work but there were others on the pit bank who conveyed them to a large wooden shed which had been erected for a dressing station. This shed would be about 100 feet long and about 20 feet broad. In this shed were piled up a large number of coffins in readiness for the dead bodies. A large staff of undertakers were in attendance night and day. This was the place where people had to come to identify their relatives. This identification was chiefly done by parts of their clothing, but those who were brought out of No. 3 pit bottom had no clothes on so it must have been very difficult to identify them. They were greatly disfigured by the burning and the damp.

I had three very intimate friends who were working in the south side of No. 2 pit at the time of the explosion who were killed. I thought I would not have much difficulty in identifying them, but I was mistaken in this, for had it not been for their clothes and their initials being stamped on their tools I should not have been able to identify them. I helped to carry them out. One of them was my best man when I married. His name was *John Dobbie.* These three friends of mine did not seem to be burned at all, but they were swollen and disfigured by the damp.

The worst case that I had to handle was that of a family of the name of *Brown* who belonged to the Law, near Carluke. There was a father and three sons. They had been dead for three weeks and the smell was dreadful, The men who were along with me shrank back in horror and refused to handle them, but our leader *John Pickering* made an appeal for some one of us to help him roll the bodies on to the sheets which we had with us for that purpose. I braced up sufficient courage to undertake the work. *Pickering* and I got the bodies rolled on to the sheets and then laid them upon stretchers. The other men helped us to carry them to the pit bottom. That finished my work as an explorer in that great colliery disaster of 1877.

I never received anything in the shape of a reward for my service except a copy of the Bible from the National Bible Society of Scotland, with a very appropriate inscription on it. It quotes a passage of Scripture from Matthew's Gospel Chapter xxv. verse 40:- *"In as much as ye have done it unto one of these my brethren, ye have done it unto Me."* March 4th, 1927.   HUGH BROWN.

*Rescuers wearing shaftsmen's hats waiting their turn to go underground*

*No. 3 Pit*

# THE BLANTYRE OVERWINDING ACCIDENT
## 5/3/1878

In 1878, the village of Blantyre was still in deep shock from the tragic loss of 216 men and boys, killed on the morning of 22<sup>nd</sup> October, 1877, by a series of gas and dust explosions which ripped through William Dixon's No. 2 and No. 3 pits. The gruesome and dangerous task of removing victims and making the workings safe for the reopening of the pits had taken five weeks, with the work being carried out by volunteer miners, who were determined to recover the dead.

By the time the pit was ready for production, there was no shortage of miners to take the place of the men who were killed. Miners travelled from all over the country to get a job at Dixon's colliery. In the English coalfields where comparable disasters took place all too frequently, there were always great problems trying to employ men to take the place of the dead, but for some reason, this understandable reluctance on the part of the miners, did not manifest itself in Blantyre and the jobs were soon filled.

The depth of the shaft at Blantyre No. 3 Colliery was 155 fathoms, or 930 feet and at the bottom there was an 18 foot deep water filled sump. The shaft had two divisions with a double cage being fitted into each.

The safe negotiation of the cages up and down the shaft was the responsibility of a highly skilled winding engineman. One of the enginemen at No 3 Colliery was *Arthur Clelland,* a Larkhall man who had come to work at Dixon's during December, 1877.

On March 5th 1878, the day shift was almost over and 95 miners who had been working in the Splint seam had already returned to the surface. At the pit bottom, another seven men were waiting to ascend the pit and *James Brannigan,* pit bottomer, gave the usual signal of three strokes on the bell, indicating that men were waiting and received the signal back, "*that all was right*" from *Arthur Clelland. Brannigan* then gave the second signal when the men were on the cage and the cage was raised.

Up on the surface, *John Tracy* was standing outside the door of the smithy waiting to hand over his picks to be sharpened, when he heard a loud crash and saw the cage go over the "whorles." At the point when *Tracy* became aware of the accident, there were only three men left in the wrecked cage and he watched in horror, as one of them was thrown almost one thousand feet down the shaft and the second man fell to his death as he desperately tried to jump to safety.

The third man, *Robert Garrity,* was crouching down and desperately clinging on to the remnants of the cage which by now, were jammed in the framework. *John Tracy* ran into the smithy shouting to *James Paterson* the works engineer that the cage was over the "whorles" and *Paterson* and *John McMillan* another engineman sprinted the short distance to the engine house for a rope to rescue *Garrity.* When they arrived there they found *Arthur Clelland* standing looking out of the window at the scene of the accident. Asked by *Paterson* what had happened, he replied that "*something has gone wrong with the indicator.*" As the works engineer walked over and touched the indicator, *John McMillan* noted that it was very loose and that it was not where it should have been. *James Paterson* then left with the rope, to rescue *Robert Garrity.*

When *Arthur Clelland* found out that six men had fallen to their deaths, he was unable to accept the enormity of the accident and went to pieces. Despite advice, he left the colliery and went home, changed his clothes and started walking in the direction of Glasgow, but he was soon arrested by the police.

The bodies of the six victims were recovered from the bottom of the sump by grappling irons. *Patrick Houghney,* (36) 16 Ann Street Burnbank and his 16 years old son *Martin*, had come from County Durham to find work and had been working at the colliery for only eight days, as had *Patrick Hopkins,* (20) their lodger, who was about to marry *Patrick Haughney's* daughter.

*Thomas Murdoch* (48) 1 Dixon Street Blantyre and his oldest son Robert (20) also died. Thomas had lost a son in the October explosion four months earlier. He left a widow and several children.

*Michael Currie,* (40) Gardiner's Place, Auchintibber had also only recently come to Blantyre and he left a wife and three children. There was also the added tragedy that his wife was blind and the family were left destitute.

*Arthur Clelland* was charged with culpable homicide and committed to prison, where he spent almost two months awaiting trial.

In court, evidence was produced by several men, which pointed to a fault in the indicator. *Andrew Forsyth*, engineman, Hamilton, told of how he had worked a shift at the same engine prior to the accident and said that he noticed that a new brake block was required. He also spoke about how the vibration on the floor caused by the looseness of the brake, often altered the indicator, although he could not say by how much. He had complained about the brakes, but nothing had been done until after the accident.

*John McMillan* confirmed that when Paterson touched the indicator it was loose and *Michael Flanagan* a furnaceman, spoke of how when he entered the engine house, the indicator was further down than it should have been and when he asked *Arthur Clelland* "*what was the matter?*" Clelland replied that "*the indicator was wrong.*" *James Dunlop,* engineer, Greenfield, spoke for the defence and told of how he thought that the indicator was likely to go wrong by the very nature of its construction. He said that it might get slack on the spindle, the end being fixed with a pinching pin. In his opinion, this mode of fastening was not proper and would lead to loosening. He explained, that when there was a great deal of vibration, the tendency of an indicator such as he found at Blantyre, was to loosen and loosen without being noticed. If an engine were set to work after such a loosening, it would go all right until it came to the bottom, but it would slip back in coming up the other side. It would not surprise him if the engineman was deceived by such an indicator, as to the position of the cage in the shaft.

*Alexander Gillespie*, engineman at Eddlewood Colliery, gave evidence that he had examined the indicator at Blantyre and the machinery connected with it. The mode in which the handle was fastened to the spindle, did not appear to him to be the best mode known to engineers. He also spoke of how he had known the accused for seven or eight years and testified to Arthur Clelland's good character, as did *William Paterson,* an engineer from Messrs Baird & Co.

The court also heard of how the markings on the indicator were only chalked instead of being painted on, which meant that they could be easily removed by cleaning.

*James Paterson,* engineer at the colliery, told of how after the accident, a joist was put in the floor to correct the vibration and a new block had been put on the brake. A pinion wheel had already been altered and alterations were to be made to the indicator after the trial.

*Robert Garrity*, the only miner to survive the accident, told of how he entered the cage with the six men who were killed. He noticed nothing unusual about the speed at which the cage was travelling, however, as it neared the top he began to sense that something was going wrong and was filled with *"a fear he could not express."* The cage failed to stop at the landing place and when it hit the crossbeams of the headings, the top of the cage was ripped off and it was turned on its side, precipitating the six other men down the shaft.

When cross examined, he stated that *"there was no cross-bar on the cage. If there had been one, he believed that the accident would not have happened."* He added that *"Dixon's was the only colliery he had ever worked in which did not have cross bars on the cages."*

*Arthur Clelland* was a man whom everyone had testified to being a *"steady sober man, who had a high reputation for caution and steadiness."* At the time of the accident, he was also a very frightened man and had taken flight to get away from what had happened. Based on the evidence given by the witnesses, he was also an innocent man, but the establishment appear to have been looking for a scapegoat. The jury, who were part of the establishment, could not bring themselves to find him not guilty. They found the case against him not proven, thereby attempting to cast doubts on his innocence.

The overwinding accident at Blantyre could have been and should have been avoided. Devices were available which prevented such accidents, but many of the coalmasters were reluctant to pay for them to be installed. In the North of England, a detaching hook was already being extensively used and it had been the means of saving many lives, by preventing the cages colliding with the whorles. The Government Inspector for Mines for Durham in a report went as far as stating that *"Walkers Detaching Hook is most efficient for the purpose intended and no winding rope should be without it."* Several of the local collieries had installed the hooks, including Auchinraith Colliery and only ten weeks previously, on 18th December, 1877, at the new Earnock colliery being sunk by John Watson, a demonstration of King's Patent Detaching Hook was given to workers and mining officials from many of the Lanarkshire mines. During the demonstration, a kettle filled with stones was deliberately over-wound and *"the Detaching Hook attached to the rope, passed through the catch plate and the rope at once disengaged, leaving the kettle securely suspended, without the slightest shock being apparent."* The demonstration was a complete success. There were no representatives of Dixon's Collieries present at this demonstration.

*Alexander Macdonald* M.P. and founder of the Coal and Iron Miners' Association of Scotland, knew of the danger's of over-winding and in a letter of sympathy to the *"sufferers by the fearful explosion in Blantyre"* printed in the Hamilton Advertiser on 27th October, 1877, he pointed out that men had lost their lives at Wigan in an overwinding accident and remarked that *"this is an unpardonable neglect, and the owners ought to be severely punished."* He wrote of how at Wellington Colliery, where men had also died in an overwinding accident, the owners had brushed aside his advice to adopt the simple contrivance to prevent the possibility of such an accident happening again, but were eventually compelled to fit the device, when the miners, on *Macdonald's* advice, refused to go underground until it was fitted. Little did he know when he wrote this letter that four months later, miners' lives would again be sacrificed at Blantyre.

*Macdonald* had also addressed a mass meeting of Wigan miners on 1st November, 1877, and he had spoken about how the provisions of the 1882 act were being imperfectly carried out. He went as far as saying, that *"during the last twenty years, ninety five per cert of the miners lost in colliery accidents were traceable to neglect on the part of the managers of the mines and bad regulations."*

Despite the loss of lives of six men at Blantyre, *Ralph Moore* the Inspector of Mines for the district, in his report on the accident, failed to recommend that the detaching hook be put in place and William Dixon Limited, did not see fit to spend the small amount of money required on such a preventative measure.

It would appear that *Arthur Clelland* was an innocent man who was put through an indescribable ordeal in an attempt to cover up the neglect of the owners and management of the colliery. Some time after the trial, he left Blantyre and returned to Larkhall, where he continued to work as a colliery engine man, until his death some twenty five years later.

# THE EXPLOSION IN DIXON'S NO.1 COLLIERY
## BLANTYRE
## 2ND JULY 1879

Words could never describe the conditions endured by the 19th century rescue teams involved in the aftermath of a fire-damp explosion. With no electricity, modern rescue equipment or breathing apparatus and working in almost pitch darkness, rescuers had to rely on their knowledge of the workings, brute strength and unbelievable bravery. The only "protection" from deadly after-damp gas was a scarf covering their mouth and nose and staying as close to the ground as possible.

This story tells of the heroism of the rescue parties involved in the race to save miners known to be still alive after an explosion in Dixon's No.1. Pit, Blantyre in July, 1879. This pit, now long gone, was situated behind Priestfield Cemetery on the strip of land that lies between the East Kilbride expressway and the Hillhouse Road

Blantyre No.1 and No.2 Pits 1953.
Photograph by Antony Small, courtesy of George Hay (son-in-law)

In Blantyre and surrounding towns, the name of Dixon's Collieries is synonymous with the word explosion and even although the actual incidents took place in the late 19$^{th}$ century, such was the impact on the inhabitants of the small coal mining community, the disaster story is still being passed on down through the generations. In Blantyre there was hardly a family who wasn't affected in some way, by one or both of the two major disasters in Dixon's mines.

The first explosion occurred in the fiery splint seams of the No.2 and No.3 Pits on the 22$^{nd}$ October, 1877, and resulted in the death of approximately 216 men and boys.

The second explosion took place less than two years later, on the evening of the 2$^{nd}$ July, 1879, in the Ell seam of Dixon's No.1 Pit and a further 28 miners lost their lives.

The men who died were night shift brushers, whose job was to advance and repair the roadways for the colliers coming in on the day shift the following morning. The 31 men working that evening were experienced men and prior to descending the shaft; the underground workings had been examined and declared safe and free from gas by the duty fireman.

At ten minutes past nine, two surface workers, engineman *James Bennet* and pit-headman *Alexander McMillan* were startled to hear a loud rumbling noise, followed by a sound like "*the sharp detonation of a charge of dynamite*" coming from the shaft. The communication bell from the Ell seam to the pit head rang urgently, as if it was being pulled by a desperate hand and the wire ropes attached to the cage rattled violently against the side of the wooden lined shaft.

The men looked up in horror towards the headings, as the whorles or pulley wheels trembled and shook as the force which had travelled the length of the workings like a giant fiery breath, terminated; its rage spent. The shocked men knew instantly that an explosion had taken place and the plume of smoke emerging from the mouth of the shaft, announced that Blantyre had been plunged once more, into the nightmare of a mining disaster.

The sound made by the explosion was heard all over the town and it was recognised by some people as trouble at the mine, but many who heard it did not associate it with the colliery; among them 32 year old Dr *William Grant,* Blantyre's highly respected family doctor who was playing bowls at Stonefield Bowling Green. When he heard the peculiar sound made by the explosion he casually remarked to his companions "*that was a shot"* and continued with his game until a messenger arrived to inform him that Dixon's No.1 Pit had blasted.

First on the scene was *John White* an oversman at No.1 Pit. *John* had been standing at his front door when he heard the noise and saw the whorles shaking. Grabbing his jacket he ran to the pit and questioned the two anxious surface men about what they had just witnessed. Taking a calculated risk that there may be survivors at the pit bottom *John White* ordered *Bennett* to start lowering the cage slowly down the shaft. The cage moved down the shaft without any problems, but six feet from the bottom it stuck fast in debris from the blast.

With the cage unusable, *White* ran to No.3 shaft where he found that No.3 oversman *John Pickering* and miner *William Gilchrist* had also heard the noise and were already in the cage, and on their way down underground.

At the bottom of the shaft, the two men were met by an extremely anxious pit bottomer who informed them that approximately ten minutes before, he had heard the sound of a *"fearful explosion,"* and although he had no idea where it had come from, he was convinced that whatever had taken place had not been in his section of the workings.

*Pickering* and *Gilchrist* were joined by *John White* and together they headed down the communicating passage between the two pits. In the north side of No.1 Pit, they found no damage; but on moving towards the south side, the unmistakable smell of explosion hung heavy in the mine and wreckage lay everywhere. The bratticing used to direct the air flow had been destroyed in the blast and thick, dangerous, poisonous pockets of after-damp were now present throughout the roadways.

Disregarding the danger, the men pushed on until they reached the lamp cabins situated at the south side of the pit. The cabin furthest from the shaft had taken the full force of the blast, with its door shattered and torn from the hinges. Inside, lying on the floor gravely injured was *Thomas Irvine,* the pit bottomer. He was given immediate assistance by his rescuers, but they could see that he was not going to last much longer. Although conscious and lucid, *Irvine,* before he died, only managed to tell them that he had been in his cabin when the explosion blew the door down and flames entered the room.

 The men moved further into the workings and found alone in the stables, a frightened pit pony whose tail, mane and body hair had been singed off by the blast. They took a few minutes to feed and water the animal before they continued their dangerous journey.  By the time they travelled 200 fathoms down the gas filled tunnels, they had discovered nine bodies. The position and condition of some of the bodies indicated that the miners had survived the explosion, but had been overcome by gas as they made for the shaft.

With the ventilation getting worse by the minute, *White, Pickering* and *Gilchrist* turned to head back for the shaft and purer air. Suffering from severe after-damp poisoning, the exhausted men chalked their initials on the roof of the roadway to show how far they had penetrated into the mine and then with their legs buckling from below them, headed for the pit bottom.

Arriving at the bottom of No.3 shaft, they reported their findings to officials organising the rescue. Among the men gathered there were manager *James Watson, James Watson Jun.*, oversman, fireman *James Malone* and numerous other firemen, oversmen and miners.

The rescuers were split into teams and allocated tasks. Men were sent to inform miners working the night shift in No.3 Pit of the explosion and to help them up the pit and others set about removing roof falls, with the remaining men replacing the badly damaged air course.

With the volunteers working flat out, the ventilation was improved just enough, for *James Watson, John White* and *Patrick Lafferty* to move forward. Making their way slowly through the wreckage of the mine, the rescue party became aware of faint moans coming from the direction of the headings. Shouts of encouragement received no reply, indicating to the rescuers that the men were unconscious. Manager *James Watson* and *Patrick Lafferty* volunteered to go forward to see if they could reach them.

Crawling on their hands and knees they moved into the deadly gas filled roadway. They had gone only a short distance when *Watson* collapsed unconscious and *Lafferty* barely conscious himself, only just managed to crawl back to inform *John White* of what had happened.

*White* immediately ran into the workings and found *Watson* almost moribund from the effects of the gas. As he started to drag the unconscious man towards purer air, he began to feel the sudden overpowering effects of the after-damp and collapsed on top of him. Drifting in and out of consciousness, *John White* with his last drop of energy managed to drag himself back down the roadway towards safety. There he found the three men he had left only minutes before also badly overcome by gas and the one man who could still walk, was instructed by *White* to make for the pit bottom and summon help.

At the surface, word reached *Dr Grant* that some of the missing miners were known to be alive, but only just and that the lives some of the rescue party hung in the balance. *Grant* at once requested that he be taken down, knowing full well, that once he entered the mine, his own life would be in serious danger.

Accompanied by several miners, this exceptionally brave family doctor picked his way through the devastated workings until he reached the unconscious rescue party. He treated the men and then accompanied them to the surface, where, after handing their care over to another doctor, he went back down underground.

When *John White* regained consciousness many hours later, he found he was lying in his own bed with his wife looking after him. The manager, *James Watson* was rescued with great difficulty by the assistant manager, *Robert Robson* and fireman *John McMillan* who, with remarkable courage, had crawled into the gas filled tunnel and dragged his unconscious body out. *Watson*, critically ill from after-damp poisoning survived after being given medical treatment underground by *Dr Grant.*

Because the explosion had taken place in the late evening, many people were already in bed and the news of the accident took more than an hour to pass from the colliery to the town. As the news spread, panic stricken relatives ran towards the mine and the long vigil began.

Women waiting for news of their men stood shivering at the pit head with shawls draped around their thin bodies. Their faces were etched with suffering and their emotions out of control and spiralling ever downwards into the depths of despair; only to soar again, at the sight of the cage rising to the surface. Peering into the gloom with hope filled eyes; they were plunged back into the depths once more, as the weary black faced miners emerging from the cage looked towards them and slowly shook their heads.

Miners from Blantyre and Hamilton started arriving at the colliery to offer assistance with the rescue work. Men who could repair the air course were taken underground to work at replacing the damaged bratticing. When they collapsed from the effects of the fumes they were taken to the surface and replaced by a fresh team of volunteers. The ventilation slowly improved as the rescue teams worked non stop to carry out the repairs.

As they advanced further into the mine, eleven more bodies were found, but it was seven hours after the explosion before rescuers finally reached the men who had been heard moaning. *John Newton, Charles Lafferty, James Owen, Bernard Cairns* and *Bernard O'Neil* were all unconscious and critically ill when found. Despite the efforts of *Doctor Grant, John Newton* died en route to the surface and *Bernard Cairns* died in the engine house soon after being brought up the shaft. The other three men survived.

Shortly after the men were found, all rescue work was suspended due to an increasing accumulation of after-damp and rescuers concentrated on restoring the ventilation.

A temporary mortuary was established at No. 3 Pit, under the charge of *Inspector McKay and Sgt. Gordon*, with *Chief Constable McHardy* in charge of the arrangements. As the dawn came up on the Thursday morning, the heart breaking task of identifying the 24 bodies began; 12 men had died from after-damp poisoning and their bodies were quite easily recognised. Identification of the other 12 victims proved more difficult as the men had been severely injured and burned. It was seven o'clock that night before the last body had been positively identified. Most of the victims were Irish and the local priest *Father Frawley* helped to identify his parishioners.

At the pit head, relatives of the four missing men watched as rescue parties entered the cage. Each time it returned to the surface the crowd surged forward desperately hoping to see the missing men coming out alive, but they waited in vain. It was the following day before the pit could be searched and the bodies of *John McGuigan, Thomas McDuff* or *Duffy, Henry Duffy,* and *Patrick Lynch* recovered.

Three of the men appeared to have been smoking pipes at the time of the explosion and one of them, *John McGuigan,* still had a pipe in his hand and this was witnessed by ordinary miners who were in the rescue team. Both *Thomas McDuff* or *Duffy* and *Henry Duff* had pipes lying beside them; all three pipes were half smoked. *Lynch* was the only one not in possession of a pipe, tobacco or matches. His lamp however, which by law required to be locked when in use underground was found to be closed but unlocked and a lamp key was found in his pocket; a serious breach of rules. No one was allowed to carry one of these keys past the lamp cabin, not even the manager.

Several of the dead miners' lamps were unlocked and several more illegal lamp keys were found. Many of the men had tobacco, matches and pipes in their clothing, despite warning notices forbidding these items to be taken any further than the lamp cabin being prominently displayed both on the surface and underground. Some of the matches found on the miners had been used. Coats and jackets belonging to the men were strewn about their work areas and in several pockets, more pipes, tobacco and matches were found. Of the 31 men who went down the pit that night only two *McArthur* and *Harvie* were non smokers.

At the public enquiry held in Hamilton Sheriff Court, on 4th and 5th September, 1879, the reason given for the explosion was the illegal use of a naked light igniting a pocket of fire damp. It was suspected that the fire-damp had either been displaced from the roof by the firing of a shot or had accumulated due to an interruption in the ventilation. The enquiry found that although it could not be proved conclusively where the explosion had originated, it had definitely not originated from shot firing. The evidence pointed to the fire-damp being ignited by an open light in the vicinity of No.1 and No.2 headings, the area where the three men were known to have been smoking at the time the explosion had occurred.

 The report found, that the fireman who lost his life in the explosion had been in charge of the nightshift for two years and had been considered a careful fireman, but on the night of the explosion, discipline was found to be lax. The Inspector of Mines had come to this conclusion due to the unlocked lamps and the amount of tobacco, pipes and matches found on dead miners or in their clothing.

Despite the major disaster and appalling loss of life such a short time before, a number of miners were still not paying attention to the special rules which had been brought into force for their own safety. Miners still appeared in court on quite a regular basis charged with using a naked light, having an illegal key or smoking underground. The day before the disaster, Burnbank miner John McLean had been fined £2 at Hamilton Sheriff Court, for having his lamp open in the same colliery.

Letters were appearing in local newspapers pointing out that many of the men who were being employed in the mines, had previously worked as agricultural labourers and were illiterate, with no understanding of the complex gasses found in coal mines. The letters called for schools to include mining in their curriculum and for miners' to have training before being allowed underground, but it was to be the mid 1930's before the first training courses for young boys entering the mines were to be put in place.

Dixon's No.1 Pit had the reputation of being the best ventilated and safest of Dixon's five pits, but it still contained fire-damp, although not as in such great quantities as some of the other pits. Nevertheless, it had the potential to throw out large blowers of dangerous gas from the workings.

Quite a number of the men involved in the explosion that night had placed themselves and their workmates in great danger by breaking the safety rules. By smoking pipes underground, it was suspected that the miners themselves had provided the catalyst for the disaster which cost the Blantyre mining community another 28 lives.

# LIST OF THE DEAD

1. Peter Berry. 58. Brusher. Dixon's Rows. Married, 6 Children.
2. Tague Boyle. 22. Brusher, Dixon's Rows. Single.
3. James Bryson. 58. Brusher, Dixon's Rows. Married, with family.
4. Bernard Cairns. 25. Brusher, Dixon's Rows. Single.
5. Henry Duffy. 35. Brusher, Dixon's Rows. Single.
6. John Harvey. 44. Brusher, Dixon's Rows. Single.
7. Michael Howitt. 27. Brusher, Dixon's Rows. Single.
8. Thomas Irvine. 60. Bottomer, Dixon's Rows. Married with adult family.
9. Edward Jardine. 28. Brusher, Dixon's Rows. Widower.
10. James Lafferty. 46. Fireman, Dixon's Rows. Married with family.
11. Patrick Lynch. 30. Brusher, Dixon's Rows. Single.
12. Alex, McArthur. 40. Brusher, Dixon's Rows.
13. Thomas McDuff or Duffy, 24.  - Dixon's Rows. Single.
14. Patrick McGarvie. 55. Brusher, Dixon's Rows. Married.
15. Edward McGarvie. 23. Brusher, Dixon's Rows.
16. Patrick McGribben. 58. Brusher, Parkhead. Married, adult family.
17. John McGuigan. 38. Brusher, Dixon's Rows. Married 2 Children.
18. John Malone. 38. Brusher, Dixon's Rows. Married, 5 children.
19. Robert Mullen. 28. Brusher, Bowie's Land Stonefield. Single.
20. John Murphy. 24.   --- Dixon's Rows. Single.
21. John Newton. 60. Brusher, Dixon's Rows. Single.
22. Bernard O'Bryne. 28. Brusher, Dixon's Rows. Married, 1 Child.
23. John O'Neil. 32. Brusher, Dixon's Rows. Married, 3 Children.
24. Richard Rinn. 31. Brusher, Barnhill. Married, 6 children.
25. Alex Symington. 24. Brusher. Larkfield. Single.
26. Edward Thomson. 31. Brusher, Larkfield. Married, 3 Children.
27. Patrick Vallelly. 21. Brusher, Dixon's Rows. Single.
28. John Wilson. - Brusher, Stonefield. Single.

# THE
# SURVIVORS

1. Charles Lafferty. 16.  His father James Lafferty was killed.
2. Bernard O'Neil. 27. His brother John O'Neil was killed.
3. James Owens. 52. Widower. Auchinraith.

# SOME OF THE MEN INVOLVED IN THE RESCUE.

John Bowie. Oversman. No.4.Pit. *
James Bowie. Fireman. No.3 Pit.
Edward Burns. Roadsman.
William Gibson. Fireman. No.3 Pit.
John Gibson.**
Edward Gillan. Miner
William Gilchrist. Oversman. No.4 Pit.*
Dr. William Grant. Local Family Doctor. *
James Howie. Fireman. No.3 Pit.
Thos Laidlaw.*
Patrick Lafferty. Fireman. No.1 Pit.
James Malone. Fireman. No.1.Pit.
John McMillan. Oversman. No.2 Pit.
Dougald McNicol. Fireman. No.3 Pit. *
Robert Peel. Miner. *
John Pickering. Oversman. No.3 Pit. *
Robert Robson. Assistant Manager.
Joseph Thomas Robson. Assistant Inspector of Mines.
Shenton Thomas. General manager.
James Torrance. Oversman. No.3 Pit
George Watt. Fireman. No.3 Pit. *
James Watson.  Manager.
James Watson Junior. Oversman.
John White. Oversman. *

Numerous unnamed miners also voluntarily risked their lives by going underground
to assist with the rescue work. For every rescuer who was brought to the surface
overcome and at times seriously ill from the effects of after-damp, more men stepped
forward and volunteered to take his place.

* These men were known to have been in the rescue party at the 1877 explosion in
Dixon's No 2- 3 Pits

**John Gibson another of the rescuers had also taken part in the rescue at the 1877
Dixon's disaster and later in 1887 he took part in the rescue of survivors at the Udston
Colliery disaster where 73 men and boys died. In 1905 he is known to have been
living at Whitehill Road Burnbank. Ref. Hamilton Advertiser. 27/5/1905. –Page 4.

\*        \*        \*

Photograph of some of the rescuers from the 1877 Blantyre disaster.
Eight of the men in this photograph were known to be among the rescue parties at
both the 1877 and 1879 explosions.
These men were *John Pickering, Robert Peel, John White, William Gilchrist, John
Bowie, Dugald McNicol, John McMillan, Thomas Laidlaw and George Watt.*

Photograph courtesy of Hamilton Advertiser.

*Front Row*
 *L. to R. William Struthers, John Pickering,* Hugh Brown (1), John McMillan (32),*
*Robert Peel (35),* Walter Nelson, Thomas Cook, John White (39),* Thomas Laidlaw**
*Back Row.*
*L. to R. John Nelson, William Watson, George Watt,* William Gilchrist, (29)**
*Donald Morrison, John Bowie,* Thomas Forrest, John Henderson,*
*Dugald McNicol (24),* John McKinlay, Daniel Hendry and John Brown.*

\* Denotes men who were present at both the 1877 and 1879 Blantyre explosions.
Age included when known.

*(1) Hugh Brown* who wrote an eyewitness account of the disaster in 1927

One of the rescuers *Robert Peel* eventually followed his large family to Maryland
U.S.A after the death of his wife.

# THE BELOVED PHYSICIAN

## WILLIAM GRANT

No reference to the Blantyre Disaster would be complete without including the story of *William Grant,* the village doctor. Born in Bellshill in 1847 and educated at John Donald's School, Glasgow, he went on to study medicine at Glasgow University, graduating in 1871. In 1874 he set up practice in the rapidly expanding village of Blantyre and it was here the young doctor was to spend the remainder of his life.

After the disastrous explosion in Blantyre Collieries in 1877 with the loss of approximately 216 lives, Dr Grant was not content to wait for the survivors to be brought to the surface. He was among the first rescue parties to go underground to search the workings in indescribably dangerous conditions. He had volunteered because he knew that early medical intervention could make all the difference to the survival of the injured. Hugh Brown's description of Dr Grant as a *"hero of the very first magnitude"* was well earned. The same bravery was displayed less than two years later, when a second explosion killed 28 men in Dixon's No. 1 Colliery and again, he joined the rescue parties underground. Present at the Udston Colliery disaster in 1887 when 73 men and boys lost their lives, the Greenfield colliery boiler explosion and the Burnbank dynamite explosion, William Grant's experience of trauma injuries could not be surpassed. He was the also foremost authority on the treatment of afterdamp poisoning, having both personal and clinical experience of its destructive powers.

The pit accidents which plagued the mining industry: --- explosions, roof falls, runaway hutches, the accidental amputation of fingers toes and limbs, the injuries caused by machinery etc, were treated by him on a daily basis. He also witnessed and treated, the diseases linked to the appalling underground working conditions which struck miners down, in what should have been the prime of their lives.

A wise physician, Dr Grant knew that no matter how much he tried, he could never restore many of the men to health and, as he walked the streets of Blantyre visiting his patients, he always found time to stop and talk to the villagers. He was very much aware, that sometimes, a kind word could go further than a bottle of medicine.

The contribution made by William Grant to the lives of the Blantyre villagers was incalculable and not only in the practice of medicine. A man of great principles, his services were much in demand and he was elected a member of the School Board very soon after he arrived in the village. For twenty four years, he was appointed and re-appointed chairman by his colleagues, who felt that in him, was a man whose sound judgment could be relied upon. In the 37 years he served on the School Board, his foremost thoughts were on the education of the children of Blantyre; he was also a Justice of the Peace and president of the local National Bible Society of Scotland.

Despite the incredible demands made on his time, he never wavered from his high ideals and he never made a hurried or rash judgement. His mind would be made up, only after calm and mature deliberation. William Grant never turned away anyone who needed him, no matter what time of the day or night the call came.

Found in one of his notebooks after his death were these words written many years before — *"I shall pass this way but once, therefore if I can show any kindness to my fellow creatures, let me do it now. Let me neither neglect nor defer it, for I shall not pass this way again".*

He retired from general practice in 1911 and died six years later at the age of 70. On the day of his funeral, as the cortege took him on his last journey through his adopted village, the people of Blantyre lined the streets as a sign of their affection and respect to the man who had spent his life helping them.

William Grant, Blantyre's *"Beloved Physician,"* was laid to rest only a few yards from the mass grave containing the remains of the majority of the miners who had lost their lives in the 1877 explosion.

*This obelisk in Blantyre Cemetery marks the last resting place of Dr. William Grant. The expanse of grass in the background contains the mass grave where most of the miners who died in the 1877 disaster were buried.*

# THE HAMILTON MINERS' MEMORIAL

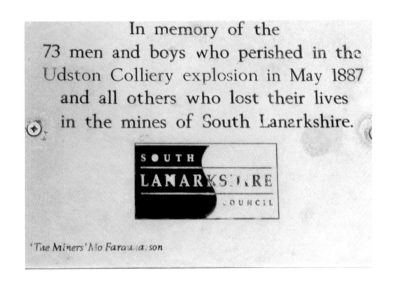

In memory of the
73 men and boys who perished in the
Udston Colliery explosion in May 1887
and all others who lost their lives
in the mines of South Lanarkshire.

SOUTH
LANARKSHIRE
COUNCIL

'The Miners' Mo Faraurason

*Plaque on base of the miner's statue situated in Brandon Street Hamilton*

# THE UDSTON COLLIERY DISASTER
## HAMILTON
### 28th May 1887

*The Glasgow Herald, 30th May, 1887.*

Situated at the very top of Hillhouse, behind where Townhill Road is now situated was the Udston Colliery owned by the Udston Coal Company and opened in 1875. It was a small pit, employing approximately 200 men and boys working in three seams at depths of up to 1000 feet. The workings of the colliery extend for 150 acres and bordered on three sides with Blantyre, Earnock and Greenfield Collieries.

Today, the site of the colliery is now a housing estate and part of Hamilton's western expansion programme, the last remaining colliery buildings and the pit waste bing were removed in 2002 and nothing was left to bear witness to the fact that this is the site of Scotland's second worst coal mining disaster.

The disaster happened on the morning of Saturday 28th May 1887 and the morning had dawned with the promise of a beautiful sunny day, however for the 184 men and boys working underground there was no time to enjoy the sunshine. There was coal to be hewed and a living to be earned.

At 9am, having been hard at work for almost three hours, many of the dayshift downed tools for their breakfast. It was during this break at approximately 9.07am, an explosion ripped through the Splint seam destroying everything in its path. The explosion manifested itself in a volume of flame and dust at the number two or downcast shaft, followed seconds later by a volume of flame from the upcast or number one shaft which set fire to the wooden sheds or headings above it.

The sound of the explosion was heard in Greenfield Colliery through a 135 foot barrier of solid coal. In the Blantyre Colliery (where an estimated 216 men had lost their lives 10 years earlier) miners working that morning were temporarily blinded with the dust thrown up by the vibration of the explosion.

Word of the disaster soon spread throughout the district and explorers or rescue parties converged on the scene coming from all the mines in the area. When disaster struck, there was never any shortage of volunteers from the mining community anxious to assist with rescue, with many miners tramping the back roads on foot to get to the colliery to offer their services.

The fire at the wooden sheds above the number one shaft was quickly extinguished by the prompt use of a water hose which was to hand at the pit head, but it soon became obvious to the men on the surface that the miners underground were entombed. A rapid examination had revealed that both compartments of number one shaft and one of the compartments in number two shaft were blocked by cages which had been working in them at the time of the explosion. It was also found that a cage was stuck in number two shaft. After a superhuman effort by the rescue team the cage was brought to the pit head and found to contain two injured survivors, *Edward Torley* and *Archibald Muir.* A young miner, 17 year old *James McGourty,* who had been travelling with them, was projected up through the top of the cage by the force of the blast and killed when he struck the winding gear.

The colliery manager *James Gavin, James Gilchrist,* Manager of Earnock Colliery, *William Watson* main coal roadsman at Udston and *Daniel McPhail* a roadsman at Earnock colliery climbed into the cage and slowly began to descend the shaft. One hundred and fifty feet down, they were stunned to find a miner named *James Rankin.* In his desperation to live, James had climbed almost 700 feet up the vertical shaft in pitch darkness.. He was pulled to safety and taken to the surface.

Once again the cage began its descent and 300 feet down a further three miners, *James Muirhead, William Gaw* and *William Elliott* were found climbing to safety. The terror of being entombed or dying from suffocation due to firedamp had given them the almost superhuman strength which would have been required in order to attempt the horrendous climb of almost 1000 feet.

A request for volunteers to go down the shaft to carry out repairs was made to the crowd standing at the pit head and three men immediately stepped forward, a joiner called -----*Robertson* and another two men *John McBride* and -------*Bowie.* These three brave men descended the shaft not knowing if there was going to be another explosion or what they were going to find. With a great deal of hard work they managed to repair the shaft down as far as the Main coal seam allowing the rescue work to begin

The scene at the pithead was indescribable. Miner's wives, children and relatives, most of whom were distraught with grief, were straining to see what was happening and listening for every scrap of information they could pick up.

The crowd was getting larger by the minute with people coming from all over the county, some just to watch the rescue work and many to offer their services

Three hundred police reinforcements were brought to the disaster site in order to control the crowds. An explosion of this magnitude drew thousands of curious onlookers and it was estimated that 15,000 people observed the rescue work.

Underground men were fighting for their lives. Desperate to escape, the miners in the Ell seam headed for the shaft, only to discover that they had to pass through large areas of roadway filled with deadly fire damp fumes.

One miner named *James Weir,* knowing that he was running for his life, had managed to reach the safety of the shaft where the air was good. There he found three miners *Archibald Sneddon*, and brother's *Richard* and *Thomas Cowan*.

While he was running for the shaft, *Weir* had passed twelve men lying collapsed unconscious on the roadway after having been overcome by fire damp while trying to reach safety. Although exhausted themselves, *Weir, Sneddon* and the *Cowan* brothers repeatedly ran back into the deadly fumes and by sheer effort of will, managed to carry the helpless men out. All twelve unconscious miners escaped certain death when they were dragged for some distance to an area containing a good current of air. Among these men was *James Weir's* own son. When James found him, he put his arm round the unconscious boy's waist, lifted him up and carried him under his arm for many yards to safety.

The shaft below the Main coal seam was so badly damaged the cage could go no further. A chain with a large iron bucket called a kettle was attached to the cage and lowered into the shaft. Into this kettle went three miners, *Daniel McPhail, John McBride* and *James Boyd* who got as far as the source of the explosion the Splint seam, but found it difficult to get in to the roadway. Further rescue parties eventually managed to gain access where they found a pony driver named *Alexander McLean* alive in the lamp cabin near the shaft. Further down the roadway *James Lang* was also found alive. The two men were badly burned but both survived. Every other miner in the Splint seam was dead.

The day after the disaster *James Lang*, a young unmarried Burnbank, man was able to give an eyewitness account of the moment of explosion. He said had been working near the pit bottom when he saw the flames and then he was blown over with the force of the blast. He was thrown some distance away where he lay unconscious for up to eight hours. When found his hands and arms were swollen from lying so long in the cold.

Evidence of the extreme violence of the explosion was visible throughout the workings. A train of loaded hutches was found broken up with some of the hutches blown 60 feet away. Every door was down and there were roof falls on five different sites of the roadway including one fall 90 feet in length.

The deadly afterdamp fumes which were always present after an explosion permeated the roadways, making progress very difficult for the rescue teams. Every so often one of the men would collapse from the effects of the poison fumes and he would be carried back to where the atmosphere was purer.

Installing the props and brattice clothes to guide pure air to where it was needed became a very difficult job, as the men installing them had to keep their heads as near the floor as possible where the air was purer. One rescuer, a big brawny Burnbank man called *Peter Gibson,* who normally worked at the Clyde colliery, was just giving a wooden prop the finishing blow with his hammer, when, on lifting his head just a little bit too high, he got a whiff of afterdamp and collapsed unconscious. Taken to the pithead and attended by the doctor, he then staggered round a field at the side of the colliery till his head was clear. Once he felt better he went back down underground to continue with the rescue work.

Of the 184 men who descended into the pit that morning 73 died. Although the official enquiry stated that they had all died from suffocation and burning this was not the case. A large percentage of the men were horribly mutilated by the explosion and in the case of one boy, his head was never found. Most of the dead, 69 in total, worked in the Splint seam where the explosion had taken place, the other four victims were from the Main coal seam.

The disaster almost destroyed many of the mining families. It was customary for the miners to work alongside their sons, brothers and other extended family members. Therefore when an explosion of this size occurred, many families lost more than one family member.

Auchentibber became a village of widows and fatherless children, almost all of its working men and boys were killed. The village, stunned by the disaster, was awash in a sea of tears. Women could be seen sitting on kerbstones in the street, so overcome with grief, they could neither speak nor function. An old man was going round comforting groups of silent children who were standing at the hedgerows.

One resident, an agricultural worker named *John Boyce* lost his three sons, his two daughters were left widows, his son-in-law's brother was killed and his nephew also died. A total of seven young men from this one family died. *Mary Harrison* one of his daughters gave birth to twin boys some months after her husband *William Harrison* was killed. Mary named them *Christopher* and *Joseph* after two of her dead brothers. She was left with eight fatherless children. Mary herself was to die six years later and her eight children were left orphans.

Ironically the *Boyce* family had moved from the small hamlet of *Tartaraghan* near *Portadown* in *County Armagh* in the north of Ireland to Auchentibber around 1872, to obtain work and a better standard of living.

Another family the *Cooks,* (originally from Newton in Lancashire but resident in Greenfield, Burnbank) consisted of the father *Richard* aged 50, three sons *Thomas* aged 21, *James* aged 17, both of whom worked underground with him, another son aged 8 and a daughter aged 12. When the two younger children heard of the explosion they ran panic stricken for more than a mile to the colliery.

After waiting at the pit head for almost 14 hours, they were called to the makeshift mortuary to identify the bodies of their father and two brothers. As their mother had died some years previously, these two distraught young children were now orphans. It is not recorded what became of them, but they did have an aunt who lived in Burnbank and who may have cared for them.

The explosion at Udston Colliery was a major mining disaster, only at the Blantyre disaster ten years earlier had there been a greater loss of life. It is interesting to note that in both of these disasters the Splint seam exploded. The area where the detonation occurred at Udston Colliery was less than a quarter of a mile from the Blantyre Colliery.

This particular seam was known to be gassy, however, in the investigation that followed, it was established by H.M. Inspector of Mines *Ralph Moore,* that although a small amount of gas had been detonated by illegal shot firing, the main reason for the catastrophic explosion had been the ignition of coal dust present in large quantities within the workings and roadways. Legislation passed after the explosion was instrumental in preventing further disasters. Never again in Scotland did an explosion claim such a high loss of life.

The bravery of the miners was almost beyond belief. The *Cowan* brothers *Richard, Thomas* and *George* were underground during the explosion and had escaped with their lives only to put them at risk again by volunteering to return underground in the most extreme of conditions. *Richard Cowan* and *Thomas* and *James Weir* who also returned underground, had already rescued twelve unconscious miners before they themselves were rescued.

*Robertson, McBride* and *Bowie* the three men who volunteered to go down the shaft and by repairing it allowed rescue work to begin, did not work in Udston colliery. They were among the many colliers who flocked to the disaster scene to offer their services, without any reward or payment expected, or given. An appeal was made to the Home Office by Mr *Stephen Mason* M.P. suggesting that the Albert Medal for bravery be awarded to one or more of the rescuers. All chance of a medal being awarded was blocked by a letter from Mr *Ralph Moore* who had arrived at the colliery five hours after the explosion and unbelievably, he said in the letter, that in his opinion, *"None of the men in anything they did were subjected to more than the ordinary risks of mining. I have most respectfully to state that there is no cause in my opinion for awarding a medal to anyone."* No medals were awarded but there could never any doubt about the outstanding bravery of the rescuers.

Lanarkshire people are proud of their mining heritage, rightly so, Scottish miners were a fiercely proud, independent and hard working breed. Their working conditions were appalling, however their indominitable spirit shone through. Each miner knew that he was responsible for not only his own safety but for that of those who worked alongside him. Indeed this was the case with the Udston disaster, as many of those who survived, only did so due to others risking their own lives to save them.

The pits are all gone now and for that we should be thankful. No longer do men and boys risk their lives going down into the bowels of the earth to earn a pittance. The 73 men who died at the Udston disaster were paid on average 3/3d (16p) per day or 17/6 (86p) per week.

Social conditions have improved beyond the wildest imagination of any 19th century miner; however, we should never forget the sacrifice made by these men and boys to achieve this progress.

More than a century has passed since the explosion and in the relentless march of progress, all trace of Udston colliery has vanished into the mists of time to make way for new housing.

In December 2001, at the suggestion of Wilma Bolton, South Lanarkshire Council finally acknowledged the disaster that had taken place on that May morning and a plaque in memory of the 73 men and boys who lost their lives and also all others who died in the coal mines of South Lanarkshire, was placed on the miner's statue standing outside Brandon Gate council offices in Hamilton's Brandon Street.

Accepting the plaque on behalf of the victims was Hamilton's oldest surviving retired coal miner, 96 years old *Jimmy Glen*. In 1917 at the age of 13 years, Jimmy started work at the screening tables in the Bent Colliery. On Armistice Day, 1918, his 14th birthday, he went underground to work as a collier and spent his working life at the coal face.

Present at the ceremony were Mrs *Netta Stewart* and her daughter *Allison*, direct descendants of *James Crichton* and his wife *Elizabeth Boyce*. *James Spiers* another of the dead miners was represented by his great grand niece *Wilma Bolton* with her daughter *Lesley Farnan* and grandchildren *Alishia and Dylan Farnan*, direct descendants of James's brother, *John Spiers*. The following year, a memorial plaque dedicated to the six East Kilbride miners who died in the disaster, was unveiled in the memorial garden at Priestknowe roundabout East Kilbride.

*Bottom row. Hamilton's oldest surviving retired miner Jimmy Glen (96) receiving the plaque from South Lanarkshire's Provost Allan Dick*
*Top row. Councillor Jean McKeown, Wilma Bolton and the Rev. Arthur Barrie*

# KNOWN UDSTON COLLIERY DEATHS

| DATE | NAME | AGE | CAUSE OF DEATH |
|---|---|---|---|
| 22.05.1879 | JAMES STEWART | 17 | ROOF FALL (Fractured skull) |
| 17.04.1882 | SIMON TAYLOR | 28 | NO DETAILS |
| 15.05.1882 | WM. ARCHIBALD | 53 | EXPLOSION (Afterdamp poisoning). |
| " | CHARLES MORRISON | 35 | EXPLOSION (Afterdamp poisoning) |
| " | WM. MORRISON | 13 | EXPLOSION (Afterdamp poisoning) |
| 10.12.1885 | WM. RENNIE | 65 | CRUSHED BY WAGONS |
| 28.05.1887 | JAMES ALLISON | 44 | EXPLOSION |
| " | HUGH AUCHTERLONIE | 41 | " |
| " | WILLIAM BABES | 41 | " |
| " | THOMAS BERRY | 25 | " |
| " | WILLIAM BERRY | 22 | " |
| " | CHRISTOPHER BOYCE | 20 | " |
| " | JOSEPH BOYCE | 18 | " |
| " | WILLIAM BOYCE | 23 | " |
| " | WM. JOHN BOYCE | 23 | " |
| " | WILLIAM BROWN | 53 | " |
| " | ISAAC CAMERON | 35 | " |
| " | RICHARD COOK | 50 | " |
| " | JAMES COOK | 17 | " |
| " | THOMAS COOK | 20 | " |
| " | JOHN CREWE | 23 | " |
| " | WASHINGTON CREWE | 25 | " |
| " | DAVID CRICHTON | 21 | " |
| " | JAMES CRICHTON | 31 | " |
| " | JOSEPH CUMMINGS | 28 | " |
| " | GEORGE DAVIS | 32 | " |
| " | THOMAS DENNISTON | 17 | " |
| " | WM. DENNISTON | 23 | " |
| " | GEORGE DINSDALE | 23 | " |
| " | WILLIAM DRAIN | 19 | " |
| " | JOHN DODDS | 13 | " |
| " | DAVID FLEMING | 27 | " |
| " | JAMES GAW | 13 | " |
| " | GEORGE HARKNESS | 30 | " |
| " | JOHN HARKNESS | 25 | " |
| " | W. HARRISON | 36 | " |
| " | WILLIAM HOUSTON | 44 | " |
| " | JAMES JARVIS | 31 | " |
| " | EDWARD JONES | 15 | " |
| " | JAMES KAIN | 14 | " |
| " | WILLIAM LAWSON | 41 | " |

| | | | |
|---|---|---|---|
| " | ANDREW LAWSON | 16 | " |
| " | JAMES LEADBETTER | 39 | " |
| " | GAVIN R. MALCOLM | 15 | " |
| " | WILLIAM MURDOCH | 26 | " |
| " | JAMES McCULLOCH | 40 | " |
| " | JAMES McCULLOCH | 14 | " |
| " | JOHN McDADE | 21 | " |
| " | MICHAEL McDADE | 32 | " |
| " | JOHN McGINNIS | 16 | " |
| " | PETER McGINNIS | 22 | " |
| " | FRANCIS McGOURTY | 49 | " |
| " | JAMES McGOURTY | 17 | " |
| " | ALEX. McLEAN | 50 | " |
| " | ROBERT McNIVEN | 25 | " |
| " | JAMES McTAVISH | 19 | " |
| " | JAMES NAVALL | 31 | " |
| " | JOHN NELSON | 16 | " |
| " | JAMES NELSON | 14 | " |
| " | JOSEPH NELSON | 22 | " |
| " | MICHAEL QUINN | 21 | " |
| " | WALTER PENMAN | 22 | " |
| " | THOMAS PENMAN | 20 | " |
| " | JOHN REID | 24 | " |
| " | JAMES RICHMOND | 58 | " |
| " | DANIEL ROBERTSON | 15 | " |
| " | TERENCE ROONEY | 55 | " |
| " | DAVID SHANKS | 45 | " |
| " | DAVID SHANKS | 13 | " |
| " | JOHN SMITH | 34 | " |
| " | JAMES SPIERS | 38 | " |
| " | FELIX TORLEY | 43 | " |
| " | ALEX. TORLEY | 26 | " |
| " | ANDREW T. WATSON | 48 | " |
| " | JAMES  WILSON | 40 | " |
| " | JOHN WILSON | 20 | " |
| " | WALTER WINTER | 22 | " |
| 20.12.1889 | MICHAEL DALY | 31 | ROOF FALL |
| 10.12.1891 | JOHN KERR | 51 | INTERNAL INJURIES |
| 15.12.1892 | JAMES DUNSMORE | 46 | ROOF FALL (12 tons) |
| 05.12.1903 | GEORGE BOYD | 16 | ROOF FALL (Fractured skull) |
| 24.02.1904 | JAMES BARR | 36 | ROOF FALL |
| 16.01.1012 | HEINRICH BOSEBECK | 35 | RUN DOWN BY HUTCHES |
| 25.09.1916 | JAMES GOURLAY | 34 | ROOF FALL (1 ton, neck injuries) |
| 10.05.1923 | JAMES HOGG | 31 | NO DETAILS (Multiple injuries) |

# THE SURVIVORS

James Allan, James Benson, John Bolton, James Borland, John Boyd, John Broadly, James Cameron, William Cathcart, Thomas, Richard, George, William and Robert Cowan, William Crewe, Michael and James Daily, Patrick Dorrington and son, James Eadie, William Elliot, William Eden, William Fotheringham, John Gall, William Gaw, George Grant, William Haggarty, John Haggarty and his son, Charles Horne, James Jack, Patrick Kane, John Kerr, James Lang, Gavin Laird, Robert McCrum, James McIlvennie, James McKendrick, Alexander McLean, Donald and William McLean, William McMillan and son, John and Bernard Madden, James Mann, Archibald Muir, Archibald, Charles, John and William Muirhead, John Miller, Thomas Paterson, James Rankin, Thomas Redpath; John Richmond, John Sharp, James Smith, Harry Smith, James Smith, James Smith Jnr, James and Charles Sneddon, Peter Scott, John Toner, William Queen, John Ward, William and James Watson, James, Robert and John Weir, Francis Wilson.

The above survivors came from Auchintibber, Blantyre, Burnbank, Dykehead Rows, Greenfield Rows and Udston Rows.

# LIST OF THE EXPLORERS OR RESCUERS
## AT THE
## UDSTON COLLIERY DISASTER

These men had left the colliery before the disaster but returned to offer their services.

*James Gilmour, James Kennedy, Thomas Watson, Robert Watson.*

The following men were in the pit at the time of the explosion but having escaped uninjured, volunteered as explorers.

*John Broadly, George Cowan, Richard Cowan, Thomas Cowan, James Eadie, William Fotheringham, John Kerr, Gavin Laird, Bernard Madden, Robert McCrum,\* John Sharp, Harry Smith, Charles Sneddon, James Sneddon, William Watson, James Weir, Alexander Ward.*

*\*Robert McCrum died some time after the disaster from head injuries received during the rescue. Ref. May McTaggart, (Hamilton) granddaughter.*

From a total of 193 miners known to be involved in the rescue work, 21 were from Udston Colliery. The remaining 172 were drawn from 21 other collieries; each and every man was a volunteer and a HERO.

## AUCH INRAITH COLLIERY

*John Anderson, J. Beecroft, James Canning, J.B. Croft,\* Joseph Emmerson, John France, David Gibson, George Gibson, William Irvine, D. King, John Kyle, William McCall, George McCall, Hugh McKechnie, James Murray, Thomas Murray, David Russell, Henry Semple, Alexander Shaw, William White, George Wilson, Andrew Wilson, D Williamson.*

*\*Possibly Beecroft*

## ALLANSHAW COLLIERY

*George Gray, William Lawson, William Lawson Jnr,\* Peter Lawson, James Lees, M. McDonald, Robert McNeil, John McNulty, John Millburn, George Murray, James Nimmo, George Pritchard, John Shorthouse, Walter Stewart, William Wilson.*

 \*In the Blantyre Gazette 23rd Oct. 1937 page 5, an article on William Lawson states that he was working in the mines at the age of seven, earning 6s a week and spent 72 years working in the pits. He retired in his 80th year. He contracted blood poisoning while working with the Udston rescue party and was unable to work for three weeks. The last survivor of the rescue team he was still alive aged 94 and living at 67 Arden Road Hamilton, on the 22nd Nov. 1941. Ref. Hamilton Advertiser, page 9. (William Lawson died at above address on the18[th] Jan. 1945, aged 97 years.)

## BENT COLLIERY

*James Adams, Archibald Blyth, James Cullen, Alexander Cuthbertson, John Donaldson, Robert Dunn, James Forsyth, Richard Marshall, Patrick McGuire, Alexander Rankin, Thomas Sorbie, Joseph Whiteford, John Williamson.*

## BOTHWELL PARK          BOTHWELL CASTLE

*Thomas Watson.*          *Robert Cavannagh.*

## BLANTYRE

*John Archibald, John Berry, John Bowie,\* George Bowie, William Brodie, Thomas Cook,\* Hugh Conway, William Kirkwood, Arthur Lamont, Alexander Matthew, George McLachlan, Robert Orr, Alexander Peat, Robert Robertson, John Watson, John Wotherspoon.\**

*\*John Bowie,\*Thomas Cook and John Wotherspoon* had both been involved in rescue work at previous explosions. *John Bowie* had been involved in the rescue work at the 1877 and 1879 Blantyre Disasters. *Thomas Cook* and *John Wotherspoon* had been at the 1877 Blantyre disaster.

# CLYDE COLLIERY

*Robert Beith, Isaac Collinson, James Dunsmore, John Gibson,* David Gibson,* Peter Gibson, Robert Keays, Isaac McCullop, Archibald McNeil, William Miller, John Moran, David Ross, William Smith, Robert Smith, Hugh Service, Patrick Thomson, Thomas Turnbull, John Wilson.*

*John Gibson* also took part in the rescue work at the two Blantyre explosions in 1877 and 1878. He was originally from Ayrshire.
*David Gibson*, brother of above, found and brought out survivor *James Lang*. Ref. Hamilton Advertiser 27th May 1905, page 4.

# CADZOW COLLIERY

*Edward Kelly, Peter Lamb, Hugh McGuire, John Millburn, Walter Stewart.*

# CRAIGHEAD COLLIERY

*Hugh Anderson, James Boyd, David Dickson,* Andrew Frame, Thomas Fraser, Thomas Gibson, John Hill, William Hill, Peter Livingston, James Maxwell, David Neilson, L. Nimmo, John Paterson, James Wood, James Strachan.* *

* *David Dickson* died on 29th December 1937 at Stonefield Rd, Blantyre aged 74 years. Ref. Blantyre Gazette. 30th December, 1937 page 5.

James Strachan

* *James Strachan* had taken part in the rescue at a previous explosion in Udston Colliery on 15th May 1882, when three men were killed. He was also one of the rescuers at the Blantyre Disaster. 1877. On the Monday after the Udston disaster he started work in Udston Colliery as a fireman. He lived at High Blantyre. Ref. Hamilton Advertiser, 2nd July 1887, page 2.

# EDDLEWOOD COLLIERY

*James Baird,* John Clarkston,* Edward Murphy, Thomas Ramsey, William Reid, William Robertson.*

* *James Baird* was still working in Eddlewood and Neilsland Collieries in 1924. Ref. Hamilton Advertiser 2nd August 1924, page 6.
* *John Clarkson* had been a miner working in the pits of Coatbridge since he was nine years old. His own father was killed in a pit-accident. He was responsible for bringing the bodies of the Udston victims up to the surface. He died aged 83 years in Kirkholm, Wigtonshire. His death was reported in the Hamilton Advertiser on 6th January 1934, page.6.

## EARNOCK COLLIERY

David Anderson, John Calligan, R. Carmichael, John Dailly, James Dick, James Gilchrist,* Alexander Gillespie, John Holmes, John McBride, Alexander McDowell, James McFadden, M. McDonald, Daniel McPhail,* Samuel Mowbray, William Morton, J. Peters, John Williamson, James Wyper, Andrew Waddell.

*James Gilchrist and Daniel McPhail were in the first rescue party consisting of four men to be lowered down the shaft.

## *GREENFIELD COLLIERY*

Walter Cullan, James Hastie, Henry Hunter, William Jardine, Alexander McRoy, James Morrison, Hugh Richardson, William Robertson, William Rainnie, Daniel Stalks, Robert Wilson, James Wood.

## GARIBALDIE COLLIERY

## HIGH BLANTYRE COLLIERY

John Hilley, Peter Lawson.

John Lee.

## LETTERICK COLLIERY

George Pritchard.

## NEWTON COLLIERY

Andrew Aird, William Frame, Robert Grosset, George Howie, Robert Isset

## NORTH MOTHERWELL COLLIERY

John Hogg, Dougal McNeil, John White.

## QUARTER COLLIERY

James Snow.

## ROSS COLLIERY

David Hendry, William Lindsay, Thomas Nisbet, Alexander Paterson, John Pollock, Wm Twaddle, Jnr., William Weir.

# SPITALHILL COLLIERY

*Daniel Crane, Robert Crane, Walter Gibb,\* John Symons, Wm. Symons,*
*James Todd, James Watson.*

\* *Walter Gibb* sen., The Manse, Gaerlaverock Dumfries writes under date 10.1.1934.
"In Hamilton Advertiser of January 6th there is a paragraph about Mr *John Clarkson*
who had died at Kirkcolm, Wigtonshire and it  you state that he is believed to be the
last surviving member of the rescue party at the Udston Colliery Explosion. That is
not so because I was one of the first batch of the rescue party who went down after
the explosion. I am living with my son at the above address. Ref. Hamilton
Advertiser 13th January 1934, page 6. (*Walter Gibb died on the 1st June, 1935.*)

# SILVERTONHILL COLLIERY

*George Morrison.*

\*        \*        \*

One month after the disaster a letter written by the Udston Coal Co. Ltd. appeared in
the Hamilton Advertiser thanking eight coalmasters or companies and their
managers, the doctors who were in attendance, the St Andrews Ambulance Corps, the
clergy, police, mining engineers, and Mrs John Cunninghame of Blairston, Bothwell
for supplying clothing and mournings for the bereaved widows and families.

Not one word of thanks was given in this letter to the volunteer miners who had
worked unpaid for three weeks to recover the bodies and repair the pit.  Ref.
Hamilton Advertiser 25th June 1887, page 4.

*James Crichton with his wife Elizabeth Boyce.*
*Photograph courtesy of Netta Stewart, great grand-daughter of above.*
*James* and his brother *David* died in the disaster. *Elizabeth* lost her three brothers, two brothers- in- law and her cousin, as well as her husband.

# LEFT WITHOUT A FATHER
# THE HARRISON FAMILY

*Photograph courtesy of Netta Stewart*

This family of eight lost their father *William Harrison* plus five uncles and a cousin in the Udston disaster.

Middle front and top second from left are twins *Christopher* and *Joseph Harrison* who were born approximately six months after their father was killed. The boys were named after two of their mother's brothers, *Christopher* and *Joseph Boyce* who were also killed in the blast. The eight children were left orphans when their mother died six years after the explosion.

*The buildings in the middle of the picture are all that remains of Udston Colliery prior to demolition in 1999.*

*Udston colliery bing 1999.*

*The colliery buildings can just be seen behind the two clumps of trees to the middle right of the picture.*

*The white cottage and the building to the right are original Udston Colliery buildings. The centre white building is a modern extension. The pit buildings were demolished in 1999 to make way for Hamilton's new "Western Expansion, Westcraigs Housing Estate"*

*Udston Colliery building, possibly the smithy where injured were taken after the explosion. Demolished 1999.*

*Tree covered Udston Bing in the centre of the picture. 2001.*

*This photograph taken in 2003 from the same car park in Hillhouse Road, Hamilton shows that the Udston Bing has gone*

*Photograph by Lesley Farnan, 2002*
*Earth moving equipment sitting on top of Udston bing during removal.*

*Photograph by Lesley Farnan.*
*All trace of Udston Colliery has gone. 2003.*
*By 2005 this area had been developed and now contains a large housing estate.*

# THE COMPANY STORE

Of all the injustices carried out by the coalmasters on the miners, the abuse of the truck system comes high on the list as an example of a total disregard for the rights of a working man or woman. Many workers were paid not in cash, but in goods or credit. The 1831, Truck Act was intended to protect workers against the refusal of payment of wages otherwise than in coin. Unfortunately the Act did not cover the refusal or omission to pay wages or any part of wages, nor the making of any deduction from wages.

A collier could work for twenty years at many pits but would never accumulate any savings because every penny he earned was clawed back by coalmasters who, by their manipulation of the terms of the 1831 Truck Act, bled them dry and kept a stranglehold on their hard earned wages.

The survival of the company store depended on the frequency of payment and the inability of the miner to survive in between pays without assistance and the practice of working "two weeks lie time" and fortnightly wages meant that the miner received no money for the first four weeks he worked at the colliery, he was then forced into debt. He would be given credit at the company store where overpriced goods were on sale, with the sum owed being paid back on pay day. Of course as he was always four weeks behind with his wage the system perpetuated itself, for paying the initial credit meant that he would have no money left and would have to rely on the company store to feed his family after he paid his bill. The miner could apply at the colliery cash office for an advance on money already earned, but then he was charged exorbitant interest on what he had borrowed. For every shilling he borrowed he would pay back 1d in interest. In many collieries if he requested cash for his wages he would have a percentage (again a penny for every shilling) deducted from his cash before he received it. In many collieries it was also compulsory for the miner to spend his hard earned wage in the company store.

A letter to the Hamilton Advertiser in September, 1879, signed by a *James Hardie*, secretary of the Lanarkshire Miners' Association highlights that the truck system was "*still as rampant as ever*" in Lanarkshire. Hardie spoke of how in one colliery "*in our immediate neighbourhood*" people were "*compelled to pay the highest price for -----well for not the most superior articles that can be got.*" He went on to describe how the "*workmen dare not pass the store with a penny of cash, under pain of having their cash stopped, or being instantly dismissed*" which of course meant that the collier and his family were thrown out on the street when the company repossessed their tied house that very same day. The letter also detailed how the miners, dependant "*on their Saturday pay to buy their wives and helpless weans their supper*" were deliberately deprived of their wages until the Monday. The letter appears to have been written after an action was brought against a mine owner in Hamilton Sheriff Court the previous week. The mine owner "*without legal cause deliberately kept the men's money in his office until Monday,*" thus forcing them to obtain goods on credit at the company store. The Sheriff decided that all the compensation the body of men whose wages were thus illegally held were entitled to, was "*the interest on the money so kept.*" The colliery operating the truck system referred to in *Hardie's* letter was the Udston Colliery, owned by The Udston Coal Company and the following week, another article appeared in the Hamilton Advertiser written by *John Dunn* a union official at the Udston Colliery, confirmed what *Hardie* had written. *John Dunn* went on to describe in detail the system of payment to the miners. He wrote of how the system carried out in the colliery store was *"detrimental to the working men and the manner in which it was carried out unbearable."*

*"Every alternate Saturday is cash day, Mondays and Wednesdays also, each man is provided with a cash-book, which he takes to the office. On the left hand page is entered the amount in cash received. This book is taken to the store and on the right hand page is set down the amount of goods purchased. When the book goes back to the office for cash, the clerk sees it at a glance if all the money paid out last time was laid out in the store; if not there is no more money advanced to that party. It is also well known that every farthing the men work for is expected."*

Dunn also goes on to compare the prices at the store against the prices in Stonefield, Burnbank or Hamilton and states that *"every article is priced 25% higher at Udston."*

The following week the Hamilton Advertiser printed another letter from John Dunn, informing the readers of a meeting at Udston Colliery between the manager, *Mr Ure* and a deputation of the miners, who were accompanied by two union agents, *James Hardie* and a man called *McLaughlin*. Ure agreed *"to give his men cash twice a week, with liberty to spend it where and in what manner they choose."*

His letter starts with the following verse.

> *"What might be done, if men were wise,*
> *What glorious deeds, my suffering brother;*
> *If we unite in love and right,*
> *And cease our scorn of one another.*

*Dunn* in the letter encourages all miners to join the union saying " *Shake off your fear, and say, as you have worked for the money no man has the right to choose for you the manner or market in which you are to spend it."*
He finishes the letter with lines from *Moore*.

> *Where is the slave so lowly?*
> *Condemned to chains unholy,*
> *Who would not burst his bonds at first,*
> *Not pine beneath them slowly."*

In the weeks following the publication of the letters, every union member at Udston Colliery was sacked and evicted from their tied homes.

The *James Hardie* whose letter in the Hamilton Advertiser drew the public's attention the unjust truck system being operated at Udston Colliery was in fact, *James Keir Hardie*, one of the founding fathers of the Labour Party and the first real working man to become a Member of Parliament. At the time of writing the letter he would have been 23 years of age and just setting out on his journey through the political quagmire of the nineteenth century. To achieve this *Hardie*, who in his teens was still illiterate, learned to read and write under the tuition of his mother. Gifted with a marvellous intelligence he soon mastered the art and began to voraciously read newspapers. It was from these newspapers that he became aware that some men were trying to improve the conditions of the workers, by starting unions. From then on *Keir Hardie's* destiny lay with improving the lives of the working classes. He was a man with strong religious and temperance views and despite tempting offers he refused, as suffragette *Sylvia Pankhurst* wrote in 1920 *"to prostitute his talents in the service of the ruling caste."* He was a man who could not be bought and he was true to himself and to the working classes. His favourite saying was *"Our day will come."*

*KEIR HARDIE.*

Make the chain of Union stronger,
Binding man to brother man,
Till short time and sweet restriction
Triumph over all the land;

Till the miners of this nation,
Bind together firm and sure,
Shall throw off their present fetters,
Slavery no more endure.

"Let us then be up and doing,
With a heart for any fate,
Still achieving, still pursuing,
Learn to labour and to wait."

*James Keir Hardie, circa 1880*
*58 Low Waters, Hamilton.*

*This poem was written during a period when the miners, fed up with wage reductions, reduced their output in an attempt to increase the price of coal.*

# THE ROOT
# OF
# ALL EVIL

*Greenhall bing, Blantyre. Photograph courtesy of George Hay.*

When trial bores discovered the rich, thick seams containing millions of tons of coal under Lanarkshire the local landowners must have been, to say the least, delighted; standing to gain as they did, vast fortunes from the royalties obtained from coal brought to the surface. Previously coal had been mined in Lanarkshire only where it was easily reached and it was sold to a small local market. However, the advances in engineering technology allowed deeper coal mines to be sunk, to meet the increasing demand for the coals needed to fire the industrial revolution.

The first deep coal mine to be developed in the Hamilton area, was Greenfield Colliery, which was sunk to a depth of almost 800 feet on the lands of Greenfield Farm. The first turf was cut by Provost *James Nisbet,* Coalmaster, in May 1859 and the pit eventually employed 1100 miners; but not before it had bankrupted *James Nisbet,* who had already developed *Ferniegair Colliery* and had bitten off more than he could chew.

Mines began to spring up all over Hamilton and there was no shortage of labour to develop and work in them. The years 1845 to 1849 and also 1879, saw potato blight destroy the potato harvest in both Ireland and Scotland and this had resulted in starvation on an unimaginable scale. The outcome of the famine was the mass migration of starving people to the industrial cities of Scotland and England searching for employment.

Prior to the arrival of the Irish immigrants, Scottish miners had enjoyed a relatively good wage, but with so many unemployed looking for work, it was inevitable that the coalmasters would take advantage of the situation and employ workers at the lowest possible rate. As a result the miner was thrown into a spiralling poverty, which was never to be resolved.

There was to be no prosperity for the hardworking men who mined the coal; that was reserved for the coalmasters who leased and developed the mineral fields and the landowning Dukes, Lords and Lairds, who received royalties of between 1/- and 1/6d for every ton of coal produced. Vast fortunes were made by these already wealthy men, but it was at the expense of the miners. In the News of the Week section of the Hamilton Herald dated January 4th, 1895, a small article quotes Councillor *John Ferguson* as saying that *"£200 of coal royalty is paid to the Duke of Hamilton or Earl Dudley, by Atlantic liners, for every voyage to New York and back."* The money made by these men from coal must have been staggering.

The obscene greed of the landowners hungry for their share of the spoils meant that they would stop at nothing to see the black diamonds and ironstone being brought up from beneath their property. To them, it was a road to riches beyond their wildest dreams and nothing, or no one, was allowed to stand in their way.

Typical of the contempt they felt for the working classes, was the treatment of a tenant farmer called *George Barclay,* who farmed Greenhall Farm, Blantyre. Without consulting *Barclay*, the landowner, *John Wardrope Moore of Greenhall House, Blantyre,* leased the mineral rights to Colin Dunlop & Co., Ironmasters, Quarter. *Barclay* got his first intimation of the mining operations to be carried out on his farm when workmen from Colin Dunlop & Co. turned up in one of his fields and began to sink a pit and excavate the land to build a railroad.

At Hamilton Sheriff Court on 13th June 1874 *George Barclay* sought to obtain an interdict against both the landowner, *J.W. Moore* and Colin Dunlop Ltd. He claimed, that as tenant and occupier of the land, the respondents had no right whatsoever, to interfere with the surface of these lands. The case for the defence was that the minerals being *ex lege* the property of the landlord, who had the power to work them. They contended that they had been all along ready to pay *Barclay* surface damages.

Sheriff Substitute *Spens* refused to grant *Barclay* the interim interdict and appointed parties to meet with the Sheriff Principal on Tuesday 9th inst, in order that the record may be adjusted and closed. He added the following note. *"In the decision Smith v Hamilton McGill in 1786 it was found that the heritor had the right to searching and put down sinks for coal in lands set in tack, upon satisfying the tenant for the damage that may be there-by incurred."* The Sheriff did not consider himself entitled to disregard the judgement of the Court of Session with reference to the precise points at issue between the two parties.

Several days later, the judgement was appealed to Sheriff Principal Dickson, who adhered to the decision of Sheriff Spens. In a note added to his interlocutor, he said that *"the only question on which he had any difficulty was as to the railway which it was admitted the defenders had constructed on the pursuer's farm. He had considerable doubt, without express power reserved in the leases, whether a landlord could make a railway through lands which he had let for agricultural purposes; but it was unnecessary to decide that question at present, because admittedly the railway had been completed."*

Some time after this judgement *George Barclay* called it a day and moved out of Greenhall Farm, no doubt a lot poorer because of the court case and also a lot wiser, having learned that the men who made the laws of the land were also the men who owned the land and the laws were made to protect their own interests.

# THE COALMASTERS' HORSES

A statement oft repeated among the mining communities was that the coalmaster thought more of his horses, than he did of his miners. How well the miners knew their masters.

From 1857 onwards letters written by outraged members of the public began to appear in the Hamilton Advertiser condemning the living conditions the miners were forced to live in. One letter published on the 10th October 1857 spoke of *"seeing coal lords making fortunes in a few years and driving their carriages with liveried servants and themselves living a life of ease and luxury, while little concern is paid to those whose lot is to toil and build up their fortunes and, who after their toil is over, go to their miserable dwellings."* The same writer goes on to say that *"the coalmasters' horses have more comfortable habitation."*

*James Merry*, coalmaster and Member of Parliament and *"chief of the art"** of robbing his colliers blind, was the proud owner of some of the best racing horses in the land. His horses won the Derby in 1860 and 1873, the St. Ledger in 1858 and the Two Thousand Guineas in 1855 and 1870. He was known to have frequently paid 950 guineas for a horse, an incredible sum at the time when comparing it with the sum of less than £1 per week being paid to his miners. When he retired from the turf in 1873, his stud was generally considered to be one of the best which had ever been collected by a private individual.

*Merry* achieved notoriety among the mining community for the way he bled his miners dry by his application of the truck system and his deduction of off takes like the house rent, the coal supplied, medical attendance, school fees, the chimney sweep, blacksmiths fees, explosives, fines etc. All deductions were obligatory, the miners had no choice, whither they used the services or not. Paying his miners fortnightly, he deducted as much as he possibly could before handing over what little was left of their hard earned wages. His workmen were forced to ask for advances on the work they had already carried out and this he gave them, but at a cost; he added interest of 1/- (5p) in the pound when the advance was being deducted from the miner's wage. His workers were obliged to spend every last farthing earned at his store and had to consent to live in hovels of houses which he had chosen for them, or *"not be employed at all."* In 1873 his company was valued at an incredible £1,500,000 the equivalent of more than £100,000,000 at today's value when it was floated on the stock market.

The coalmasters' homes reflected the fortunes they had made from coal, (John Watson's Earnock House had 42 rooms) while the miners and their families were squeezed into one and two roomed houses with no running water and not even a kitchen sink. The stark contrast in the cramped living conditions of the miners and the living conditions of the coalmasters horses, is vividly outlined in the following article describing the new stables being built at Earnock House, Hamilton, home of *John Watson*, coalmaster, (later Sir John Watson Bart.,) and was published in the Hamilton Advertiser in 1878.

# EARNOCK STABLES

"During the last two years, extensive stables have been in the course of erection by Mr Watson, at Earnock and are now about completed. A short description of them may not be uninteresting to many of our readers.

The site selected by Mr Watson is in the park, and about 200 yards from the old Mansion House of Earnock. The east approach leading towards Neilsland passes near to the principal entrance to the stables, which consists of a splendid façade 40 feet in breadth and 65 feet in height, supported on one side by a beautiful tower, with pinnacled roof and loopholed. In the centre of the façade is a noble archway, 15 feet in width and 17 feet in height, on passing through which we find ourselves in a magnificent covered court, 50 feet, by 36 feet width and 40 feet in height, with gothic roof, supported on massive laminated brackets of pitch pine.

On either side of the covered court are roomy coach-houses, lined with pitch pine and sliding doors. Further on we enter into an open court, 40 feet square, with bronze fountain in centre. Around this court is placed the principal buildings. First, on the left are a harness and cleaning room, both beautifully finished in pine, with roof of the former panelled in walnut and floors laid in marble. The principal stable is 70 feet in length and 20 wide and is divided in stalls and loose-boxes. The whole of the wood-work in this stable is of the finest description. The roof, which is 15 feet in height, is panelled in pitch pine and walnut of exquisite design. At the head of each stall the whole width are mosaic tiles, with neat Greek border; the back wall is of white enamelled brick. Patent ventilators are introduced which can be opened and shut by an ingenious contrivance. There are also chutes from the hay lofts above for letting down the corn and hay to different stables. Close to this stable is a convenient place for washing horses, with boilers for hot water; on the opposite side is a hospital for sick horses, and other conveniences.

A coachman's house and ample accommodation for grooms have also been carefully studied. On the outside, but connected by a passage, is a finely fitted-up stable and coach-house for visitors' horses. All the floors and courts, with the exception of harness-room, are of artificial stone, grooved and radiating from a centre. The whole is well supplied with water. Provision has also been made in case of fire, by introducing fire-plugs and having hose always in readiness, and instructing the men how to use them.

Although the stables are upwards of 600 feet from the mansion house, an electric bell and speaking tube have been introduced between those extreme points. We understand that previous to Mr Watson commencing to build, he visited most of the principal stables in England taking notes. He has also introduced as fastening, on some of the doors, locks from Damascus, brought by him during his late tour in the East.

The whole of the buildings, now that they are completed, form a very handsome block. The style is what we might term mixed Scotch baronial and as seen from a distance, with its crow stepped gables and pinnacled tower, nestling amongst the trees, adds another feature to the landscape of old Earnock."

# THE COAL MASTERS

*Sir John Watson, Bart.*

Born in Kirkintilloch, on the 9<sup>th</sup> July, 1819, *John Watson* was the son of a builder and contractor who afterwards became a successful coalmaster. Watson was originally trained as a stonemason; he also studied mathematics and architectural drawing, however his father became very successfully involved in the coal trade and it was to this line of the business that John Watson decided to concentrate.

In 1846 he rented some fields on the Wishaw Estate belonging to Lord Belhaven where his first pit the Victoria was sunk and he subsequently leased Parkneuk Colliery, Dalzell. He then extended his business into the Slammanan district of Stirlingshire.

In the early 1870's Watson acquired Neilsland Estate and a few years later the estates of Earnock and Eddlewood. He bought Eddlewood Colliery and developed Earnock and Neilsland collieries.

In 1893, John Watson donated a fountain to the town of Hamilton. It was erected at the junction between Cadzow Street and Muir Street. In the centre of the fountain was a woman who represents and commemorates the finding and working of coal. In her right hand she held a miner's pick and in the other hand a miner's wire gauge Davy Safety Lamp. The fountain cost £10,000 and is still there today, although the miners pick and lamp are missing. In 1895 the coalmaster was created *Sir John Watson, Bart. of Earnock* in the Queen's honour list.

Watson was always ready to contribute to charity and of course was always willing to be seen contributing to charity but, when it came to his own miners he appeared to have a different policy. On Tuesday 8<sup>th</sup> February 1897, Keir Hardie, spoke to a large audience at the Cambuslang branch of the Independent Labour Party, and told of how an appeal had been recently launched to help famine victims in India. He informed the audience, that one of the subscribers to the fund was *"Sir John Watson, Earnock. That gentleman was away in the Mediterranean at a place called Nice, where the flowers were blooming and everything that was beautiful surrounded him. Sir John Watson, the Christian and Liberal had been so greatly touched by the sufferings of the Indian people, that he telegraphed to Provost Keith, Hamilton, to place his name down for £100 to be sent to the people of India. That night he (Keir Hardie) believed that Sir John would go to his bed with the feeling that he had discharged his whole duty as a man, as a Christian and as a Liberal friend of the working classes. Last week however, in the Hamilton Court, a poor man was brought in leaning on crutches. He was a miner who had been injured at one of Sir John Watson's pits. As miners' always do, a "lift" was taken for the poor fellow, but what did Sir John Watson do but seize the money collected for the "lift" for the rent of the house in which the poor fellow lived. After that, he sent the Sheriff Officer with an eviction order and turned the poor man out of his house. The Liberal and the Christian did help the people of India, but what about the poor miner of Lanarkshire who was turned out of house and home after receiving injuries at one of Sir John's pits."*

Sir John Watson's £100 donation was equivalent to the wages of one hundred and twenty miners for one week's work. The famine fund's published list of subscribers, shows that the average donation was between one and two guineas.

The man involved in the accident *Keir Hardie* was referring to was *Walter Mackay,* a pit bottomer, who had been seriously injured in July 1896 while he was replacing a truck on the rails at the bottom of No.1 Pit, Earnock Colliery. The cage, without any warning, began ascending and his breast was caught by the end of the cage and his body was partially forced up the shaft. He was severely crushed and left permanently disabled. He sued John Watson (Limited) and lost. The court ordered the case to proceed against *John Bolton,* engineman and one month later Mackay sued him and was awarded £25 damages. *Bolton's* lawyers were obviously not as expensive as his employers. In 1897 John Watson Ltd made a profit of £95,166 1/6d, the equivalent of approximately £5,000,000 at today's values.

Then as now, "money talks" a fact which was so obvious when, before the marriage of his daughter *Henrietta* on 10th December, 1896, the streets along the route of the bridal carriage were carefully swept by men using brushes; a distance of almost 1 ½ miles.

Sir John Watson, coalmaster and entrepreneur was not the worst of the Scottish coal barons and he was most certainly entitled to make a profit from his business. He was also a safety conscious coalmaster, never hesitating to invest money in equipment, if he thought it could cut down the appalling accident rate. However, like the rest, he paid his workers as little as he possibly could.

When he died on 26th September, 1898, at the age of 78 years, he left a large fortune in money, property, jewellery and other possessions which had been obtained from the blood and sweat of his miners. He died in the comfort of his own bed at Earnock House. That same day *Edward Curwood* (41) was crushed to death by a 3 hundredweight piece of coal in Watson's Neilsland Colliery; he had been working for a wage of 16/4d (82p) per week.

*42 room mansion house situated in extensive grounds.*

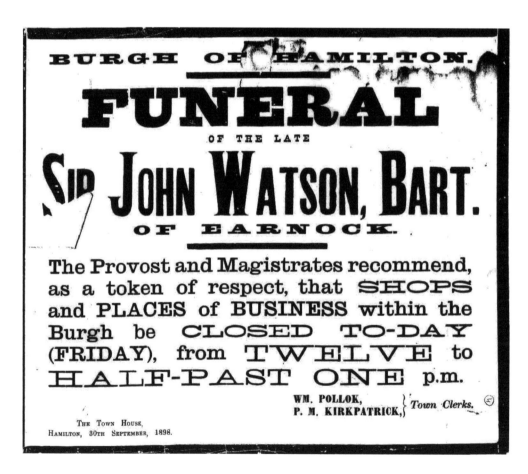

*Courtesy of Hamilton Town House Reference Library.*

# THE WATSON FOUNTAIN

*The last remnants of an industrial empire*

# ARCHIBALD RUSSELL
## COALMASTER
### 1831-1904

Born in Govanhill in 1831, *Archibald Russell* was the son of Archibald Russell one of the earliest pioneers in the development of the coalfields of the west of Scotland. Although he was associated in business with his father from an early age, he was also a farmer and farmed Flemington Farm, Cambuslang as a tenant of the Duke of Hamilton's Estates.

On his father's death Archibald Russell gave up farming to devote all his energies to mining. He was a very successful businessman and he possibly had only one failure in his life when, in 1872, Glasgow City Bank collapsed and as a large shareholder he had unlimited liability for the banks debts and had to meet claims amounting to what was a large fortune. Russell met his obligations and managed to continue in business; many of the other shareholders lost everything.

In 1882, Archibald Russell bought Greenfield Colliery, Hamilton and from then on he acquired and developed colliery after colliery, amassing a fortune on the way. He died on 11th April 1904 at his home, Auchinraith House, Blantyre and at his funeral; the chief mourners were his four sons and six grandsons. His estate amounted to £715,028 13/- the equivalent of approximately £50,000,000 today.

*AUCHINRAITH HOUSE, BLANTYRE.*

# THE RIGHTS OF MAN

*Not all the money made*
*   By companies on the Clyde*
*Can give men confidence in trade,*
*   If pay they won't provide.*

*Men have a right to live,*
*   To work, and to get good*
*For what they work, and what they give*
*   To gain a livelihood.*

*But Capital is King!*
*   So Labour is crushed low;*
*Some companies hardly care one thing*
*   How poor their men may go!*

*These companies are so large,*
*   Their men they seldom see;*
*They leave their businesses in charge*
*   Of some shameful Legree!*

*These companies combine*
*   To keep the wages low;*
*Men only ask a living wage,*
*   Yet masters answer "No."*

*Tis hard to have to toil,*
*   And see the lion's share*
*Go to those who ne'er toil nor spin---*
*   Good God! Is this act fair?*

*Away with sham programmes!*
*   Justice will ne'er be got,*
*Nor, will the people gain their rights,*
*   Till each man gets a vote!*

*Then, then industrious men*
*   Will have themselves to blame*
*If they don't cause the upper class*
*   To recognise their claim.*

*Unknown*
*Circa 1895.*

## ON A CERTAIN LADY'S SUGGESTION THAT ALL MINERS SHOULD BE KEPT UNDERGROUND

Oh, sable stalwart hapless wight.
Know that a certain lady
Would banish thee from God's daylight,
Far from her much exalted sight,
Within thy workplace shady.

"Much trouble," say's our dainty foe.
"Could so wise be averted,
The filthy fellows kept below".
And why not let their families go!
Then all would be diverted.

No need for them to be seen
Outside their working place,
They pass my gates and spoil the scene,
Their raucous voices sound obscene,
And, oh!  What dirty faces.

Thus comrades, would I humbly ask,
Thy pardon for my action,
Though silence is a simple mask,
Thy thoughts are mine, and mine the task,
To seek for satisfaction.

Then lady to thy human plea,
Wouldn't read a humble letter!
Our ideals, true, might disagree.
But chivalry remains with me
To say thine are the better.

But since unburdening thy mind
With weighty words expounding
The vileness of the miner kind
I hope that you will be resigned
To see the ball rebounding.

The air is free the sun, the sky,
God's gift to all bestowing,
He made the ant, the butterfly,
Both live their lives, yet one can die
Without the other knowing.

The butterfly in languid ease,
Evades the shadowed places,
The sunlight shimmering on the trees
Kissed by each sensuous wand'ring breeze,
Is where its course it traces.

And as the red glow fires the west,
It scans its meted measure
In listless languor, deep depressed,
Its gaudy wings at last find rest,
It lives and dies for pleasure.

The lowly ant in toiling haste
Ne'er stops to gaze about it,
Scant time has it to work or waste
Its love of fresh air's not a taste,
It cannot live without it.

*"Rhymer"*
*Circa. 1922*

The above poem illustrates the contempt of the upper classes for the miner. It was written after a Larkhall "lady," irritated by the colliers passing her gate as they went to and from their work, made the suggestion that it would be better if they could stay underground and not come up.

*Young miners with lamps in hand ready to go down the pit.*
*Photograph courtesy of Scottish Mining Museum.*

# THE EDDLEWOOD EVICTIONS

During the nineteenth century, many of the miners and their families had no choice but to live in houses tied to the colliery where they were employed. This story tells of how, in October 1897, during a strike about a threatened wage reduction in Neilsland Colliery, John Watson Ltd., evicted 750 men women and children from their homes at Eddlewood Rows and Meikle Earnock village.

 The story is dedicated to all the pit wives; our mothers, grandmothers and great grand-mothers; who, down through the years, fought a daily battle against poverty, dirt, disease and exploitation.

Meikle Earnock village

From scenes like these, old Scotia's grandeur springs,
That makes her lov'd at home, rever'd abroad;
Princes and Lords are but the Breath of Kings,
'An honest man's the noble (st) work of God'

The Cottar's Saturday Night.
Robert Burns.

*Eddlewood Hall, 1964 prior to its demolition Photograph by kind permission of Hamilton Town House Reference Library*

The Eddlewood Colliery was situated just off the junction between Eddlewood Toll and Strathaven Road, Hamilton. Opened in 1874 it was a medium size pit, employing 336 men underground and 104 men on the surface.

Eddlewood estate was bought by coalmaster John Watson, on 3rd February 1886 and although he had ambitions to purchase the colliery, it did not become his property until 1890. Included in the sale, were five rows of colliery houses known locally as Eddlewood Rows and also houses in the tiny hamlet of Meikle Earnock. Some time after Neilsland Colliery opened in December 1895, access to the Eddlewood workings was gained via the Neilsland shafts.

Early in August 1897, Mr. *Thomas Thomson*, General Manager of John Watson Ltd, notified the miners union of a   proposed 2d per ton reduction in the rate paid to the men in Neilsland Colliery's Main coal.  The price offered was well below the agreed fixed rate for all seams and sections and the proposal infuriated the miners. A meeting was arranged between Messrs. Smillie, Gilmour and McAleer the union representatives and Mr. Thomson without any satisfactory agreement being reached. Numerous meetings followed with management which only resulted in claim and counter-claim.

Gilmour claimed that the Eddlewood rate was already 6d below the county average and the manager maintained that according to a calculation made by the oversman the miners earned from 4/- to 5/5d (20 to 27p) per shift. This was hotly denied by Gilmour who insisted the average was 3/4d (17p) per shift. After further fruitless meetings the miner's withdrew their labour and two days later the dispute had escalated with pits in Burnbank, Blantyre, Cambuslang, Larkhall, Motherwell, and Wishaw idle. Other miners were being asked to contribute 6d of an advance to the Eddlewood miners.

*David Gilmour*

That evening, at Eddlewood toll, the men were informed that the manager had refused offers of arbitration and a vote was taken to continue the strike.  It was also confirmed that the checkweighman's book showed that no miner had earned more than 3/9d (19p) per day during the previous six months despite Thomson's claims of a higher rate.

The strike continued for some weeks with each side blaming the other. On Monday 13th September, a notice posted at the pit head, warned that ejection notices were being served on the 150 Eddlewood and Neilsland miners who rented company houses.  The notice, dictated by Thomson read… *"As it has been resolved to stop No.1 pit for an indefinite period, notice was put up to this effect on 25[th ult]. and the 9th inst. requesting that you to remove your graith\*.  I now hereby give you notice to remove from the house you occupy belonging to the company by Thursday 16th instant, failing which, immediate steps will be taken to have you removed. Trusting you will save me this disagreeable course, yours truly,* Thomson."

At Hamilton Sheriff Court the following Tuesday, a lawyer representing John Watson Ltd submitted an application for 100 summonses of ejection. Representing the miners, Mr. F. Armour argued against the suggestion made by Watson's counsel, that the men could get work and accommodation in other collieries and accused the coal company of conspiring with other Coalmasters to prevent strikers being employed elsewhere. Watson's Representative, Mr. W. Hay denied this and alleged that only 10 -14 men were involved in the strike.

The pleas put forward by Armour, fell on deaf ears and the Hon. Sheriff Substitute Patrick granted 91 eviction orders, to be carried out in five days time. The other nine cases were adjourned till Thursday. The only way now to halt the eviction process was to present a medical certificate from Dr Robertson the company doctor declaring that there was a serious illness in the home, but these certificates were almost impossible to obtain.

No one knew this any better than *John Adamson* and his wife *Jane* who lived at 31 Eddlewood Rows. For several weeks they had been nursing their baby daughter *Elizabeth,* only five months old and desperately ill. Despite all the loving care John and his wife were giving her, she was slowly fading away in front of their eyes. Nearly out of his mind with worry, John had gone to Hamilton Sheriff Court three times to beg Sheriff *Patrick* not to evict them but because he had no medical certificate *Patrick* refused. He told him that no Doctor would withhold a certificate if a child was as ill as he said.

Despite *John Adamson's* pleas, *Dr. Robertson* is reported in newspaper accounts of the strike, as having refused to issue a medical certificate, maintaining that if he did, he would lose his position with the company when strike was over.

With the evictions due in four days, the scramble was on to find alternative accommodation and by the time Thursday arrived, almost fifty families had moved out of the rows and into temporary accommodation with other family members. A few of the men managed to obtain work outside the district and moved away with their families.

The miners' union had purchased three large wooden huts at a cost of £300 and had erected them in the grounds of Cadzow Chapel and *Willie Agnew's* lorry had been hired to take the evicted miners and their possessions to the huts.

At seven o'clock on Thursday morning *George Kemp,* Messenger-at-arms and six assistants arrived at the Rows to carry out the evictions. The only people about at that time in the morning were union officials *Gilmour, Robertson* and four miners who had been watching for the Sheriffs' Officers. Kemp gave the 27 families on his list until twelve o'clock to vacate the houses and if they didn't comply, then he would forcibly evict them.

Word of their arrival spread like wildfire through the Rows and a large crowd gathered. The miners were using delaying tactics and as time dragged on George Kemps nerves became a bit frayed and as a result he began to lose his temper and became quite abusive towards the miners. His assistants began to infiltrate the crowd taunting and intimidating them. One of them waved a brown paper parcel shaped like a crow bar about. Another one called *Sandy McIntosh* insisted on entering houses with *George Kemp* although as an assistant, he had no right to enter and only stopped doing so after *Gilmour* threw him out of a house in the back row.

*George Kemp*

The assistants, sensing that the tide was turning against them, took to their heels and headed for Hamilton, leaving only *McIntosh* who mistakenly continued to act the big man. He was stopped in his tracks by a group of young miners, who slapped him about, threw him over a hedge and left him bleeding, battered and hatless. It was then he realised then he wasn't just quite as big as he had thought and headed off down the Strathaven Road.

Finding his assistants gone, *Kemp* called it a day and went to have a discussion with the manager at the colliery office. The crowd followed shouting and booing, but they moved on, after the chairman of the strike committee, *Robert Jack,* stepped forward and appealed to them to refrain from violence.

With negotiations deadlocked, it seemed inevitable that the evictions were going to be carried out. A petition signed by Provost *Keith,* local traders, the clergy and merchants failed to make any difference; the evictions were going ahead. Over the next few days, six families abandoned their homes, rather than subject their children to the horrors of an eviction.

Lookouts were posted throughout the district and on the Thursday morning, the eviction party were spotted heading for the Rows. Runners were sent ahead to warn the families that the evictions were going ahead. Father *McAvoy* the local R.C. priest went from house to house counselling the people to be brave, but law-abiding.

Sheriff Officers Mr. *T.H. Bell* and Mr *F. Cassels* arrived with men from Coatbridge and Glasgow to enforce the court orders. As soon as they set foot in Rows, they were pelted with cinder ashes and anything else the crowd could lay their hands on. A telephoned request to the County Police Headquarters for assistance, resulted in the arrival of twenty-four police constables, accompanied by Superintendent *Anderson* and Inspector *Middleton.*

*Harry* and *Annie Burgoyne's* house was the first on the list and this was no coincidence. *Harry* was a member of the strike committee and the sheriff's officers were set to make an example of him; but Harry had made up his mind that he wasn't going to go quietly he was going to make sure that they would have to work for their money. The usual six knocks were given at the door by Bell, but Harry was not for opening it. Barricaded from the inside, Bells assistants had to break the door down with a heavy hammer. Every time the hammer struck its target, a roar would go up from the watching crowd and it took almost half an hour before the door was breached. When Bell stepped over the doorway, *Annie Burgoyne* who had been waiting in the crowd ran forward. Her nerves were shattered; she hadn't shut her eyes the whole night. The moment she had dreaded was here and she was shaking like a leaf; but wee Annie was not going out without a fight. Armed with a bag of pepper she threw a handful over the top of Bell and each time he made a move to enter the house, Annie would throw another handful. Only when his assistants made a run for her and physically dragged her away from the door, did he gain access.

Stepping into the house, another surprise was waiting for him. *Harry Burgoyne* was standing with a smile on his face and a pail of sour milk and dirty water in his hands, which, with precise aim, he emptied over Bell. Harry was eventually overpowered and forcibly ejected from his home and then both he and his wife were arrested and charged with assault.

Bell cleaned himself up as best he could and continued with the evictions. At No 140 *William Brown* and his wife were evicted after his door was broken down by a sledge hammer, the eviction of *Robert McElroy* and his family followed in quick succession.

When it was the *Kerr* family's turn, *Gilmour* informed *Bell* that *Mrs Kerr* had a serious heart condition and that he would be held responsible for the consequences. *William Kerr* a large powerfully built man had already barricaded the door and could be seen at the window with a hammer in his hands and a look on his face that said he would have no hesitation in using it.

*Bell* appeared to have second thoughts about evicting this family and went to the colliery offices to speak to the manager. On his way, there he was booed and pelted with stones. One man, *William McKay,* was arrested and the crowd charged the police, in an attempt to rescue him. The police had to run for safety as the mood of the crowd changed and the simmering resentment of the miners and their families surfaced, and it appeared that a riot was about to break out.

*Father McAvoy.*

This was an unwanted turn of events prompting *Father McAvoy* and three elderly miners, *Terence Murphy, John Boyle* and *William Berry* to move among the crowd, in an attempt to calm the people down. The police then drew their batons and viciously attacked the old men, with *Murphy* and *Berry* being severely cut about the head. They then struck out in all directions, causing a panic among the crowd, as people stampeded along the rows in an attempt to escape the blows. The more fearless of the strikers stood their ground to challenge the police and the situation was becoming more explosive by the minute.

*Father McAvoy* stepped forward and pleaded with the crowd to allow "*things to go along quietly just now,*" and the crowd, heeding his word, began to calm down, allowing the police led by Inspector *Middleton,* to go through the colliery gates with their prisoner in front of them.

A meeting then followed between the union officials and the crowd, who afterwards dispersed quietly to their homes.

Early the following Thursday, *Superintendent Anderson* arrived at the rows accompanied by 40 police constables, who had been brought in from all over the county and they cordoned off the streets. No one was allowed in or out until the evictions were carried out. Sledge Hammers, crowbars and hatchets were being used to burst the doors down. After a skirmish, *Robert Crookston* and his family were evicted, followed by *Robert McVey* and his family.

At the next house *John Connacher* put up quite a fight but he was eventually overpowered. Once his belongings had been dumped outside, his wife stepped forward and demanded that they finish the job, as there was still one item of furniture left. One of the assistants with downcast eyes entered the house and came out carrying a baby in a cradle. The crowd surrounding the house stood in silence as he put the cradle down beside the furniture. The assistant, who was visibly affected by what he had just done, walked away after apologising to the family and remarked that he had children of his own.

Once the families in Eddlewood Rows had been evicted, the police and Sheriff's officers turned their attentions on the small hamlet of Meikle Earnock.

At the home of *Ned Harkins* they were informed his wife was seriously ill. One look at the old lady confirmed what her husband had told them and a temporary respite was granted.

*Alexander Crookston's* home was the next target. The police surrounded two houses, but were unsure as to which house was *Crookston's*. A plea to the large crowd fell on deaf ears; no one would point the house out. It took almost an hour to locate the Eddlewood local Police officer, Constable *Forrest* and eventually, when he did arrive and identify the house, the eviction proceedings began; but *Alexander Crookston* had made a good job of barricading his door and access was gained, only after sledge hammers and crowbars were used to smash it down. An inside door received the same treatment and after ten minutes of backbreaking pounding on the doors with the sledgehammers, entry was finally gained and the family and their belongings, were out in the street.

Approximately 750 men, women and children were evicted or forced to leave their homes; many of them moved to other areas to live with relatives. Most of their names are lost in time, but the following names are of eleven families with the number of children in each household, who were living in the huts in the grounds of the Cadzow R.C. chapel.

*Harry Burgoyne (9) John Connacher (8) Alexander Crookston (2) Robert Crookston (8) John Hendry (5) John Kenny (2) James Laird (4) Robert McElroy (2) Robert McVey (5) Charles Menzies (5) and John Reeves (4)*

The eviction of the *John Adamson* and his wife was put on hold, thanks to *George Kemp* who using common sense and compassion, visited them the morning after baby Elizabeth died and reassured them that although he had the ejection order, he would delay the eviction as long as he possibly could.

The trials were held at Hamilton Sheriff Court and *William McKay* was found guilty of striking a police officer with a stone and sent to prison for 20 days.

The *Burgoyne's* were found guilty of assault. Harry was fined £1 or 14 days imprisonment, his wife *Annie* was fined £1. 10/- or 21 days imprisonment. They were a respectable, good living couple, both members of Hamilton Baptist Church and had no previous convictions. The thought of eviction had left them distraught. The baby of the family aged 18 months was suffering from whooping cough and was not fit to be moved. They had nine children, all still at home. Where could they go with nine children? Who'd protect them? Not the law! The law protected the men with the money; the coalmasters.

The miners eventually resumed work when the dispute went to arbitration. Returning on the old rates of pay they immediately suspended their subscription to the company doctor demanding his removal, despite Dr Robertson strenuous denials that he had refused to issue the Adams family with an exemption certificate. Each Eddlewood and Neilsland miner contributed 3d per week subscriptions to the company doctor and collectively this amounted to approximately £300 - £400 per year. By refusing to pay the doctors subscription, the miners eventually won the right to appoint a doctor of their own choosing, with the choice of four doctors, including Dr. Robertson.

In November 1892, two years after *John Watson* purchased Eddlewood Colliery; he erected a recreational hall and reading room for the use of the company's miners. At the opening ceremony he recited all 21 verses of The Cottars Saturday Night by *Robert Burns* and it is said that he excelled himself, so great was the depth of feeling in his voice.

Watson's miners and their families lived in grossly overcrowded conditions in one and two roomed homes, most with no running water or kitchen sinks and with the outside dry toilets shared by numerous large families. The size of the one roomed house a "single end" was 15ft x 10 ft. or 11ft. x 9 ft. plus two set in beds on the wall opposite the fireplace, there was one window in the house. The size of the two roomed houses was not much better.

A miner's wife had to be a financial genius to clothe and feed her family on the pittance that was her husband's wage; 19/- or 95p per week, less deductions. Money was deducted for the blacksmith, for sharpening or repairing tools, whither or not his services had been used, explosives, the doctor, the check weigh man, schools, the rent the chimney sweep, fines and anything else the coalmasters could think up. She would cook, bake, scrub, clean, knit and hand sew, patching, mending and altering clothes outgrown by one child and fashioning them into acceptable clothes for a younger sibling. First out of her bed in the early hours of the morning to see her husband out to work, she was invariably the last one in the house to retire at night.

Life was a constant battle, living as they did in these grossly overcrowded and unsanitary conditions. Outbreaks of measles, chickenpox, whooping cough, diphtheria, typhoid, cholera and polio regularly claimed the lives of her children, despite her vigilance.

Before the erection of outside wash houses, these women would be out in the back courts at three or four o'clock in the morning, boiling the family wash in a cast iron pot suspended over an open fire. After boiling, the clothes would be scrubbed and rinsed in a wooden bine and finally wrung out. Hail rain sleet or snow the washing was done outside over these fires.

Many of the women went to an early grave. Undernourished and worn out with the daily struggle to survive, there were no reserves left to fight many of the common illnesses so prevalent at the time.

John Watson with his wife and family lived a life of unimaginable luxury in a 42 roomed mansion house, with servants to take care of their every need. In Hamilton and surrounding areas, he was master of the estates of Neilsland, Eddlewood, Earnock, Meikle Earnock, Earnockmuir, Beechfield, Whitecraigs, Hollandbush, Sheriffaulds and Broomhouse.

In 1890 an inventory of his Hamilton estates showed that he owned 1,900 acres of arable land and plantations. There were 500 head of cattle and sheep and 49 horses and 6 foals on the Earnock and Neilsland estates.

In the 1895 Queen's honours list, John Watson was created Sir John Watson, 1st Baronet of Earnock, an honour which he no doubt accepted with more genuine feeling than that displayed at the opening of Eddlewood hall. *"Princes and Lords are but the breath of Kings!!!"*

He died on the 26th September 1898 aged 78 and left in his will, a trust fund worth £400,000 for his children, the equivalent of approximately £26,000,000 today. The total value of his estate could not be estimated, because in addition to cash, there were shares, property, annuities, valuable jewellery and estates in other parts of the country. His son, also named John, inherited his title and much of his wealth, becoming the second Sir John Watson, Bart. of Earnock and a director of John Watson Ltd, the company who reduced the miners' rate by 2d a ton and evicted approximately 750 men, women and children from their homes...TO INCREASE COMPANY PROFITS.

*      *      *

Miners known to be working in Eddlewood's No. 1 Pit, Main coal No. 2 section, between 13/3/1897-31/6/1897. *James Bonnar, John Bonnar,* * *Frank Brown, James Brown, Samuel Green, Andrew Hamilton, Edward Harkins, Wm. Hill,* * *Robert Hill, John Howe, Wm. Jack,* * *James Jack,* * *Wm. Malcolm, James Mathie, John Mathie,* * *Antony Miller, N. Middleton, W. Middleton, Patrick Mullin, David McAllister, Robert McVey, Joe Pollox,* * *Wm. Rodger, Thos. Rutherford, Alexander Smith, John Smith; George Ward.* * After name denotes a Polish miner.

*      *      *

# KNOWN EDDLEWOOD COLLIERY DEATHS

| DATE | NAME | AGE | CAUSE OF DEATH |
| --- | --- | --- | --- |
| 24.01.1882 | JAMES HARPER | 41 | CRUSHED TO DEATH IN SHAFT |
| 06.03.1883 | GEO. WILSON | 24 | FELL 66 ft. DOWN SHAFT |
| 15.04.1887 | THOS. C. LAIRD | 58 | ROOF FALL (Crushing injuries to legs feet and head) |
| 12.10.1887 | ROBERT YOUNG | 40 | JAMMED BETWEEN ROOF AND HUTCH.(Chest infection) |
| 26.12.1888 | JOHN McNAMARA | 15 | RUN DOWN BY TUBS |
| 16.08.1889 | HENRY BROWN | 45 | ROOF FALL (Buried 3 hours) |
| 06.08.1890 | JAMES GOWANS | 46 | ACCIDENT IN SHAFT (Severe head and leg injuries) |
| 08.08.1890 | WM. GRAHAM | 15 | CRUSHED BETWEEN BUFFERS |
| 27.02.1891 | JOHN BROWN | 15 | CRUSHED BY HUTCHES |
| 01.01.1892 | WM. RENNIE OR WILSON | 40 | CRUSHED BY BUFFERS |
| 28.04.1892 | PAT. McINTYRE | 38 | NO DETAILS (Injured spine) |
| 24.05.1892 | ALEX. PEACOCK | 21 | CRUSHED BETWEEN HUTCH AND DOOR-HEAD OF CAGE |
| 19.02.1896 | JOHN MILLER | 36 | FALL OF 3 cwt. FACE COAL (Fractured pelvis) |
| 07.07.1897 | JOHN McLAUGHLIN | 25 | RUN DOWN BY PUG ENGINE |
| 21.04.1900 | WM. MURPHY | 50 | FALL OF STONE FROM FACE (Loin injury) |
| 12.05.1902 | WM. RANKINE | 20 | DRAGGED 48ft. DOWN SHAFT (Multiple fractures) |
| 26.08,1904. | MICHAEL McGUIRE | 28 | HUTCH ACCIDENT (Fractures of ribs, both clavicles and cervical vertebrae) |
| 01.12.1904 | WM. SHAPTOCH | 37 | FALL OF FACE COAL (Fractured skull) |

# EDDLEWOOD RAW

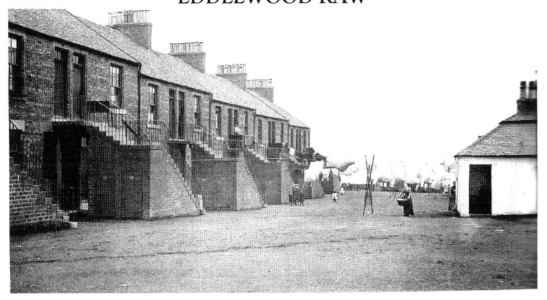

There was auld *Mrs Davidson* who smoked the clye pipe
And auld *Mrs Crookstane* was always in sight;
Auld *Mrs Frew* wha' stopped no far awa'
We were aye happy in Eddlewood Raw.

There was *Killiecum, Rankin, Hamilton* and *McGraw*
And a' the *Forrests* at the fit o' the Raw;
And auld *Harry Gray*, the poet an' a'
We were aye happy in Eddlewood Raw.

There was auld *Solly Calder* and *Bummer Brownlie,*
Who worked in the pit boattum frae seven tae three;
When the men goat their wages, as little they goat,
They made fur *John Craigs* tae hae a wee tot.

When they played at the bools in Eddlewood Green
The trophies they won could always be seen;
For the miners in Eddlewood were always sae braw
We were aye happy in Eddlewood Raw.

Auld *Wullie Ross* we ca'ed Royal Blood
He'd come bawling and shouting, we could hear every word;
We'd scamper inside till he went awa'
Yet we were aye happy in Eddlewood Raw.

We played fitba' in the park for oors at a time,
*Campbells* and *Johnstones* and *Kerr's*---they were fine;
And after the gemme there was nae fightin' at a'
For we were a' happy in auld Eddlewood Raw.

There was *Bender Simpson* and *Willie McKay,*
*Tully Lyons, Red Wilson* and others forebye;
They played cairds oan the wee green for a penny or twa'
Yet a'body was happy in auld Eddlewood Raw.

Auld *Granny Shaw* made candy galore,
When the weans goat a penny they made fur her door;
They'd chow and they'd chew till their wee gums did gnaw
But the weans were a' happy at Eddlewood Raw.

There wis wee *Tammie Collins* an auld *Francie Young,*
They kept us a' laughin--- and great wis the fun;
We'd staun' at the corner and listen in awe
We had some coamics in Eddlewood Raw.

In the twenty-wan strike things werna sae guid,
And *Mr Hamilton** was gettin' some wid,
He loast his life in sic a guid cause
He'll aye be remembered in Eddlewood Raw.

There wis *Hawthorn Murray* who had the Boy Scouts,
We'd gaither at the hall and you could hear his shouts;
He'd tak the salute an' dismiss us an' a
Oh we were so happy in Eddlewood Raw.

There were *Hughes, O'Neill's* an' also the *Wynnes,*
*Greenhorns, Chow Gray,* who always caused dins;
There were *Lindsays* and *Clellands* and also the *Scads;*
An' wee *Ned Torrance* who wis ca'ed bike mad;
There were *McCrums* and *McGurks,* I remember them a'
And we were aye happy in Eddlewood Raw.

There wis *Jock Mairtin* the polis, who'd gie us a chase,
We'd keek roon the coarner an' see his big face,
We'd a' rin like hell tae we couldnae rin at a'
But we were a' happy in Eddlewood Raw.

Wee *Sunny Forrest* came up oot the pit,
He'd gae hame in the moarnin' some breakfast to git,
He'd gae back doon the pit an' he'd shout and he'd craw,
But he wis weel liked in auld Eddlewood Raw.

We played fitba' oan the road fur oors at a time,
*Clellands* and *Johnstones* and *Kerr's* they were fine.
An efter the gemme there wis nae fightin' at a'
For a'body wis happy in auld Eddlewood Raw.

My pen has gaun dry an' I'm sleepy furbye,
Wi thochts o' them a' I heave a great sigh,
So I'll gae tae ma bed an' dream about a'
The happy auld days in auld Eddlewood Raw.

*Unknown.*
*Circa 1930's*

*William Hamilton, colliery fireman.*
*Photograph courtesy of Janette Cameron, great grand-daughter.*
*Killed in Neilsland Glen during the 1921 miners' strike after he was*
*struck on the head by a large boulder dislodged by people scavenging for*
*coal on Neilsland Colliery bing. He had been collecting wood for the*
*striking miners' and their families. He was highly respected in the*
*locality and was always referred to as Mr Hamilton.*

# THE SIEGE OF CADZOW ROWS

*Cadzow Colliery miners, circa 1900. Photograph courtesy of William Walker,*
*grandson of oversman William Walker, back row second right.*

Hamilton was an unusual town in having two bridges with the same name. One Cadzow Bridge spanned Cadzow burn in Cadzow Street, but the real Cadzow Bridge, as any local would tell you, stood at the top of the Low Waters Road. Under this Cadzow Bridge ran Cadzow Colliery's branch of the Caledonian Railway Line.

Cadzow Bridge was the meeting place for the Low Waters and Cadzow communities. All miners meetings were held at the colliery storehouse adjacent to the bridge. People arranging to go out would meet at Cadzow Bridge and all the local news and gossip could be heard and exchanged there.

Seven hundred local men were employed by Cadzow Colliery, the entrance to which lay between gaffers row (a block of houses reserved for colliery officials) and Cadzow Bridge.

*The former entrance to Cadzow Colliery*

The sinking of the pits or shanks commenced in 1872. There were three pits; No.1 the pumping pit measured 24½ feet × 7 feet, No.2 pit 21½ feet × 6 feet and No.3 pit round and brick lined measured 13 ½ feet in diameter. From the onset water penetration proved to be a serious obstacle being encountered at a depth of only 12 feet from the surface. By the time bed rock had been reached, one of the largest Cornish engines in Great Britain had been installed, pouring 6000 tons of water every 24 hours into the Meikle Burn. Coal was eventually reached in February, 1876. The deepest pits, numbers 1 and 3, were sunk to a depth of 888 feet.

Cadzow coalfield extended 500 acres from Strathaven Road to the River Avon, with most of its workings lying under the High Parks. At its peak, 1500 tons of coal was mined every day. The lowest level, the Splint seam, was notoriously gassy and the colliery was closed twice in 1877, when a series of violent explosions damaged the underground workings, fortunately with no loss of life.

To house their workforce, the colliery built and acquired approximately four hundred houses. Inside the colliery was *Smithy Row* and on the opposite side of Low Waters Road was *Field Street; Hall Street; School Street; Cadzow Square* and up past Cadzow Bridge and to the left of *Strathaven Road* stood Cadzow Rows. The streets were named after directors of the Cadzow Coal Company. The fore row looking onto Strathaven Road was called *Wilson Terrace* followed behind by *Moore Street; Austine Street; McCreath Street; Aitken Street; Landale Street; Bishop Street and Simpson Street.*

Like every other colliery, Cadzow had had its labour disputes, but in July 1900, the discontent which had been grumbling away for almost a year, came to a head. Despite an agreement to the contrary, the management had in its employment, 8 non union miners. Seven of these men were eventually persuaded to join, but one man, *John Kennedy,* had continued to refuse offers of union membership. Allegedly, Kennedy had some months previously joined the union and then failed to pay his dues, denying that he had ever joined.

On Monday, 23rd July, almost seven hundred miners downed their tools and came out on strike. Four days later, at Hamilton Sheriff Court, Cadzow Coal Company applied for and was granted, summonses for the eviction of over two hundred mining families living in company houses. This news sent shockwaves spreading throughout Hamilton. Three years earlier, in 1897, *John Watson* and company Ltd, owners of Eddlewood, Neilsland and Earnock Collieries, had evicted over seven hundred men, women and children from Eddlewood Rows during a strike over a reduction in wages, now once again the spectre of eviction was looming over their heads.

*Huts for the evicted miners*

Later that day, at a meeting of miners in the Victoria Hall Hamilton, *David Gilmour,* secretary of the Lanarkshire miners union, outlined the problems the miners were going to face. For once, the union was in a strong financial position and would be able to pay strike pay. He assured the miners that even though Cadzow Coal Company was determined to fight women and children by evicting them, the union would provide temporary homes to accommodate every man, woman and child who was left homeless.

At seven o'clock the following morning Mr *T. H. Bell* or 'Bell the Sheriff' as he was known, arrived at Cadzow Rows accompanied by an assistant and two police officers. Having only 48 hours in which to serve the eviction summonses, he was going to be a busy man. The mining families, knowing of the deadline had been up most of the night in anticipation of his visit.

*CADZOW ROWS*
*The sheriff officer's last stand*

Beginning at the front row (Wilson Terrace) he began to serve the summonses.

The traditional knock was given but not one door opened, the summonses were then pushed under the doors. With most of the front row visited, he went round the back. Up the first stair he went and on entering the porch, found to his surprise a door was opened and he was invited in. He duly served the summons on the occupier, but when he tried to leave, he found the stairway blocked by miners. One look at their faces and he knew he was never going to walk down the stairs. Turning, and running back into the house, he got out of the building by opening a window, dreeping down onto an outhouse, then jumping to the ground; he wasn't on his feet for long. In the scuffle that followed he was pushed to the ground by a woman in the crowd. Getting up and trying desperately to hold onto his dignity, he elbowed his way through to the front of the building and proceeded to serve summonses on the remaining downstairs houses.

By this time the crowd had turned into a howling mob and they were forced to make a run for the policeman's house in the front row. To add to his misery, Bell's assistant had just informed him in no uncertain terms, that there was no way he was going to try to serve another summons.

For almost an hour they remained in the police house, until loud booing coming from Cadzow Bridge, heralded the arrival of reinforcements in response to their frantic telephone message. Several Burgh police constables had arrived on their bicycles, followed soon after, by Superintendent *Ritchie*, Inspector *Gracie* and a dozen county constables. With his assistant steadfastly refusing to cooperate *Bell* had no choice but to call a halt to the morning's proceedings.

*Gilmour* the union representative advised the crowd to let them depart and soon they were beating a retreat down the Low Waters brae, with the cheering of the residents of Cadzow Rows, ringing in their ears.

Five days later, on the Thursday, workmen arrived at the Rows and started to remove the doors from the head of the stairs leading to the upstairs houses. This was a ploy to prevent the Sheriff's Officer being locked in the porch on their next attempt to serve the summonses. Many of the men folk were at a meeting in Hamilton and it fell upon the women to defend their homes. Aided by residents of Eddlewood Rows who had been hastily summoned, the tradesman left after some angry scenes.

*John Robertson,* vice chairman of Lanarkshire Miners Union, who had appeared on the scene, soon organised new doors to replace the ones removed by the workmen and to add to the Sheriff Officers misery every door number in the rows was carefully obliterated with paint.

All was quiet for a few days, and then insider information was received from a sympathiser revealing that the next attempt to serve the eviction summonses was to be made early on Monday. Again the man in charge was to be Bell the Sheriff with a dozen Glasgow assistants.

The miners union offered a cash prize for the best barricaded house; first prize being one pound. This was won by a pyramid arrangement of furniture at the door topped with a curtain draped cradle, containing a large doll. Another house displayed a Union Jack inscribed "Mafeking" (a comparison with the famous siege).

*First prize,*
*Barricaded house*
*(We shall not be moved.)*

Cadzow Square was the first port of call reached by *Bell,* his assistants and fifty police officer, at eight o'clock in the morning. Seven Glasgow Sheriff Officers and twenty five police officers were dropped off and the rest continued to Cadzow Rows, followed the whole way up, by loud booing.

*Cadzow Square. Waiting for the sheriff 'officers*

At Cadzow Square, the officers proceeded to the first close accompanied by the jeering crowd, many of whom were women, who jostled them, caught them by their arms, knocked their hats off and danced in circles around them.

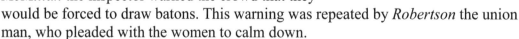

Police trying to protect the Sheriff Officers got their helmets knocked off and scenes like this continued until *McMillan* the inspector warned the crowd that they would be forced to draw batons. This warning was repeated by *Robertson* the union man, who pleaded with the women to calm down.

The Sheriff Officers succeeded in pinning only 35 summonses to doors before they were forced to make a run for Cadzow colliery office to seek sanctuary.

At Cadzow Rows, Bell had fared no better, having been greeted with a fusillade of stones. Surrounded by twenty five police officers, they started in Moore Street. Inspector *Gracie* warned the excited crowd to calm down, or face the consequences. One man *John Davidson* was arrested for head butting Sheriff's Officer *John David Anderson* and knocking him to the ground.

Because of the jostling of the crowd, it was almost impossible for the Sheriff's Officers to pin the summonses to the doors. Identity was also a problem; they didn't know who lived where, as the door numbers no longer existed.

One Sheriff Officer found a back stairway completely blocked by a whole tree, complete with branches and leaves. Undeterred and with great dexterity and skilful manoeuvring, he succeeded in climbing over the obstacle. After pinning the summonses to both doors, he descended to the cheers of the crowd who had obviously appreciated his athletic skills.

In Austine Street, miners and their friends blocked doorways, preventing the officers from reaching the door to serve the warrants. With one exception when a number of miners were arrested, the police present did nothing to assist, saying that they couldn't interfere by removing people from their own doors.

Tempers became frayed and *Bell* the Sheriff took offence to a remark addressed at him by *David Gilmour*, the miners union secretary. *Bell* threw a punch at *Gilmour* striking him on the shoulder. In an instant, *Gilmour* had *Bell* by the throat. The watching crowds began to cheer at the prospect of a punch up, but the two men returning to their senses refrained from continuing the fight. *Bell* however, had had enough, calling off his men; they retreated to the colliery office at Cadzow Bridge where he found the Cadzow Square officers already there. In the safety of the office they began to count their bruises.

Still reeling from his Glasgow kiss, *Anderson* was nursing his head, while another Sheriff's Officer laughed as he described how he also had been reeling, but in a different way. Captured, he had been danced and birrled from Cadzow Square to the Cadzow bridge by a group of young women. His only fear was that a press photographer may have immortalised him with a tell tale photograph.

One man displayed a large bruise on his head from a stone thrown at him. Another Officer had escaped by leaving one of his coat tails in the hands of his captors. Most of their legs had been kicked black and blue.

While in the office, a telephone message had been sent to Mr *Aitken*, Managing Director of Cadzow Coal Company, requesting further instructions. At two o'clock and none having been received, they informed the police surrounding the office that they wished to leave. *David Gilmour* was informed of their decision by the police and on his instructions, the crowds dispersed, allowing the Sheriff's Officers to leave unhindered.

The following day, the press hung about Cadzow Bridge for some hours hoping for further developments, but as all was quiet they left to walk to Hamilton. Some distance down the hill, to their utter astonishment, they met one of the Glasgow Sheriff Officers heading for Low Waters. On stopping to enquire what he was doing, he replied that he was going back to revisit the scene. Unable to persuade him to change his mind, the reporters followed at a discreet distance. As he turned into Cadzow Square, he was instantly recognised by a group of women, who danced around him and jostled and pushed him about. His plea that he was only looking fell on deaf ears and the women, taking him by the arms, rushed him down the brae.

Halfway to Hamilton, they destroyed his hat and tied him to a lamppost with his torn coat-tails. Asked by his tormentors if he would ever come back, he swore at them. For his language, he was slapped about by the women and then chased into Hamilton where he was taken into protective custody. He was given a police escort to the railway station where, on boarding the train, his clothes in tatters, he almost collapsed with relief at his escape.

The following Thursday, the Sheriff Court was packed to the door with miners giving their support to some of their own who had been charged with various offences. The first man in the dock was miners' agent *David Gilmour*, charged with assaulting bricklayer *William Miller*, whilst the latter was employed repairing the stair landings (removing the porch doors). He was alleged to have seized him by the collar, dragged him about and threatened to throw him down the stairs. *Matthew Keith* or *White* was accused of assaulting Glasgow Sheriff Officer *Robert Wilson* by striking him on the head with a stone. *John Davidson* was accused of assaulting *John David Anderson* (Sheriff Officer) by head butting him. *John Robertson, William Cox, Hugh Morton, James Robertson, Miles Welsh* and *Luke McGowan* were all charged with having maliciously removed and destroyed with picks and shovels 140 square feet of newly laid cement on three stairs at Cadzow Rows. This charge was also related to the doors. All the accused pleaded not guilty.

Several days later, *John Cunningham, John McCarroll, John Davidson, John Phillips, Robert Cochrane, Patrick Powell, William Jones, William Gillon* and *Andrew Ramsay*, all but two residing at Cadzow Rows, appeared in the same dock. They were charged with standing closely packed together upon the steps of a house occupied by *Thomas Nailon*, blocking the door and kicking Sheriff Officer *Thomas Taylor* on the left knee, thrusting pins or needles into his legs, cursing and preventing him from serving a warrant. The case was adjourned till a later date.

The Cadzow Coal Company, in a last desperate attempt posted the summonses. All but two were returned by the postman marked house blockaded, refused, closed and gone. No further attempts were made to serve the summonses.

Two weeks later the strike finished when *Kennedy* joined the union.

All eviction proceedings were unconditionally withdrawn. Rent arrears were to be treated sympathetically and every miner was to get his own job back.
On Tuesday 28th August 1900 Cadzow returned to normal when the miners resumed their work.

### Gilmour and Robertson
Of the eighteen miners who had been charged with offences in only one case (*Matthew Keith or White*) was the charge withdrawn. In September 1900 the other eighteen miners appeared in court and the verdicts were mixed. *David Gilmour* was fined a pound or ten days imprisonment. The case against the six men accused of destroying the newly laid cement was found not proven. *John Davidson* was acquitted of head butting the Sheriff's Officer. Nine men were found guilty of assaulting *Thomas Taylor* with pins

and needles and were fined 30/- (£1.50) or twenty-one days imprisonment. An appeal to the High Court failed to change the guilty verdicts. The union paid the fines.

Life was hard for coal miners, the work was back breaking and dangerous. When their men folk left to start their shift the women who stayed behind in the home knew that before the day was finished, they could be widows and grieving mothers.

Many of the improvements in conditions and safety had been hard won by the miner's union, the miners having learned that their strength lay in unity and where there was division, conditions would never improve. The inhabitants of Cadzow Rows knew this, and as a community they had acted as one for the common good, making it known, that no longer were they prepared to allow the threat of eviction to be used as a sword to be held above their heads. They had seized the moment...... AND WON.

*GAFFERS ROW,*
*CIRCA 1900*
*Photograph courtesy*
*of Wm. Walker.*

*Gaffers Row 2005*

133

# THE NAMES OF THE MINERS WHO WERE TO BE EVICTED

## AITKEN STREET

*James Canning, John Brannigan, Thomas Hanson, Gilbert Hansen, Joseph Hanaten, James Hislop, William Kane, James McLaughlan, Edward McCarrol, William Walker.*

## AUSTINE STREET

*William Barker, Thomas Brannigan, Henry Brown, Henry Burns, James Dougan, William Gillon, Henry Gray, Bernard Hughes, William Hutchison, Bernard Kellachan, Charles Lawless, John McCreadie, Arthur McGhie, Frank McKay, Daniel McLaughlin, Daniel Miller, John Neilan, Thomas Neilan, James Nicol, Patrick Pollack, George Radcliff, John Reid, Allan Scott, James Swift, John O'Neil.*

## BISHOP STREET

*William Burns, John Burns, John Cole, John Donnelly, George Gardiner, John Green, Robert Gillespie, Charles Miller, R. Halliday, Edward Larkins, Thomas McCreish, John McCarroll, James Martin, Patrick Monachan, John Norton, John Stanley, Archibald Smith, Gavin Taylor, Joseph Tyndall, William Queen.*

## CADZOW SQUARE

*John Adamson, Robert Aird, John Barker, William Bell, Thomas Bertie, John Burns, Patrick Casey, John Donevan, John Ferguson, Robert Hill, John McGucken, Denis Moran, Thomas Small, Archibald O'Brien, John O'Brien, Archibald Tutton.*

## FIELD STREET

*Arthur Brannigan, Walter Bulloch, James Clark, John Dunn, Thomas Docherty, James Donnelly, Charles Gorman, John Hayes, James Marin, Bernard McDonald, James Paterson, James O'Neil, Robert Selfridge, Anthony Stewart, William Walker.*

## HALL STREET

*Frank Donnovan, Ralph Early, Edward Gilmour, William Handlay, William McGillvray, Peter McGillvray, Charles Mallows, William Murray, Patrick Murray, Frank Starrs, Andrew Taylor.*

## LANDALE STREET

*Thomas Archibald, Thomas Cairns, Robert Cochrane, James Coravay, Thomas Cornish, Peter Devine, Matthew Fleming, Richard Fitzpatrick, William Jones, John Jenkinson, Frank Kane, William Kinstray, William Kelly, James Robertson, Thomas Scott, William Stratton, David Stewart.*

## McCREATH STREET

*Hugh Collins, Thomas Cowan  Bernard Hughes, Richard Johnstone, Robert Kane, Hugh Martin, Matthew Madden, Bernard Murray, Wm. Mullholland, James Mulligan, Thomas Moore, Arthur Rafferty, Francis Reilly, David Smith.*

## MOORE STREET

*Wm. Cowan, James Clark, Wm. Cox, James Davis, John Dickson, James Ellis, Wm. Gebbie, James Gebbie, John Gibson, Patrick Gaynor, Alex. Hamilton, Matthew Henry, Thomas Jardine, Frederick Kane, David Kellachan, Patrick Lenard, Robert Lees, Wm. McCallum, Robert McLaren,  Robert McDougall, John Phillips, James Polland, Andrew Ramsey,  Joseph Reid, Wm. Thomson, Archibald Weir, John Wilkie.*

## SCHOOL STREET

*James Callington, John Cardie, Thomas Cavanagh, John Chalmers, Peter Connor, James Connor, John Early, James Harrison, John Jackson, Hugh Kerr, James Kelly, John Mackie, Charles Maxwell, John Reilly, John Simpson, Robert Stewart, George Summers, R. Thornton, Thomas Todd, William Walker, Adam White.*

## SIMPSON STREET

*Wm. Cape, John Davidson, Wm. Gray, Richard Hackett, James Lindsay, Henry Paterson, Wm. Petrie, Charles Ryan.*

## SMITHY ROW

*Charles Cornish, James Cornish, Wm. Kirk, Adam Rae.*

## WILSON TERRACE

*Alex. Archibald, Robert Barns, Daniel Canavan, Lawson Humphrey, Wm. Lennox, Thomas Lightbody, Peter McCabe, John McDonald, Robert Mathieson, Alex. McDonald, Wm. Napier, Thomas Ross, Alex Stewart, James Stewart, William Walker.*

# THE COLLIERY MANAGER

Among the miners, were highly gifted men, who, had they been born seventy years later, would not have gone down the pit, but would have gone to university and had successful professional careers. However, many of them worked their way up the colliery promotion ladder by attending night school to obtain the required qualifications.

*Hugh Logan,* General Manager of Bent Colliery Company was among the men determined to move on in life. In 1890 he started working as a boy at the coal face in the Bent Colliery, Hamilton. Three years later, he became a haulage boy, then a repairer covering all classes of repair work.

A Territorial Army reservist, he volunteered in 1900 for service in the Boer War and two years later, he returned home to resume work in Bent Colliery.

 Studying mining at night school classes in Hamilton Academy, he obtained the coveted manager's certificate in 1911 and was appointed undermanager at Bent Colliery. Later he was transferred to a similar position at the Hamilton Palace Colliery, belonging to the same company.

While working there, the First World War broke out and as he was still attached to the 6th Battalion, The Cameronians (Scottish Rifles) he was mobilised in 1914. Sent to France with his battalion, he was wounded in the carnage of the battle of Festubert on 15th June1915 and was discharged on medical grounds in 1916.

Returning to his post as undermanager at Hamilton Palace Colliery, he was appointed manager of Bent Colliery two years later and he was to remain in that position, until the colliery closed down in May 1930, after which, he was transferred to Cadzow Colliery, where he was manager for nine years.

Never forgetting his roots and his early life as a miner, Hugh Logan was always interested in miners' welfare work; he was the first president of Low Waters welfare scheme and of the bowling club connected with it.

Highly respected by the workmen, his style of management and successful co-operation with the various committees, paid dividends for both men and company and during  the nine years he was manager at Cadzow Colliery, there was not a single day lost through a dispute. In 1938 he was promoted General Manager of Bent Coal Company and remained in this position until retiring in 1942.

The position of mine manager was by no means an easy one, because he was, by the very nature of his job, the buffer between the complaining miner and the company. Had more colliery managers adopted Hugh Logan's respect for his workmen, his forward thinking policies and an open office door where any grievance, real or imaginary could be discussed, then the Scottish coalfields and the Scottish miner would have jointly reaped the benefits.

# ENTOMBED
# IN
# NEILSLAND COLLIERY
# 1916

*1895. Waiting for the first coal to come up at Neilsland Colliery.  Photograph
courtesy of Hamilton Town House Reference Library*

Neilsland colliery was one of the larger Hamilton collieries and employed more than
1200 men and boys at the height of its production. Situated off Neilsland Road, the
entrance to the colliery was approximately where the street called Laurel Bank now
begins.

The colliery, owned by Messrs John Watson Ltd,     was developed on the lands of
Neilsland estate. The managing director of the company John Watson was a shrewd
entrepreneur who had purchased the land in 1871; he also owned Eddlewood and
Earnock Collieries.

Work began on the colliery in June, 1893 when amid great
ceremony, *John Watson* junior cut the first sod of earth for number
one shaft and his brother *Thomas* cut the first sod for number two
shaft. Two and a half years later in December 1895 the colliery
went into production.

*The winding engine, Neilsland Colliery*
*Photograph courtesy of Hamilton Town House Reference Library.*

*1895. Miners going underground at Neilsland Colliery.*
*Photograph courtesy of Hamilton Town House Reference Library.*

That same year, *John Watson* was created Baronet of Earnock in the Queen's honours list, but he did not live to see the colliery start to produce coal; he died on 26th September 1895. His son also called *John* inherited the title and he became Sir *John Watson,* 2nd Baronet of Earnock.

Neilsland colliery had its share of accidents like all the other collieries in the Lanarkshire coal field, but it's record was no better or no worse than any other pit, until the morning of Wednesday, 26th April, 1916.

An advert placed in the local newspapers of that time had invited contractors to tender a price for the removal of stoops in the abandoned Eddlewood Ell seam.
These stoops or pillars of coal were the roof supports left by the colliers working the old stoop and room method of extracting coal. As the stoops were removed, the roadway behind them collapsed and this invariably led to buildings on the surface being damaged, but the cash value of the coal contained in the stoops overrode any worries or conscience about subsidence.

*Hugh Scott courtesy of*
*Jean White (granddaughter.)*

*Hugh Scott* won the contract to remove the stoops and commenced work with his team of miners, Robert *Leadbetter, Robert Robertson, George Stewart, John Shaw* and *Robert Brownlie,* all Hamilton men. Access to the abandoned workings in Eddlewood colliery was gained via Neilsland colliery. John Watson's three Hamilton coal

138

mines were all interconnected. At one time it was possible to descend the shaft at Earnock Colliery, walk through the underground workings, and surface at both Neilsland and Eddlewood collieries.

The Ell Coal had been reached by roadways and a blind pit, at a point near the abandoned Eddlewood No. 3 shaft. As a safety precaution, boreholes had been kept in advance by the men, as they approached the area where they were going to work. At midday on Wednesday 26th April, 1916, the barring of the old No.3 shaft collapsed and the refuse with which the shaft had been filled in, consisting mainly of sludge from the coal washer in an almost liquid state, burst into the Ell coal where five of the men were working.

Several minutes before the collapse, shaftsman *Robert Brownlie* had finished his work and left to return to the surface. Some distance down the roadway he heard a thunderous rumbling noise and realising that there had been some sort of catastrophic accident, started running through the workings warning miners who were working in the area to run for their lives. Brownlie knew that the pit manager *James Cook* and undermanager *James Houston* were supervising work somewhere in the vicinity and managing to find them, reported his fears to them.

The three men attempted to return to the area where the five colliers had been working but found their way blocked by a torrent of glutinous debris and liquid material which was flowing like a river of lava through the roadways, destroying everything in it's path and filling up every available space.

*Cook, Houston* and *Brownlie* ran to all the other sections where men were still working and warned them to make a run for the shaft and get to the surface before they were cut off.

Up on the surface, a huge crater had appeared where the old Eddlewood No.3 shaft had been. The material from the crater had descended down the shaft contributing to the influx of debris filling up the roadways. A fence was erected to prevent any further loss of life and work commenced to fill in both the shaft and the crater with solid material.

The Coatbridge Mines Rescue Brigade was in attendance at the colliery, as was *Robert McLaren* H.M. Inspector of Mines and *Henry Walker,* Chief Inspector of Mines for Scotland and two assistants, Messrs *A.H, Steele* and *P.McIlhenny.* Under their direction, the rescue teams continued their search, but despite their efforts, it was becoming increasingly obvious that the missing men could not have survived.

At ten o'clock that night the body of *Robert Robertson* was recovered. He had apparently been swept forward for some distance by the rush of sludge and debris from the collapsed shaft. His body was embedded in mud and he had died from suffocation
   A total of five men died and despite the efforts of the rescue teams, the search for the men had to be abandoned, four of the bodies were never recovered. The death total would have been far greater had it not been for *Robert Brownlie,* who, despite the torrent of sludge pouring through the workings, saved many men from a horrible death.

*Photograph courtesy of Mary Clydesdale, (granddaughter of Robert and Mary Robertson.)*
*Back row, Robert Robertson, killed in Neilsland Colliery 26/4/1916.*
*Middle Row, John and Mima Easton, Mary Robertson, Nancy Easton.*
*Front row, Mary, Helen and Jean Robertson.*

The part of the colliery involved in the accident was bricked off and abandoned after it became far too dangerous to continue the search and work resumed once more at Neilsland Pit.

Sixty years later the late *Guy McDermid* a retired miner of Neilsland Street, Hamilton, recalled the incident. He was he said, "*only a boy of fourteen and had been working down the pit when the shaft collapsed.*" Being young and inexperienced he wasn't involved in the rescue work and set off for home at finishing time. As he was walking down Low Waters Road, he caught the eye of *Mary Robertson* who was standing outside her home. "*Is that the shift finished son*" she enquired? "*Aye missus it is*" he replied, lifting his bunnet as a mark of respect for the woman, before walking on. Guy knew that her husband was one of the missing men, but continued down the road saying nothing to her. "*It wasn't my job to tell her that her man was dead,*" he said, "*She was still a young woman and that was the second husband she'd had killed down the pit*". "*You know, these four men are not far away*" *and* pointing over to Millgate Road, *Guy* added; "*their bodies are lying over there, almost 800 feet down*".

*Guy McDermid* had been right about *Mary Robertson* losing another husband in a colliery accident. Her first husband *Robert Easton* (29) had fallen down the shaft of Cadzow Colliery in 1906 and some years later she married his best friend and best man at their wedding, *Robert Robertson*, only to lose him to a different type of shaft accident.

*Back row Robert Easton, killed in Cadzow Colliery. 1906.*
*Front row, left to right. Mary, Mima, John, Nancy Easton.*
*Photograph courtesy of Mary Clydesdale.*

*The victims.*
*Robert Robertson,* 229 Low Waters, (body recovered.) *Hugh Scott,* 30 Low Waters, (entombed.) *John Shaw,* 136 Eddlewood Rows, (entombed.)
*George Stewart,* 187 Low Waters, (entombed.) *Robert Leadbetter,* 103 Beckford Street, (entombed,) all Hamilton.

\*     \*     \*

## NEILSLAND COLLIERY'S LAST MANAGER.

*James C. Parker M.B.E who at 28 was one of Hamilton's youngest colliery managers. He was highly respected by all who worked with him. Photograph courtesy of Margaret Stewart (Daughter)*

# KNOWN NEILSLAND COLLIERY DEATHS

| DATE | NAME | AGE | CAUSE OF DEATH |
|------|------|-----|----------------|
| 01.09.1895 | JOHN MOONEY | 26 | FELL DOWN SHAFT |
| 09.07.1897 | JAMES RICHARDSON | 20 | ROOF FALL (30 cwts) |
| 20.06.1898 | JOHN DOYLE | 50 | NO DETAILS (Fractured skull) |
| 26.09.1898 | EDWARD CURWOOD | 41 | FALL OF COAL AT FACE |
| 17.08.1899 | THOS. McKINNON | 24 | ROOF FALL( Neck broken) |
| 14.03.1901 | WILLIAM MURPHY | 19 | ROOF FALL |
| 17.06.1901 | DAVID GALLACHER | 39 | HIT BY CRANK |
| 16.07.1902 | HENRY GRAHAM | 54 | DECAPITATED |
| 12.05.1903 | JAMES MATHIE | 56 | ROOF FALL. (Chest Injuries) |
| 21.11.1904 | ANGUS MATHIESON | 23 | FALL OF COAL AT FACE (Fractured skull) |
| 13.11.1904 | JAMES MARSHALL | 26 | CRUSHED BY HUTCH (Fractured spine lived 33 months) |
| 10.01.1908 | ROBERT MUIR | 62 | FELL 108 ft DOWN SHAFT |
| 17.01.1910 | DUNCAN WILKIE | 13 | FELL 1000ft DOWN SHAFT |
| 29.08.1912 | JONAS ZAGARAUSKAS | 54 | ROOF FALL (Multiple fractures of spine, ribs, left leg)) |
| 28.09.1912 | WM. M. FORREST | 33 | ROOF FALL (Fractured spine) |
| 17.02.1912 | JAMES McFADYEN | 68 | ROOF FALL (Chest injuries) |
| 30.07.1913 | EDWARD MITCHELL | 31 | ROOF FALL (Broken neck) |
| 07.11.1913 | PATRICK LYONS | 26 | CRUSHED BY CAGE |
| 26.04.1916 | ROBERT ROBERTSON | 35 | COLLAPSE OF SHAFT |
| " | HUGH SCOTT | 45 | ENTOMBED |
| " | JOHN SHAW | 22 | ENTOMBED |
| " | RBT. LEADBETTER | 62 | ENTOMBED |
| " | GEORGE STEWART | 29 | ENTOMBED |
| 31.07.1918 | WM. McGONAGLE | 18 | MULTIPLE INJURIES |
| 18.01.1921 | JAMES RODDEN | 60 | ASPHYXIATED |
| 09.10.1922 | SAMUEL BAIRD | 21 | CAUGHT IN MACHINERY |
| 15.01.1923 | THOMAS GOLD | 36 | CAUGHT IN COAL-CUTTING MACHINERY |
| 23.01.1928 | JAMES RAE | 52 | FALL OF COAL |

*Brand New Pug Engine, Neilsland Colliery 1895*

# THE RIOT IN THE RANCHE

*Photograph courtesy of Edward Hart*

Up until the 1980's the corner at Strathaven Road and Graham Avenue Hamilton was dominated by a large red sandstone building comprising of shops, flats and on the prime corner site Hamilton's most famous public house, The Ranche. One of the features of the Ranche was the sloping floor, which was caused by collapse of the underground coal workings which honeycombed the area.

The Ranche was a favourite of the local miners and in 1926 there took place an extraordinary incident that is still spoken of today eighty years later and is known as the riot in the Ranche.

The main character in the chain of events which led to the riot was a miner called *Bob McTaggart*, a powerfully built man with neck and shoulders like a prize bull. Although Bob, who lived in Low Waters and worked in the former Cadzow pit was definitely no angel, he was well thought of in the 'Cadzow Rows' that now-demolished collection of over 200 miners homes situated off the Strathaven Road. But Bob had, as all mortals have, some failings; the main one being that after a few pints he liked to fight. You could call him the local 'hard man with the soft centre'.

On a Saturday night after a few pints, 5ft 9in Bob would weave his way down past Cadzow Bridge into School Street. By the time he arrived he would be stripped to the waist; then, standing in the middle of the street he would bellow his war cry to the tenement windows; *"Come oot and fight..... I'll fight the best man... Come oot..."* The neighbours, well accustomed to this ritual viewed it as their Saturday night entertainment, but it is doubtful if there were many who took up his offer as Bob also had quite a formidable reputation as an amateur boxer. It was this penchant for a fight that got him barred from the Ranche public house in Strathaven Road which was the local for many Cadzow Row miners.

On the evening of Friday May 7th 1926, the owner of the Ranche turned up at the County Police Headquarters with a request for a police presence at the pub. Through the grapevine, he had heard that *Bob McTaggart* intended to partake of 'quiet refreshment that very night, despite being barred from the pub. Returning to the Ranche in the illustrious company of a police inspector and a superintendent (both of whom were dropped off a short distance from the pub) the owner entered the premises and there, standing at the bar, was Bob.

At the trial, according to the evidence of the owner, he told McTaggart that he was not welcome as he had been barred. At this, Bob was alleged to have shouted: "You b......., you have insulted me. I'll murder you" and then made a run for him. The owner beat a hasty retreat out of the door and Bob, hot on his heels, ran straight into the arms of the law, who just happened to be outside;

Captured, he was returned to the pub, where he was soon on the receiving end of police batons. At the sight of this assault on one of their own, the clientele of the establishment attempted to release Bob from police custody and thus began, the riot in the Ranche.

Before it was finished, the gantry, along with every window, mirror and glass in the pub had been smashed and police reinforcements had to be brought in from Hamilton and Blantyre police stations.

With an estimated 100 men fighting inside the pub and a crowd of approximately 500 outside baying for police blood, the only way to restore public order was for the police to release a much battered but still defiant *Bob McTaggart.* This defused the situation just enough to empty the pub and calm the crowd down, but not for very long, soon the riot was in full swing again. The police and the Ranche came under fire from a fusillade of stones, bricks and anything else the crowd could get their hands on.

The arrival of the Black Maria containing 10 police officers from Hamilton Burgh Police Station and more men from the County Police Headquarters and Blantyre Police Station sent the crowd scattering in every direction; through back courts, up closes, anywhere to get them out of the clutches of the officers.

Early the following morning the arrests began. There was hardly a house in Cadzow Rows where there wasn't a man sitting waiting for the knock on the door. Police raided numerous houses in the area. Identity parades were held and eventually 11 men were charged with mobbing and rioting.

The trial at Hamilton Sheriff court lasted three days. One by one the witnesses took their stand in the witness box all anxious to give their version of the riot. The one exception was *William McMorran Symington,* the barman who had been working in the Ranche that night and for reasons known only to him (and possibly the Cadzow miners) he appeared to have developed amnesia when questioned about who was there and what took place.

At first he thought there could have been about 30 men present in the bar when the owner returned from the County Police Headquarters, but then he changed his mind, reducing the number to 20 men. Finally, he settled on only four people being present, protesting that he couldn't see, as he had taken cover during the riot!

The owner's chauffeur however, *James Robertson,* (a Blantyre man) appeared to have a photographic memory. He said that having gone into the bar, he soon left after being struck by a pint measure. Outside, finding his windscreen has been smashed, he climbed into the vehicle hoping he could at some point, move it out of the way. Identifying *Daniel (Gowdie) Hughes* one of the accused, he said that he had come running out of the pub covered in blood from a head wound and had stood cursing and swearing at the door of the Ranche. He tried to convince the jury that this Cadzow miner was shouting to the crowd outside *"come on you fellows; don't just stand there; come in and pull the whole bloody lot out. Them dirty b……. are using their sticks wholesale"* and also said that Hughes was encouraging the crowd to break down the front door which had been locked behind him.

The chauffeur also identified another of the accused, *Alexander Murphy,* as being the man who had pulled him out of the car by the throat and informed him that if he *"attempted to go for help, his car would go down the brae wanting wheels..."* *Robertson* said that the crowd by this time was throwing a hail of stones at the building and Superintendent *Taylor* came outside and appealed to them to stop. The reply was more stones and he saw one hit the superintendent on the jaw.

He described how at this point *Taylor* drew his baton and then watched with amazement on his face as a wee man dressed in blue, marched up and down the pavement in front of him firing questions at him. (The bar room lawyer?)... The chauffeur identified this man as *Owen Martin*. Another man *Robert (Bobby) Mount* was identified as also being in the vicinity when *Superintendent Taylor's* baton was pulled from his hand. (It was never recovered.) *Robertson* told how the officer had started to chase the culprit, but he was knocked down, surrounded and then attacked by the crowd, eventually being rescued by *Inspector Mutch* who came to his aid and managed to get him back into the Ranche.

Having done his best to jail half of the accused, *James Robertson* was allowed to stand down from the witness box.

Some of the defendants pleaded alibi and produced witnesses to prove it. One, *James (Wee Pea) Canning* in an attempt to scale down the size of the riot, put it to the jury that the crowd outside the Ranche had not actually taken any part in the riot; they were merely passing the pub on the way home from devotions at the local Catholic Church.

At the end of the trial, 10 of the accused miners, including *Bob McTaggart*, received a six-month prison sentence, the other miner *James McGhie* got four months and the legend of the riot in the Ranche slipped into the pages of Hamilton's history.

Several years after the riot *Bob McTaggart* with his wife and children emigrated to Canada where he lived until he was in his seventies and died after losing a leg in a lift accident.

In the summer of 2003 the mystery of *Superintendent Taylor's* baton was solved when *Robert Chartier,* grandson of *Bobby Mount* told of how after the riot, his grandfather had arrived back at his house with the baton up his sleeve and his grandmother, (a quiet, decent wee woman,) terrified that the police would arrive at the door, grabbed it and threw it into the fire. The baton failed to burn, so she pulled it back out of the fire and throwing it at her husband, told him to get it out of the house.

Ducking and diving through back courts and over fields, *Bobby Mount* arrived at Cadzow forest where he buried the baton, making sure that it could never be used as evidence against him and there it remains, to this day,............ IN AN UNMARKED GRAVE.

## THE ACCUSED

The following men, all miners, appeared in court on a variety of charges relating to the riot. *Robert McTaggart, Richard Hutchison, William Pollock, Joseph Allison,, Alexander Murphy, Patrick Martin, Owen Martin, Daniel Hughes, James McGhie, Robert Mount, Robert McBride*

## DEFENCE WITNESSES

*John Burns, James Canning, Mrs Mary McLeary, Arthur O'Neil, Archibald Peffers, Richard Thomson*

## PROSECUTION WITNESSES

Inspector *Alexander Mutch,* Superintendent *Alexander Taylor, James Robertson,* motor driver, *William McM. Symington, James Francis McDonald*

*Photograph courtesy of Robert McTaggart, great grand nephew of Bob McTaggart.*
*1910-1911 Hamilton's Cadzow St. Anne's R.C. church football team with Bob McTaggart*
*top row, second from left.*

146

# THE RANCHE HOLIDAY CLUB

*Photograph courtesy of Charlie Lawless son of John Lawless 2ⁿᵈ right middle row.*

 The men in the photograph with the exception of two (middle top and bottom rows) are miners who were regulars at the pub. At least one of the men shown in the photograph, (*James Canning*, top row, fourth from right) was called as a witness at the trial of the eleven men charged with rioting and assault.

Contrary to the public's perception of the miner, the photograph illustrates how beautifully turned out the men were, with white shirts and shoes polished and fit to see your face in.

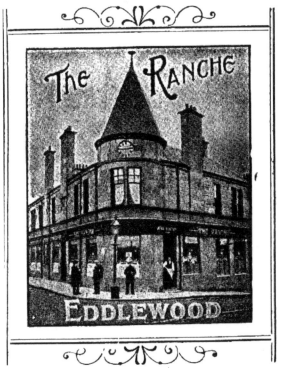

# "HERE'S THE POLIS"
# CADZOW ROWS
# 1927-1935

Some of the collieries had a police officer living in the colliery "Rows" and it was his job to keep the peace, safeguard company property and keep an eye on the residents. The constable at Cadzow Colliery Hamilton lived at Wilson Terrace, Cadzow Rows, which was the fore row facing on to the Strathaven Road and the local pub, "The Ranche."

In 1929, there was a worldwide depression and many pits were closed down or on short time. Life was harder than usual and the mining community never missed an opportunity to make their burden a bit easier. Such was an opportunity presenting itself to the locals on the afternoon of 13th April, 1929, at Cadzow Rows, when four single apartment houses at the corner of Simpson Street and Bishop Street were being demolished.

For most of the morning many of the residents of the rows had been hanging about watching the demolition squad in action. Standing on guard at the demolition site was the company policeman and he was watching the locals. He was under strict instructions that the wood which was being removed from the roof was required by the company and he was told to keep the residents away from it.

However at lunch time, the workmen left the site to go and eat their "piece" and the officer, unable to ignore the pangs of hunger, soon left to go home for a meal. As he walked towards his house, little did he know that there were many pairs of eyes following his every movement.

As soon as he was through his front door, there was a stampede of men, women and children running for the demolition site and soon they were swarming over the roof, stripping the wood linings off with saws and axes. A short time later, the constable returned to find to his horror that fifty square yards of wood had all but vanished and the place was alive with looters. At the sight of the law the crowd fled carrying their loot.

A telephone call for reinforcements resulted in another two constables appearing on the scene, but by the time they got there, much of the wood had been sawn into "clugs," or chopped into firewood. Off they went, up and down the "Rows," looking for tell tale signs of sawdust outside doors. Three houses were visited, but by that time the general alarm had been sounded and when they came out of the third house, the sight which met their eyes must have put paid to their dreams of promotion. Lying scattered on the pavements and roads up and down the "Rows" were pieces of wood which had been hastily pitched out of doors and windows. Sawdust had also been liberally thrown about and it was well nigh impossible to prove which of the houses the wood had come from.

The residents of the houses searched by the police soon found themselves appearing in court on a charge of reset. Two women and one man pleaded guilty, using the excuse that their children had brought the wood into their homes without their knowledge. The judge however was having none of it and fined them 10s (50 pence) each.

Had the police gained access to the rest of the houses before the evidence was thrown out, many of the residents of the "Rows" would have found themselves standing in the dock. The unfortunate accused who appeared in court were, *Mrs Margaret Harkins*, 16 Bishop Street; *Mrs Catherine Dickson,* 14 Landale Street and *John Reid*, 16 Bishop Street all of Cadzow Rows.

\* \* \*

Always on the lookout for an arrest, the Cadzow police constable showed no mercy after an accident which took place on the afternoon of Sunday, 18th August, 1935, at Cadzow Rows during a heavy thunderstorm. Eleven young men had entered a condemned house in Aitken Street to get out of the rain and were having a game of cards, when, without any warning, the roof collapsed, trapping some of them under the heavy debris. Soon the miners from the rows were frantically pulling at the rubble to reach the trapped youths. Three of the most seriously injured had to be taken to the Glasgow Royal Infirmary while the rest were treated by a local doctor.

The following youths were injured *John Walls* (18) labourer (fracture of left thigh bone and body bruises) ; *Alfred Rinaldie* (13) a Govan boy, (abdominal injuries); *Thomas McGhie* (23) ashman, (fracture of the left thigh bone and exterior bruises.) The other eight, *Thomas McGilvary* (18) clerk, *Arthur Hughes* (18), carter, *Owen Corns* (22) miner, *Joseph Murray* (21) miner, *William Walker* (16) stable-boy, *James McGhie* (15) *Robert Allison* (15) and *Joseph Stewart* (13) all had suffered shock and a variety of injuries to back, head, legs and arms.

Two months after the accident, nine of the injured (two were still being treated in hospital) appeared at Hamilton Burgh Police Court, charged under the Trespass Act 1865, with "*lodging in premises without permission.*" Fortunately for all concerned, one of their lawyers had done his homework and he put it to the bench that, as they had not been charged until more than one month after the incident and the Act stipulated an interval not exceeding one month for citing respondents, there was no case to answer. The judge, faced with a good lawyer, was forced to discharge the accused.

\* \* \*

Pit refuse bings were a bone of contention to both the mining community and the police. Desperate for coal, many people took the chance to look for some which had been thrown out with the pit waste. This led to frequent raids on the bings by the police when people were scavenging for coal.

On the 24th October 1927 at Hamilton Burgh Police Court, Justices Mr *W.B. Thomson* (Wishaw) and Mr *Alexander McIntosh* (Stonehouse) sentenced *James McIntyre*, Meadowhill Rows, Larkhall, to forty days imprisonment with hard labour for taking coal from the refuse bing at Dykehead Colliery. The same day *William McDonald*, Eddlewood Rows and *Robert Thomson*, Meikle Earnock were given fourteen days with hard labour, for taking coal from Cadzow bing and *Bernard Fitzpatrick* and *Edward Torrance*, Eddlewood Rows were both sentenced to ten days with hard labour, for taking coal from Neilsland bing. There was an outcry at the sentences but an appeal was turned down.

# CADZOW COLLIERY
## 10/10/1929
## "ARE YOU RIGHT ALL RIGHT BOB?"

For weeks, miners working in No.1 Pit Cadzow Colliery had been searching for coal in the Kiltongue seam and finally on the 9th Oct, 1929, they found it.   The following day the night shift went down the pit at ten o'clock to start working the seam.

Although there were quite a few men working in the colliery that night only six men were working in the immediate area, *John (Jock) Whitton, Robinson (Robbie) Foster, Robert (Bob) Mathie, Terence (Terry) Murphy* and two younger men *Charles (Charlie) Russell* and *Robert Stein.*

The men were working at the face and blasting was required to bring the coal down, so having drilled three holes and set the shots in preparation for blasting, they moved back along the roadway to safety.

*Russell* and *Stein* moved further up the roadway to carry out some work and the remaining three men took the chance for a rest and settled themselves down on their hunkers at a "gable" some distance away waiting for the sound of the blast when *Jock Whitton* plunged the handle of the charger. The shot was heard to go off and a few minutes later Whitton who as fireman was responsible for safety and shot firing went off to connect the wires for a second shot.

The miners sat about waiting on the fireman coming back to fire the second shot but after a few minutes and there was still no sign of him, *Bob Mathie* shouted *"How did the shot go Jock?"* His voice echoed down the silent mine but there was no responding answer.   Getting to his feet *Matthews* said to his mates "I'd better go up and see what's wrong" and off he went in the same direction as *John Whitton.*

Up until that point the thought of something being wrong hadn't crossed the minds of the other miners but after *Bob Mathie* left there was the same ominous silence. *Terry Murphy* stood up and shouted *"Are you all right Bob?"* and, in the silence as he listened for an answer, he heard a groan from the workings.

 At this point *Robbie Foster* jumped up and said *"he must be gassed"* and ran forward to see what he could do and he had only gone short distance, when, in full view of his workmate he started staggering and collapsed on his face.

*Terry Murphy* then ran towards him and getting him underneath the armpits, managed to pull him back up the roadway for a distance of 18 feet, before he also collapsed. However *Murphy* who by this time was seriously affected by black damp gas, managed to shout out a warning just as he was losing consciousness.

*Charlie Russell* and drawer *Robert Stein,* who had been working in the vicinity at the time, heard the echoing cry and they ran along to see what was up. Spotting *Terry Murphy* lying on the roadway, *Russell* sprinted forward and grabbed him and managed to drag him back up to where the air was clear.

*Terry Murphy* who, by this time was semi-conscious, managed to tell them that there were still three men in the section. Leaving him with *Robert Stein, Charlie Russell* went back into the gas filled workings, but only went a short distance when he started to feel light headed and his legs started giving way, and he had to turn back.

Help began to arrive from other parts of the pit and fireman *George Rodger* went in to the workings with his dampened cap in his mouth in an attempt to protect him from the gas, He noticed that the "air was clear and inviting" and different from anything he had ever encountered before. As he ventured down the flame of his safety lamp warned him that there was gas in the roadway. He stopped and taking his shirt off wafted it about in an attempt to clear the air. With some of the gas cleared he ran eyes nipping from the fumes and found *Robbie Foster* still alive. Dragging him up the roadway, he reached clearer air, where despite desperate efforts by local doctor *Nora Steel* to resuscitate the unconscious miner, he died underground, at the bottom of the pit shaft.

Undermanager *James Sloan* managed to obtain a smoke helmet and entered the workings where he found *Bob Mathie* lying face down and beyond any help. He then went back in found *Jock Whitton* lying on his back six feet from the coal face and he also appeared to be dead. Despite this, *Dr Steel* attempted to resuscitate the men but finally had to pronounce them both dead.

When *Dr Nora Steel* returned to the surface it was obvious the amount of effort she had put into her attempt to save the men. Her clothes were damaged and both of her knees were badly bruised.

The mining community was stunned by the loss of the three miners. The men were well known and respected, both *John Whitton* and *Robbie Foster* were married with families and *Robert Mathie* was due to be married in a few months. *Robbie Foster, Terry Murphy* and *Charlie Russell* all entered the workings knowing that they were filled with gas. *Terry Murphy* tried his best to recover the unconscious Robbie Foster and he would have lost his own life, had it not been for the bravery of *Charlie Russell.*

*Robbie Foster* was the first miner to recognise that gas was the problem, but in spite of this, he ran straight into the workings to see if he could help. *Robbie* had been a miner in Cadzow Colliery until 9th September, 1914, when he left the pit and joined the army after the outbreak of the First World War. He had seen active service on all the chief battle fronts with the exception of Mesopotamia. He had gone out to the Dardanelles on July 1915 and had been in the retreat from Serbia. He had fought in Egypt and Palestine and returned from there to France in 1918. He had seen the all the horrors of the battlefield and had himself displayed an exceptional courage, far beyond the call of duty.

On 18th October, 1918, *Robbie Foster*, by then a Lance-Corporal in the Royal Munster Fusiliers had been ordered to withdraw to a new position when he noticed a wounded comrade lying at the front of the line. Running back under heavy artillery fire, he managed to reach the wounded soldier, bandage his wounds and then carry him back to safety. For this action he was awarded the Military Medal.

Less than three weeks later he was reconnoitring on the left of the line on the railway embankment near La Chapelle when he saw a party of about 30 German soldiers armed with several machine guns taking up a position about twenty yards away. Knowing that they would use the guns with devastating results on the British soldiers, he ran back, seized a Lewis gun and returned to where he had seen the Germans, turned the gun on them causing them to retreat. He then rushed forward, capturing two prisoners and a machine gun.

This action allowed his battalion to reorganise and advance without giving the enemy time to consolidate. For his bravery he was awarded the Distinguished Conduct Medal. He was also awarded the French Croix de Guerre.

*Robert Mathie* was buried in his home town of Motherwell and both *John Whitton* and *Robbie Foster* were buried at the Bent Cemetery Hamilton.

*Robbie Foster. Photograph courtesy of Bill Foster (Son).*

On day of the funeral the Hamilton branch of the British Legion formed a guard of honour outside Robbie Foster's home as the coffin draped in the Union Jack was lifted out through the window and gently placed it in the hearse. A firing party of Cameronians with reversed arms marched behind the cortege honouring the memory of an exceptionally brave man. A lone piper led the procession. Fireman *John Whitton's* cortege joined the procession and together the two miners started their last journey watched by crowds of silent people who lined the pavements six deep.

*Jock Whitton* and *Robbie Foster* were buried in adjoining graves, in the shadow of the No 3 Pit, Bent Colliery, situated only fifty feet away.

As Robbie Foster was being lowered into the earth, the sound of the bugler playing the last post echoed round the cemetery, and as the notes died away, the guard of honour fired a volley of shots over his grave……………… a fitting tribute to a man who was a hero ……both in war and peace.

# IN MEMORIAM

(Lines in memory of our dear departed comrades, who lost their lives in Cadzow
Colliery)

'Tis sad to think our comrades,
   Just in a single night,
Have left this world behind them,
   And vanished from our sight.
Beneath the bowels of the earth
   Their precious lives they gave,
Three gallant Scottish collier lads,
   The bravest of the brave.

To the ones both near and dear to them
   It must be a cruel blow,
But we hope they come to realise
   That the Lord has willed it so.
We know 'tis very hard to part
   With dear ones that we love,
But we hope to meet them once again
   In the better land above.

Life in this world is but a span.
   For we never know the day
That gentle knock comes to our door
   To beckon us away.
Our comrades bold went down the mine,
   As happy as could be;
And never dreamt that God's daylight
   They never more would see.

Our hearts go out in sympathy
   To the dear ones left behind,
For we know they must be troubled
   Both in body and in mind.
But still they know they never can
   Meet in this world again,
God comfort them and keep them
   Is our earnest prayers.   Amen.

Willie Gray
Low-Waters.

153

# A CADZOW COLLIERY HERO

*Terrance Murphy dragged unconscious miner
20 feet down the pit roadway before he himself was overcome by gas.
Photograph courtesy of Evelyn Stewart. (Daughter.)*

## THE FUNERAL OF ROBBIE FOSTER AND JOHN WHITTON

*Crowds line the streets to show their respects for the dead miners.*

*Robbie Foster's two small sons following behind the cortege.*

In
LOVING MEMORY
OF
OUR DEAR FATHER
JOHN WHITTON
WHO WAS ACCIDENTALLY
KILLED 10TH OCT. 1929
AGED 39 YEARS.
ALSO
OUR DEAR MOTHER
ISABELLA ORR MILLER
WHO DIED 5TH APRIL 1951
AGED 59 YEARS.

ROBINSON FOSTER
KILLED CADZOW PIT
10TH OCTOBER 1929
MARY FOSTER
7TH JANUARY 1942
HELEN GRAHAM FOSTER
16TH JANUARY 1945
MARGARET (MEG) FOSTER
11TH SEPTEMBER 1951

*Buried side by side in Hamilton's Bent cemetery*

# KNOWN CADZOW COLLIERY DEATHS

| DATE | NAME | AGE | CAUSE OF DEATH |
|------|------|-----|----------------|
| 20.04.1878 | THOMAS GILMOUR | 20 | CRUSHED BY HUTCHES. |
| 08.04.1884 | HARRY EDGAR | 40 | ROOF FALL (10 tons) |
| 13.07.1885 | PETER DUNNION | 30 | CRUSHED TO DEATH |
| 19.05.1888 | RICHARD CURWOOD | 28 | POWDER EXPLOSION |
| 15.11.1888 | ALEX. PENMAN | 20 | "PIT ACCIDENT" |
| 20.06.1890 | FELIX OAKES | 46 | CRUSHED BY CAGE |
| 09.01.1895 | DAVID IRONS | 24 | ROOF FALL |
| 11.10.1895 | ANDREW MAXWELL | 22 | ROOF FALL (Fractured skull) |
| 21.02.1896 | CHARLES REID | 20 | CRUSHED BY HUTCHES |
| 14.04.1897 | ROBERT ANDERSON | 68 | RUN OVER BY PUG ENGINE |
| 24.11.1898 | HUGH CAIRNEY | 53 | CRUSHED BY WAGONS |
| 16.05.1899 | CHARLES GORMAN | 49 | ROOF FALL (Fractured skull) |
| 18.05.1899 | JAMES RAMSEY | 52 | RUN DOWN BY HUTCHES |
| 10.12.1899 | PETER CORRIGAN | 40 | COMPOUND SKULL FRACTURE |
| 12.06.1900 | GEO. W. RENWICK | 16 | OVERTURNED CART |
| 140.6.1900. | WILLIAM CORNISH. | 17 | RUN DOWN BY HUTCHES (Multiple injuries) |
| 25.04.1902 | JAMES O'HARA | 43 | FALL OF COAL AT FACE |
| 24.11.1902 | JAMES EARLY | 35 | MULTIPLE FRACTURES |
| --.12.1902 | CHAS BARNITT OR WELSH | 50 | NO DETAILS |
| 16.07.1903 | JAMES DOCHERTY | 35 | ROOF FALL (Fractured spine) |
| 09.11.1904 | JAMES CONWAY | 51 | FALL OF COAL AT FACE |
| 12.01.1905 | WILLIAM GILMOUR | 28 | COLLAPSE OF BRICK ARCH |
| 23.02.1905 | THOMAS RIELLY | 38 | FALL OF STONE AT FACE (7 cwts) |
| 07.12.1905 | JAMES KIRK | 45 | PUG ENGINE COLLISION |
| 25.08.1906 | ROBERT EASTON | 29 | FELL 900 ft DOWN SHAFT |
| 14.06.1909 | GEORGE BROWN | 44 | MULTIPLE INJURIES |
| 02.09.1910 | ANDREW McCALL | 54 | RUN DOWN BY HUTCH |
| 14.02.1912 | THOMAS McQUADE | 31 | FRACTURED SPINE |
| 10.10.1913 | JOHN HIGGINS | 20 | RUPTURED KIDNEY |
| 13.06.1916 | ROBERT LINDSAY | 28 | ACCIDENTALLY SUFFOCATED |
| 12.01.1920 | RICHARD RITCHIE | 20 | BURNT BY ESCAPING STEAM |
| " | WILLIAM McCAIG | 66 | BURNT BY ESCAPING STEAM |
| 18.05.1923 | HENRY CALLAGHAN | 50 | RUN OVER BY WAGON |
| 13.08.1923 | WILLIAM HUNTER | 32 | DECAPITATED BY GIRDER |
| 09.04.1924 | ARCHD. BROWNLIE | 64 | ROOF FALL (1 ton) |
| 06.05.1927 | DANIEL AIRNES | 24 | INTERNAL INJURIES |
| 10.04.1928 | JOHN J. KANE | 18 | CRUSHED BETWEEN HUTCH AND ROOF |
| 07.10.1928 | JAMES RODDEN | 31 | EXPLOSION |
| " | THOMAS PATON | 37 | EXPLOSION |
| 20.12.1928 | JOHN DICKSON | 22 | CRUSHED BY A HUTCH |
| 16.03.1929 | WILLIAM SHEDDON | 34 | ROOF FALL (Asphyxia and shock) |
| 10.10.1929 | JOHN WHITTON | 39 | GASSED |
| " | ROBINSON FOSTER | 42 | GASSED |
| " | ROBERT MATHIE | 24 | GASSED |
| 22.06.1930 | JOHN SINCLAIR | 19 | SUFFOCATED BY COAL GUM |
| 16.07.1931 | WILLIAM W. GRAY | 30 | ROOF FALL (Fractured skull) |
| 14.09.1933 | ROBERT STEWART | 21 | ROOF FALL (Multiple injuries) |
| 26.03.1941 | ALEXANDER MURPHY | 52 | ROOF FALL (Asphyxia) |
| 28.11.1941 | JOHN DUNSMORE | 49 | ROOF FALL |
| 02.12.1942 | HUGH DAVIS | 43 | ROOF FALL (Asphyxia) |
| 11.05.1944 | JOHN PERCY | 49 | ROOF FALL (Fractured skull) |

# ROBERT SMILLIE
## PRESIDENT
## OF THE
## SCOTTISH MINERS' FEDERATION
## 1894-1918.   1921-1940

## PRESIDENT OF
## THE MINERS' FEDERATION OF
## GREAT BRITAIN 1912–1921

Robert Smillie was born in Belfast on the 17th March 1857 of Scottish parentage. Orphaned very young, he was brought up by his grandmother and received no education until he was nine years of age. At fifteen he came to Glasgow where he worked in a brass foundry and at sixteen he moved to Larkhall where he worked initially as a pump man, a drawer of coal tubs and then he progressed to being a coal hewer.

Very much aware of his lack of education he attended evening classes for several years and it was there he developed a lifelong love of reading with the works of Robert Burns, John Ruskin and Thomas Carlyle among his favourites.

In 1885 Larkhall miners were visited by Motherwell men who were attempting to revive the miners union in Scotland.   Robert Smillie agreed to chair the miners meeting and as a result a Larkhall branch of the Lanarkshire Miners' Union was formed with Smillie elected as secretary.

Through his union work he came into contact with other union leaders including Keir Hardie, and he was there at the foundation of the new political party the Independent Labour Party.

 Smillie made several attempts to enter the House of Commons and finally in 1923 he was elected Member of Parliament for Morpeth and continued in that capacity until 1929 when he resigned due to ill health.

Robert Smillie died in 1940 and the following obituary was published in the Hamilton Advertiser. *"So our grand old man Bob Smillie is gone! It is doubtful if we of our day will ever see the likes of him again. He was a kind and gentle soul and essentially, as was the nature of him, a man of peace and peaceful ways. Bob detested human suffering of any kind, and throughout all his long and active life he seemed to bear on his broad shoulders the weary burden of the toiling masses—refusing to be relieved of the heavy load until the complete emancipation of his people had been won. Bob was a bonnie fechter, delivering two blows for every one received in his fight to obtain for the collier and his family their just rights to a better share of the nation's wealth. He had often in his early struggles as Kipling says, to bear the hearing of the truth he'd spoken, twisted by knaves to make a "trap for fools," and watch the things he gave his life for broken, "yet stoop to build them up again with worn-out tools." Bob could also "wait and not be tired by waiting, or being lied about" he did not deal in lies; "or being hated" did not give way to hating, and yet did not "look too good nor talk too wise." If ever a man was the living symbol of Kipling's hero, that man was surely "our Bob!" Yet away from the stern industrial struggle in a social hour with his ain folk's, one found a different Bob Smillie, a man with merry twinkling eyes and a love for Doric prose and poetry."*

Bob Smillie like Keir Hardie could not be bought, he was a man true to his own conscience and to the Scottish miners, he was one of the giants of the Scottish Miners' Federation, a man of his time, an honourable man.

## ROBERT SMILLIE: FAREWELL

Until you came we did not know
    How fair the day in summer glen
The songs of life where roses grow
    Our heads were bowed in darkness then
        Until you came.

That grey-red dawn! Let Freemen tell
    The saga risen from our doom
As slaves and heirs of slaves we fell
    Until we saw the roses bloom
        That grey-red dawn.

Farewell, our friend! The cots besides
    Our mothers sing, where babies sleep,
And maids and lads tell stars and tide
    Your memory our free dreams will keep;
        Our friend, farewell.

*Edward Hunter*
*Circa 1940*

*Bob Smillie at home with his wife Anne, 1929.*

158

# WILLIAM SMALL

## 1850—1903

*William Small* as a draper, was an unusual choice for the position of paid, full time Miners' Union official and at the time of his appointment, more than a few eyebrows must have been raised.  However his sincerity, hard work and determination to improve the lot of the coalminer, soon earned him the respect of the coalminers.   On the list of the pioneers of the Miners' Union in Lanarkshire, *William Small's* name must surely be near the very top. One of the greatest authorities on mining matters in the country; he worked ceaselessly to build up an effective and strong union for the miners of the county.

Having worked initially at his own trade in Glasgow and then Cambuslang, *William Small* was introduced to the miners' union through *Andrew McCowie* an enthusiastic Scots-Irishman who thought he saw in him, signs of greatness.

For more than 20 years *William* devoted himself to keeping alive the dying embers of unionism among the Lanarkshire miners and his devotion to the cause of justice for the miners is unequalled.

The great *Robert Smillie,* champion of the miners and M.P. in his book "*My Life for Labour*", described *William Small* as a man of medium height, rather heavily built, ruddy complexion, with a short sandy beard. "*Bob" Smillie* in his memoirs has documented for posterity, a vivid description of the sacrifices made by *William Small,* in his efforts to organise the Lanarkshire miners into a credible and effective union.

In a chapter aptly named *"Under the Greenwood Tree" Smillie* describes how *William Small "lived for the miner".* He writes *"I have known him leave home at four o'clock in the morning on five days of the week, holding morning meetings in various parts of the country—at a distance of sixteen or seventeen miles from his house in Blantyre. The use of horse and trap was completely out of the question on the ground of expense, and this devoted man made those long journeys on foot and at all seasons of the year. Frequently he would be far from home holding meetings at night in summer weather, and it was no uncommon thing for him to sleep out in a field or wood with a copy of the Glasgow Herald or the Scotsman for his coverlet. In this way he was able to visit one of the collieries in the vicinity early the following morning in furtherance of the cause he had so much at heart."*

On his appointment, the reception *William Small* received from the Lanarkshire coal-masters was, as to be expected. As a full time paid union official, he found it necessary to write to or to discuss his members' grievances, real or imagined with them, but he was presented from doing so by a brick wall behind which the coal-masters maintained a stony silence. His letters to them pointing out grievances went unanswered, because they refused to talk to anyone who was not in their employment. It was to be two years, before they eventually agreed to communicate with him.

Because of *Small's* meticulous research at the British Museum on the old Scottish Mining Laws, laws which he laboriously transcribed word for word, the burden borne by the Scottish miner was gradually reduced.  Long after his death his research proved invaluable and it was also used when a Coal Commission inquiry held in the Throne Room of the House of Lords, called the Dukes to produce the title deeds of their lands.

*William Small* appeared somehow, to be swept aside as the County Union he fought so hard to establish, expanded to become a powerful and influential force for the miners.

An able and versatile man, he was also very much a family man, with two daughters and three sons. A member of Blantyre School Board he gave freely of his talents towards the improvement of the educational facilities for Blantyre's children. His death occurred very suddenly at the early age of 53 in 1903, at Olivia Cottage, his home in Blantyre, a home which he had built with his own hands in 1894 from stone obtained from houses dismantled in Glasgow's High Street.

*William Small* was a man with a vision; a vision of justice and a fair wage for the Lanarkshire miner and no one worked harder than he did for that cause.

The day of his funeral, all the local collieries stopped work at one o'clock in the afternoon and the miners joined in the funeral procession which was led by three local brass bands. The route to the High Blantyre cemetery was along Stonefield Road and Larkfield, and the pavements were lined by large crowds of people, who had come to pay their respects to a man who had given his all, to the cause of the miner.

*William Small's headstone, erected by Lanarkshire Miners' Union at a cost of £100.*

# IN MEMORIAM OF THE LATE
## WILLIAM SMALL
### MINERS' AGENT

He died on the field of battle,
   In the midst of the din and the strife;
He gave what the cause had asked for—
   His energy and his life!
He grappled with foes around him
   For Justice, Truth and Right,
And he died where they first had found him,
   In the van of a desperate fight!


If there's glory in death, he has won it!
   Let the halo shine bright round his name!
Whatever his duty he done it
   Regardless of praise or blame!
His conscience, true guide to his actions,
   Was free from the guile and deceit
That would lure honest men into fractions,
   That ever must end in defeat.


The long weary struggle is ended,
   The soul of a hero has fled;
The cause he so ably defended
   Must find a new light in his stead!
The feet of the martyrs have beaten
   A track that will ever remain,
Their sufferings may yet help to sweeten
   The long, bitter struggle with pain!


*Duncan Mathieson.*
*Castle Street.*
*Hamilton.*
*Circa 1903.*

# YOU'RE BARRED!

In the miners' continuous struggle for emancipation and a fair and living wage, many men found to their cost, that to join the union, or to become an active member, could lead to them being sacked and barred from working in every local colliery, and the effect on their families could be devastating.

Unemployment and eviction with all the associated horrors of starvation and the threat of the poorhouse was enough to keep all but the most diehard miners in check. The policy of sacking and evicting men was the one way, that management could exert total control over the workforce and root out anyone who was perceived to be a possible troublemaker.

Coalmasters and their officials also had long memories; if a man's "*card was marked,*" very often this permeated through to his sons. Typical of this type of attitude was the treatment handed out in Blantyre in the mid 1880's to *William B. Small,* eldest son of *William Small,* Miners' Agent. On leaving school he obtained employment as a miner's helper in one of the local coal mines, but at the end of his first shift, he had the bitter experience of being sacked. On being informed of his dismissal, the colliery official informed him that "*No son of William Small will work at this pit.*"

*William B. Small* junior was a highly intelligent boy and eventually he was apprenticed to a Glasgow solicitor, but unfortunately the position had to be given up when the family could not raise the indenture fees. He later found employment with his father outside Blantyre in Haughhead Colliery, Uddingston.

In 1890 at the age of eighteen years, he was appointed checkweigher at the Clyde Colliery, Hamilton. Three years later he became a member of the Lanarkshire Miners' Union county executive. His union career was to take him to the position of Miners' Agent, secretary of Lanarkshire Miners' Union and he also represented the county miners on the Scottish and National Miners' Executive Committee. He was joint secretary of Lanarkshire District Miners' Welfare Committee and was a representative of Lanarkshire Miners' at the T.U.C. Labour Party conferences.

In 1942 *William B. Small* junior was presented with a "Pioneer's Diploma" by Lanarkshire Mineworkers' Union in recognition of his long and valued services to the organisation. He died in 1944.

# A BLANTYRE MINING FAMILY

# THE RUSSELLS

*Circa 1889 Top left. Rebecca, John, William, Jean, Adam.*
*Bottom Left. Lizzie, Joanna Russell (mother) David, George, unknown female.*

In 1859 Joanna Kerr left Newtown in Midlothian, to work in Blantyre Mills. Her sister had moved before her and lived in the house where David Livingston was born. It was to this house that 12 year old Joanna came to stay. When she was 17 she married Irishman John Russell, (30) a railway platelayer and former soldier, who had fought with the 86th Foot Regiment (Royal County Down) during the Indian Mutiny. When he left the army he came to Blantyre to where his parents had settled after fleeing the mass starvation of the potato famine.

When this photograph was taken, John was already dead and one son Johnstone had left for Australia. The other five sons John, William, Adam, David and George became coal miners at the age of eleven. The three girls worked in Blantyre mills.

 Three of their sons died young men.  John died from cholera aged 20, William in his 20s and George aged 44.

The youngest child George was, like the rest of his brothers, a socialist and he was barred from every pit in Lanarkshire for his union activities. He eventually went to Glasgow to live with his sister Lizzie and was working as an insurance agent when he died.

# THE THIRTY WEEK LOCKOUT
## 1926

*See yonder poor o'erlaboured wight*
*So abject mean and vile*
*Who begs a brother of the earth*
*To give him leave to toil*
*And see his lordly fellow–worm*
*The poor petition spurn*
*Unmindful tho' a weeping wife*
*And helpless offspring mourn.*

*Man Was Made To Mourn*
*Robert Burns.*

The miners life was far from easy, the work was hot, dirty and dangerous, with death and serious injury a constant threat and a daily occurrence. In the earlier part of the nineteenth century wages had been relatively good but as deeper coal mines opened up and people flocked into the county from Ireland and Eastern Europe to obtain work, the wages were repeatedly reduced, until eventually, they were so abysmally low there was hardly enough money coming in to hold body and soul together.

Coal face workers' wages were calculated on the amount of coal mined, but calculations were weighted heavily in favour of the pit owner. Miners' wages and safety were at the bottom of the priority list. Top of the list was maximum output, at the cheapest possible cost.

Fluctuations in the price of coal meant that wages and continuity of employment were always in danger. If the price of coal dropped, wages were cut and miners were put on short time or laid off. When the price of coal increased, the men would be re-employed. However, no mater how high the price of coal went, the collier saw not one extra penny in his wage packet and this unjust method of paying wages had resulted in strikes in the past.

Efforts by the Miners Union and the Co-operative Society to improve conditions had resulted in 1908, in the passing of an Act of Parliament called the Eight hour Act, which restricted by law, the working hours for underground workers. This Act ensured that miners, who were underground for eight hours, were to work no more than seven hours.

In 1925, the price of coal slumped and once again the miner was faced with a reduction in wages and an increase in hours. The government of the day, led by Stanley Baldwin, averted a lock-out at the last minute by giving the coal masters a nine months subsidy.

This was a shrewd move by the government, as it bought time for them and the coal masters to complete extensive preparations for the inevitable conflict with the miners.

The Trade Union Congress unfortunately was not so far sighted, making virtually no preparations. When the subsidy finished, the coal masters again delivered an ultimatum to the miners; accept a 10 to 25% reduction in pay and longer hours or be locked out. To a man, the colliers rejected the terms and at midnight on April 1926, every collier in the country was locked out by the pit owners.

On May 3, the TUC called a general strike in sympathy with the miners but this lasted only nine days and from then on the miners were on their own.

*The Hamilton Tammies entertaining for funds*
*to help the mining families to survive.*

Over the next seven months, the Scottish miners stood shoulder to shoulder, despite the destitution and hardship they and their families were experiencing. Their wives stood loyally with them, for more than anyone, they knew the struggle a miner's family had to live on his pittance of a wage.

In an attempt to alleviate distress and prevent starvation among mining families,    Hamilton Parish Council granted them parish relief. This was distributed initially as cash, but an objection by a prominent local businessman led the payment to be changed to food vouchers.  The maximum value of the vouchers was set at 35/- or £1. 75 and the amount granted was calculated on the number of children in the family, 4/- (20p) per child under 14 years and 12/- (60p) for the wife.

Some of the local business and professional community within the town who viewed the miners with suspicion and anger, were enraged by this payment to the mining families.   Conveniently forgotten was the reason for the miners being idle. They were not striking for more money; they had been locked out after refusing wages which would have kept them at starvation levels. A great deal of emphasis was put on the burden the ratepayers would be faced with because of the payment of relief but also forgotten was the indisputable fact that the miners too were ratepayers.

One prominent local businessman (the same one who objected to the cash payment) led a group of like –minded individuals in applying for an interim interdict in an attempt to prevent the Parish Council paying relief to miners' families.

The hearing was held at the Court of Session in Edinburgh before Lord Moncrieff, who found in favour for Parish relief and refused the application, a ruling which undoubtedly saved quite a number of lives.

The men who had initiated the legal proceedings, while publicly declaring that they felt a great deal of pity for the miners' wives and children, failed to display one scrap of humanity towards them. All they appeared to show was self-righteous indignation and class division.

Much could have been learned, if they had only observed the quiet dignity displayed by the miners' families in the face of much suffering and deprivation. No miner would ever have gone to such lengths in an attempt to starve women and children. Miners had more respect for the lives of their fellow men.

With almost no income coming in, starvation was a real threat to most mining families. To help alleviate this, the mining communities set up soup kitchens, with soup being cooked in large copper boilers in backdoor wash houses.

*Miners and their families from Portland Square, Hamilton organised a Gala day and 500 children were treated to buns and milk; the women received pots of jam and bread. Prizes donated by Mr Cockburn of Butterburn Park Dairy.*

Local traders and ordinary working people sympathetic to the miners cause helped to keep the kitchens going with donations of bones, chicken, vegetables and pulses to make soup. The Salvation Army also supplied thousands of meals during the lockout. The generosity of these people and the desperately needed food vouchers from the Parish Council, helped to keep the miners' families alive during the long struggle. In Lanarkshire, 4,000,000 school meals were supplied to miners' children, but 1s 6d (15 pence) per week was deducted from the 4s (20 pence) a parent received in parish benefit for each child.

*JOHN STEVEN*

Most of the families had forgotten what it was like to have meat on the table and one young mining contractor, *John Steven,* could not believe his luck when his mother gave him one sausage and an egg to take home. He hadn't seen a sausage or an egg for months, never mind tasted one. He hurried home to his young wife *Barbara* in Hamilton's Burnblea Street, desperate to share his good fortune. Out came the frying pan and soon the mouth-watering smell of sausage cooking was wafting from the range. The table was laid with two plates and then the egg was gently cracked into the pan.

*Photograph courtesy of Kate Tait, daughter.*

Just as *Barbara* was about to take the pan off the range, there was a loud whoosh and down the lum fell a large pancake of soot which landed right in the middle of the frying pan. However, the soot was gently removed and the sausage and egg were washed and then eaten and never did a meal taste better, soot and all!

During the lock-out, cooking and washday became a nightmare. Most of the miners' wives used coal to fire the cooking ranges and to heat the water in the wash house boilers. With only food vouchers being received and no money coming in, it was impossible for them to buy coal. Day in and day out, large numbers of men women and children could be seen up at the pit waste bings digging for coal and wood. Many of the men wore their pit clothes carrying their graith or pit tools with them. Any coal and wood found would be carried home in Hessian potato sacks.

Occasionally, the men would get more than was required for the household and would sell the surplus. They were then able to supply a few shillings to their wives for household necessities.

However scavenging on pit waste bings was illegal and frequent police raids resulted in both men and women appearing in court charged with theft; so to try and prevent capture, lookouts were posted to warn the scavengers of a police presence. As soon as the alarm went up, men women and children looking for coal scattered in every direction, in a desperate attempt to avoid being arrested.

Emergency coal regulations brought into force on May 29th meant there was always a market for any surplus obtained. Commencing the second week in June, householders could only purchase one hundredweight of coal per fortnight and for this, a local authority permit was required. An allowance of 28lbs a week could also be purchased without a permit, but the coal had to be taken away by the buyer.

*Jimmy Glass* a Hamilton fruit and vegetable merchant was very sympathetic to the miners' cause and donated vegetables to the soup kitchens throughout the lockout. As he opened for business one morning a customer, a miner's wife, approached him and inquired if he had a banana box he could spare. Finding one in the back shop, he carried it out to the door for her and handed it over, remarking that she should get a

few good fires from it. With tears running down her face, the woman whispered that the box was for a coffin for one of her children who had died during the night. At that, she turned and with great dignity, walked down Quarry Street, leaving *Jimmy* stunned.

*Wm. Glass, fruiterer, Quarry Street, Hamilton.*

In Blantyre, several children were said to have been buried without even the dignity of a banana box. Their bodies were lowered into their graves, wrapped only in a cotton sheet.

During the period affected by the strike, the mining community in Hamilton lost 41 children. Although none of the death certificates lists poverty as the cause of death, it is well documented that poverty and infant mortality go hand-in-hand. No fewer than 39 of the children were aged two years and under, while one was aged three and another aged four.

For months the miners held out despite the acute distress being experienced by them and their families. They ignored media propaganda being fed to them, which exaggerated reports of a return to work by some miners and stood united, in their determination for a fair wage and conditions.

The coal masters then brought blacklegs in from other districts hundreds of miles away who were protected by a provocative police guard. Merry and Cunninghame

Ltd. employed 30 of these blacklegs at Auchinraith Colliery in Blantyre. On the afternoon of Wednesday, October 20th 600 miners protesting outside the colliery were baton-charged by the police and seven were arrested.

The following day, the largest meeting of miners ever witnessed in Blantyre, was held in a field next to the colliery, as a protest against the unjustifiable baton charge. The protest passed peacefully, as the police, sensing the mood of the crowd, knew better than to once again draw their batons.

After 30 weeks of almost unbelievable hardship, the Miners Federation declared the struggle over. On November, 27, the Scottish Delegate Conference, by a majority vote accepted the owners' terms.

The miners, forced by starvation into accepting longer hours, lower wages and district agreements, were plunged into the abyss of never ending poverty and hardship, with no prospect of a fair wage.

In 1894, a 13-week strike by the miners had also resulted in the strikers returning to a reduction in wages. After the strike, Keir Hardie published an article in the October 20 edition of the Labour Leader headed "A Friendly Chat with the Scottish Miners." On one side, he said, were miners, their wives and children. On the other side, fighting against them, were hunger, the masters, the law, -- backed by the police and soldiers – the government, the press and the pulpit. He asked the question; why do 50 mine owners have the power to starve 70,000 miners into submission? His answer; *"All these are rich and you are poor!"*

Just over 30 years later, nothing had changed; the miners had once again been starved into submission by powerful, wealthy men, with the blessing and assistance of the government.

As at the end of previous mining conflicts, many miners emigrated. The reasons for them going were numerous, but many left after being blacklisted. Coal masters had long memories and although there was a promise of no victimisation on return to work, the reality was the exact opposite. Miners were blacklisted for being union activists, for picketing, for speaking out against management and for numerous other petty reasons. Such was the power held by the coal masters, that once a man was blacklisted, it was impossible for him to obtain employment, so very often he had to leave, or starve.

Others, like Burnbank miner *Willie Russell*, left because they had just had

enough. Seriously injured and lucky to escape with his life after a roof fall in Greenfield Colliery, *Willie* had been idle for almost a year. Having just returned to work, he then found himself locked out.

Another long period of enforced unemployment convinced him, that for a better standard of life, he would have to leave Scotland. The Canadian Pacific Railway was at that time offering a £5 assisted passage to Western Canada, so Willie took advantage of this offer, packed up and emigrated with his wife *Jessie* and their baby daughter *Greta.*

Arriving in Winnipeg, Manitoba in April 1927, he applied for and was accepted for the first job he saw advertised and one week later he started work as a police officer in the city of St. Boniface, and during a career spanning 37 years, rose to the post of Chief Constable.

Over the years he was given many honours for his contribution to the battle against crime. The two which delighted him most were having a school named after him (The William Russell Elementary School) and being made an honorary citizen of St. Boniface. That's quite an achievement for a man who although Blantyre born had been educated in America until the age of 13, had then returned to Scotland on the death of his mother and, having added an extra year onto his age, started work in Earnock Colliery.

For *Willie Russell* and thousands of other miners the lock out had been a blessing in disguise. In their adopted countries, free from the shackles of the class system, they were allowed to develop and achieve their full potential and as a result, contributed much to the development of these new nations.

# THE MINER

IN THE MINE
     "Midst noxious gas and rayless gloom
       The miner toils with laboured breath
     To earn bread, and hew a tomb
       When jagged rocks compass his death.
                   ---Before his time.

O. CHRIST.
     Was man not made to dwell on earth,
       And not to grub like moles "within" it?
     To starve, to slave, to be a serf,
       Enriching mammon every minute.
                   ---Gold accurst.

THE ANGELS WEEP
     To see how man's immortal soul
       Is twisted, warped, and close confined;
     To see a "Temple" beg the dole,
       To see "starvation" underlined.
                 ---Is God asleep?
             *Wm. Park, Blantyre, circa July 1926.*

# LITTLE COAL-GETTERS

From the "bing," from the "bing,"
See the ragged, limping string,
See the pinched and starved wee faces
Where the hunger-demon traces
Lines and furrows with his finger
That will linger, ever linger,
Till the cups and daisies mingle o'er their
       heads.

From the "bing," from the "bing,"
See each hunched-backed little thing,
Hear the gasping, weary moan
Hear the rasping jerky groan
As the cheerless, fireless goad
Cruelly presses them with their load
Till the Home for little children opens to
       greet them.

From the "bing," from the "bing,"
See the twisted bending limb,
See the filthy bag of coal
Killing "gems" worth untold gold;
Can you sense the deep-drawn sigh?
Can you hear the Master's cry?
Suffer, little children to come unto Me.

*William Park, circa 1926*

*Scavenging for coal during a strike, photograph courtesy of Scottish Mining Museum.*

# LOCKED OUT
# AND
# NINE HUNGRY MOUTHS TO FEED

*Photograph courtesy of Ann Winkley (Spiers) granddaughter of James Spiers.*

When there was a lockout or a strike many of the miners attempted to obtain work outside the coal industry until the strike was over.

The above group of men are working at the building of the Shettleston housing scheme during the 1926 lockout. In the photograph is at least one Earnock Colliery workman; pit joiner and father of seven, *James M. Spiers* is in the second row, second from left.

## RELIEVING THE BOREDOM

Miners, who were used to working extremely hard and having very little time off, made good use of the idle time by organising Gala and sports days, with impromptu dancing taking place if someone turned up with an accordion.

*Dancing at the Palace grounds Hamilton during the strike*

# LETTERS TO THE PRESS CONCERNING THE LOCKOUT

Controversy about the 26 week lock-out raged in the letters pages of the local press, with all sorts of points of view being expressed. Members of the public not connected with the mining industry, appeared to forgot that the reason the miners were unemployed was because they had been locked out, after refusing to accept a 10-25% reduction on their already *"starvation rate"* wages.

The following two letters appeared in the Hamilton Advertiser during the lock-out and show the strength of feeling, on both sides of the divide.

## THE MINERS' STRIKE AND DESTITUTION

Sir, *Very dismal reports come from Hamilton district as to the demand for assistance from Parish Councils. Are all the ratepayers to be bled to suit the tactics of Communist Cook and Co?*

*What is wanted at the moment is courage - courage in the part of Parish Councils to refuse all applications for relief and courage on the part of the ratepayers to refuse to be victimised in this fashion.*

*If the Colliers' Union cannot afford to pay for this despicable game, let the men go to work and not "sponge" on the whole community. It is the duty to sue every idle man for failure to provide for wife and children.* **If the children must be fed**, *let the miners themselves start soup kitchens (assisted by their wives and aided by subscriptions from sympathisers.)*

*I decidedly object to be bled to death to allow a lot of men to lounge at every street corner smoking their pipes quite comfortably without worry, as they know the Parish Councils will not see them starving. Let us show determination to handle our own affairs and not remain the laughing stock of our own Colonies and other countries.—I am,* etc., JAMES WILSON. Ref. Hamilton Advertiser 29/5/1926. Page 12

## A LETTER FROM AMERICA

### THE MINERS' CASE

Sir,--*In reference to Mr James Wilson's letter in the "Hamilton" on 29th May, I wish only to say that I am sure the miners will appreciate his sentiments.*

*He talks of bleeding ratepayers to feed wives and children of "sponging miners" who smoke in "comfort" at street corners. Possibly Mr Wilson was one of the gentlemen who in 1914, did the smoking while many of the self-same miners did the bleeding.*

*Also he does not follow the teachings of Christ, who succoured the needy despite their views or cause. In closing, I wish to let Mr Wilson know that it is men of his calibre who draw criticism of other countries on Great Britain.* Mrs A. McEWAN. Benton, Illinois, U.S.A. Ref. Hamilton Advertiser, 6/7/1926 page 5

# UNEMPLOYED LARKHALL MINERS LEAVE FOR CANADA
## 1928

*Goodbye to the old country.*

*Last farewells*
*One hundred and thirteen Larkhall miners leaving for Canada*

# THE COLLIER

The collier hunkered on his heel an' dichtit aff the sweet,
For he'd tae work baith lang an' sair tae get some grub tae eat;
He had a wife an' bairnies three that couldna work or want,
An' tho' the meat wis plentifu' the siller was gey scant.

The ventilation wis gey bad, the coal wis hard tae howk,
And "Billy Fairplay" on the tap did fleece the collier fowk;
Tho "Billy" wis an honest chiel, coal managers were not,
But averaged them wha couldna howk an' roon coal never got.

Noo Jock had thocht baith lang an' sair, but nae way could he see
Hoo for tae better his ainsel', his wife an' bairnies three;
"We'd be better in the puirhoose," says Jock untae himsel',
"We'd get mair meat an' claething, an' I'm tell't they're treated
well."

Jock gethered up his bits o' tools, put them ablow the bed,
Then aff an' saw the Doctor, then ane ca'd Doctor Ned;
"Gie you a line for the puirhoose? faith that ye'll never get."
You're young an' yawl, an stuffy, much wark is in you yet."

Says Jock we'll sell oor furnitur', sell a' that we can sell',
Tae grind oot life in Scottish mines, I'd suner be in Hell;
Sae Jock sell't a' his bits o' things, which brocht him fifty pound,
Then taen passage in a liner which for Canada was bound.

Jock didna look for pit wark, but got wark upon the lan',
Wrocht twa year tae a fermer juist tae learn an' un'erstan'
Their different styles o' workin', an' aye kept twa open een,
An' noted whit wis novel juist as far as could be seen.

Noo mony years hae passed awa' since we left auld Scotlan',
Says Jock untae his partner dear, his faithfu' sonsie Nan,
"Hoo mony o' my butties are still warslin' in the mine?
Hoo mony mair hae' passed awa', dear neebors o' lang syne?"

One hundred an' fifty acres o' bonnie prairie lan'
Jock owns in Manitoba, an' ferms wi' his ain han';
His sons own ferms o' their ain, an' help their dear old dad,
An' his dochters a' are marriet weel, which mak's him unco glad.

Jock aften sighs for Scotlan', but minds it's harsh land laws,
Hoo crofters o' their ain bit lan' were ousted without cause;
Hoo lang will Scotlan' thole an' bear, how lang will Scotlan' stan'
The grabbing gang that rule the roost, ca'd owners o' the lan'?

Unknown circa 1930

# THE DEPRESSION
# 1929
# UNEMPLOYED MINERS MARCH TO LONDON

*Unemployed Burnbank and Blantyre miners setting off on the march to London.*

Cold and shivering in the blast off an east wind, thirty-one poorly clad unemployed Lanarkshire miners congregated at the Palace Grounds, Hamilton on the 18th January 1929 to walk to London. Every man carried a well filled haversack and each had a travelling canteen and a field tent. The march was organised by the Miners Federation of Great Britain and in charge of the Lanarkshire Contingent was Blantyre man *James Beecroft.* Heading the march were two standard bearers carrying a banner which proclaimed N.U.W.C.M. (National Unemployed Workers Committee Movement) National March to London. Lanarkshire Contingent. ---We demand full maintenance, not charity.

In the march were *John Edmiston* and *John Kelly* both of Greenfield Road, Burnbank and *George Teesdale, Harry Paterson,* Millar Street, *William McNulty,* 55 Victoria Street, *Hugh Devlin,* Knightswood Terrace, *James McLaughlin,* Hardie Street, *D. Kelly,* Dickson Street, *Hugh Reynolds,* Hall Street, *Peter McGinlay,* Maxwell Crescent and *D. Mathison,* 45 Hall Street, all from Blantyre.

The march was a desperate act to call the attention of the public to the plight of the unemployed miners'. In 1928, 78 Lanarkshire pits closed down, throwing thousands of men out of work. Of the pits that were still working, many were on short time, leaving mining families destitute and on the verge of starvation. The following letter published in the Hamilton Herald dated 8.9.1928, gives a vivid description of the suffering among the miners' families.

*Sir, The attention of the general public is hereby drawn to the terrible conditions prevailing throughout the mining villages of Lanarkshire. There we find thousands of men destitute, lots of cases of needy expectant mothers. Little children practically naked and their little bodies worn to a skeleton for want of proper nourishment. Such a condition of affairs requires immediate attention! Branches of the W.R.I. are being formed throughout the country and collectors will visit the different districts for the purpose of collecting funds for the immediate wants of the little ones. There are hundreds of little children who must of a certainty be provided with warm clothing and boots before the winter sets in, or the percentage of deaths amongst the miner' children will be increased considerably. Donations either monetary or gifts of clothing, boots, etc., will be welcomed A postcard notifying the secretary "re" gifts, parcels of clothing, boots, groceries, bags of potatoes etc will be attended to at once and a collector asked to call.*
*(Mrs) J. Smith, 17 Hill View, Coalburn Lanarkshire.*

# THE MINERS' RAW

When clachans are quate
On a Saturday Nicht,
And black is the grate
Ance wi' burning coals licht,
There's something ado wi' the miners—
A something that's no' very richt.

Nae clatter and clang
Frae the derlect pits;
Nae shutters play bang
Whaur the miners' raw sits;
A gey missley soond in the mornin'
Is the scuffle o' tackitty buits.

Nae mair will the man,
As he gangs oot tae fen'
Wi' the door in his haun'
Shout his Guid mornin's ben,
Nae mair will his labours be wantit
He's feenish'd—that's a' he's to ken.

The mither and wife
Has her thochts she maun thol,
For sherp as a knife
Stabbin' into her soul,
Is the fear that weans'll gang hungry
And steekless when "He's" on the dole.

Ay! Broken at last
Are the hopes that were bent;
Gey cauld is the blast
When on miner's it's sent;
And daurk is the cloud that is hinging'

Oot owre his wee world o' content.

*J.F. 1929*

Between 1913 and 1928 well over 1,000,000 men and boys were employed in British coal mines; but this was to change dramatically as the demand for coal fell.

The years between 1928 and 1936 were desperate times for the mining communities, with many of the pits closing down or idle. In 1928, 540 coal mines closed nationwide, 78 of these collieries were in Lanarkshire.

It was calculated that 25% of miners were either out of work or working short time. Unemployment was the spectre that hung above the head of every mining family and starvation was always lurking round the corner.

# GLENCLELAND COLLIERY

# WISHAW

# 1930

The following poem appeared in the "Lanarkshire" newspaper, following the revelation that the owners of Glencleland Colliery, Wishaw, had written to the Parish Council, complaining that they were unable to obtain miners to man the working places.

The letter created a considerable sensation throughout the county in view of the fact that so many miners were out of work. The implication was that the unemployed miners did not want to work.

So serious were the charges, the executive of the Lanarkshire Miners' Union instructed their General Secretary, Mr *William Small,* to investigate the circumstances.

His report to the executive, graphically explained the reason why it was difficult to get men to work in the colliery. The coal seam varied from 15 to 20 inches in height, it was damp on the roof, with water dripping constantly on to the men and running down the pavement where they were lying. The coal company did not supply waterproof oilskins, although they would have proved useless, as they soon became water-logged.

The conditions were so bad, that an adequate wage could not be earned by the men who were working eight hour shifts, soaked to the skin and crawling along the road on their stomachs; also the effort required to draw coal along the roadway was such, that only the strongest of men could have attempted it.

This was the true story of the sensational rumours wrote *William Small* after he had examined the workings and he asked the critics of the miners if they would be prepared to work under such conditions for less than 10s (50p) per day, with about 2s to 3s (10 to 15p) offtakes at the end of the week.

Very often, it appeared that criticism of the miners was a national pastime and people were very quick to condemn them. It was only when the truth about workings conditions were published, that the public realised just what the miners' were up against. But then people had short memories and they soon forgot and it was "kick the miner time again."

# THAT WEE PIT DOON THE GLEN

Fegs, if I were in the council
I wad need tae ha'e ma say
I'd see mair aboot yon letter
That they got the ither day;
For they puir, defenceless miners
I wad fecht thro' tae the en'
Till I solved the wee bit myst'ry
O' that wee pit doon the glen.

At some pits that I could mention,
Whaur condeetions aye are fair,
They don't need tae sen' for workers,
For there's aye some waitin' there;
Sae I'd like tae ken the reason
Why yon maister cries for men.
When there's plenty in the district,
Near that wee pit doon the glen.

Are the roads in good condition?
Whaur the chaps' ha'e got to draw?
Are the workin's free frae watter
Whaur men crawl alang the wa'?
Are the places safe tae work in?
Dis the air get traivlin' ben?
A' these questions I'd ha'e answered
Frae that wee pit doon the glen.

If they're ocht like whit I've mentioned,
An' the wages reach the mark,
Men will hurry ower frae Wishaw
Through yon short-cut in the park;
Then this talk o' miners slackin'
Very sune will ha'e an en'
An' the wark will get on smoothly
In that wee pit doon the glen.

*J. Maxwell. Circa 1930*

# THE JUSTICEMAN

The checkweigher, or the "Justiceman" as he was known throughout the mining industry, was to the coal miner, one of the most important men employed at the pit. It was his job to weigh the coal sent to the surface and to make sure that the miner was paid for it. Prior to his introduction, hutches of coal reached the surface for which he was deliberately deprived payment.

The Coal Mines Act of 1872 was designed to deal with safety issues, but it also granted workmen the right to appoint a checkweigher. Unfortunately, it also contained restrictions, including the owner's right to veto the appointment. The Act also stipulated that the person appointed, had to be an employee at the colliery, which left him susceptible to intimidation by the master.

It was a further sixteen years, before one of the most important pieces of legislation in the history of mining was passed. The Coal Mines Act, 1887 made compulsory, the weighing of the "*produce*" of the coal hewers, except at mines employing underground not more than 30 persons and it also gave the men a legal right to appoint practically anyone whom they desired to the position of checkweigher. The Act was the first real step forward in the miners' fight for emancipation.

The history of the checkweigher is one of the brightest in the annals of the miners' struggle for justice and the importance of his role cannot be underestimated. In law, the checkweigher existed to weigh the coal and to see that the hewer received payment for the tonnage, or in legal terminology, the *"weight of mineral gotten by his labours;"* it was also to him, that all grievances were taken.

His wages were paid for solely by the miners themselves and this independence made the checkweigher the only man in the colliery who could not be intimidated by management.

Normally a union representative, the checkweigher was responsible for the growth and development of trade unionism in the coal mines. The Miners' Federation of Great Britain was formed in 1888 and by 1893 had 200,000 members, 363,000 in 1900, 600,000 in 1908 and by 1920 membership had reached 900,000. The phenomenal growth of unionism was, in many ways, attributable to the hard work and dedication of the checkweigher, in the building up and maintenance, of the mining unions.

By the 1930's, after more than forty years of fighting *"short weight,"* the checkweigher, champion and protector of the miner, had outlived his usefulness. There were two main reasons for him becoming redundant. Technology had made vast leaps forward and the improvements in mechanical coal cutters had done away with the need for coal to be weighed. The introduction of shift work eventually sounded the death knell for the "Justiceman."

With his demise, the mining industry lost a very valuable friend and a friend who had fought and fought well, for justice for the British miner.

# SONG OF THE COALCUTTER

It's a life of roar and rattle,
Dust and danger, work and wile,
And there's never in the battle
    time to smile.

For the grinding disc is willing,
As it sends the splinters spilling,
To do a bit of killing
    all the while.

Though it's terrible it's splendid,
This squat monster and its groan,
As it tears a path through wrended
    ways unknown.

There's a certain fascination,
Just to watch the dissipation,
By our God, of a creation
    all His own.

But you'll see it if you want to,
Oh, my brother of the cash,
If your pleasures ever taunt you
    to be rash.

Toil that's carried out, and clever,
Where there's barely room to shiver,
Where a dude would hardly ever
    cut a dash.

And you'll see them, coldly civil,
Tending every whimp'ring call
Of the awesome, crushing devil
    on the crawl.

Though the rocks might fly asunder,
It's their share of this Life's plunder,
Just to do and dare, and wonder
    at it all.

*Peter Logan*
*Hamilton. Circa 1913*

# SONG OF THE "PAN RUN"

On, on with the "pans," let the cundy's ring
  With the swell of the hellish din:
Let them quiver and shake like an iron snake
  Tortured in hell for its sin,
Let them shriek and scream as the coal black
  steam
Jerks on to the big road head,
  Or sigh and moan and fret and groan
  While rocked on their cradle bed.

On, on with the "pans" though the heavens fall,
  Feed in the inky gum,
And stay the howls of the reptile's bowels
  As they clatter down the "run."
If bolts are slack, don't turn your back
  Or stay in the engine's sway---
What matters a nail if the iron snail
  Winds on his wriggling way.

On with the "pans" let the black steam leap
  To the "dredger," stark and grim,
Whose greedy maw and endless paw
  Scoops diamonds o'er the brim,
Where dusty clouds weave ghostly shrouds
  For shadowy spectres dim,
And through the gloom, like shapes of doom
  Flit demons out and in.

*W.P. Circa 1928*

By 1933, no less than 72 per cent of the Scottish coal output was machine cut. Conveyers had been developed side by side with the mechanical cutting machine and by the same year, Scotland had advanced far in the direction of complete mechanisation, with loading and conveying systems, capable of handling 1000 tons per shift. While a hand hewer could cut down only a few tons of coal per shift, an electrically driven machine was capable of turning out enormous tonnage.

The pan run was the method used to transport coal from the coal face. A pan was a long steel trough from 6 to 9 feet long. Each pan was capable of holding 3 to 5 hundredweight and the miner at the coal face, shovelled the coal into the pans. In a pan run there were from 30 to 40 pans bolted to one another and resting on rollers, so that when they were coupled together to the engine at the top of the run and the engine started, it shook the coal down the pans to the bottom of the run and into empty hutches. The pan run was 200 to 300 feet long. It was divided into equal parts, so that each man had the same amount of coal to strip and look after.

The incredible noise made by machinery and men shovelling coal, meant that the coalcutting machineman, unlike the old time hewers, could no longer hear the natural workings of the roof, or of the waste behind him and he therefore felt more vulnerable, with less control over his own safety.

# A SONG OF THE "SCREE"

Bell One! bell two! the cage ascends,
  Around the "horels"(1) hum,
The level of its journey reached
  And so the day's begun.
Drumgray,* Kiltongue,* and Virtuewell,*
The lower and the upper Ell,*
  In journeys to and fro
With empty hutches from above
  And full ones from below;
Bang on plates (2) go "round" of coal,
  The "scree" (3) receives the dross,
And merrily, we active move,
   Necessity being our "boss."

Parent of steam, child of the sun,
  Mated with fire, what ho!
Trails of your make circle the earth
  Wherever you ever may go;
Drumgray, Kiltongue and Virtuewell,
The lower and the upper Ell,
  Wombed in the earth below,
Aim of the effort daily exerted
  In face the risks we know;
But bother the risks, the danger and toil,
  The "round" (4) must come with the dross,
And down in the depths miners must move,
  Necessity being their "boss."

Bell one! bell two! the cage ascends,
  Around the "horels" hum,
A second to wait, and down it descends,
  And the half o' the day is done.
Drumgray, Kiltongue and Virtuewell,
The lower and the upper Ell,
  "Cleek" (5) still the faster must,
From level's, "dook," from "mains" and "sides,"
  The output takes its dust.
And bang! with a clang tumbles the "round,"
  The "scree" receives the dross,
And merrily, we active move,
  Necessity being our "boss."

If you could but speak of the life,
Extant in the times ere man,
What would you tell in the pantograph style
Of the thing that around you ran?
Drumgray, Kiltongue and Virtuewell,
The lower and the upper Ell,
Never, however, witnessed a stir
To equal with that they've set on the go
When they rise from the earth wi' a whirr,
Where wi' a rumble, a rattle, and tumble,
The "scree" receives the dross,
Nor yet such a movement where men are in doing,
Necessity being their "boss."

Bell one! bell two! the cage ascends,
Around the "horels" hum,
With a snort and a pant the exhaust makes acclaim
That the work of the day is done.
Drumgray, Kiltongue, and Virtuewell,
The lower and the upper Ell,
One and three quarters each have their "ben,"(6)
With a sigh o' relief the hillman (7) records
The "record" in tons of "310,"
We rest from our labours, the rattle is o'er,
The "scree" has exhausted the dross,
Silence maintains, where erstwhile had noise,
Necessity being its "boss."

*J. Sutherland.*
*Millburn, Larkhall.*
*Circa 1911.*


* *Names of coal seams.*
*(1)  Whorles/Winding wheels.*
*(2) Flat cast iron sheets or plates, laid to enable the*
     *hutches to be easily turned.*
*(3) Scree or screens, bars arranged 1-1 ½ ins. apart through which dross is*
     *separated from coal.*
*(4) Coal after the dross has been separated from it.*
*(5) Coal as it comes from the pit.*
*(6) Working place.*
*(7) Pitheadman.*

# BRITHERS'

The brusher came doon like a wolf on the fold,
His troosers were tatter'd, his jacket was old,
And for three short 'oors that he wrocht in the dook
Told the gaffer to chalk down a shift in his book.

The gaffer he swore he'd be hanged if he would;
When a fight between brusher and gaffer begood,
They foucht frae the Pyotshaw down to the Main—
Sat doon, took a smoke*, then at it again.

They struggled and foucht till far in the nicht,
Till they coupit their lamps, and oot gaed their licht;
They made for the bottom, got up tae the cage,
An' up tae the hill in a terrible rage.

Then Sanny, the lampman, they roundly reviled,
An' swore that their lamps had never been iled;
But Ishmael stepped in and ended the fray,
For the daylicht was breaking, and morning was grey;
So he clootet the tane, and walloped the tither,
And made them agree like brither and brither.

*Unknown.*
*Circa 1891.*

*Smoke was a term used by miners for a break.*

Brushers at work boring holes for shot firing. Photograph courtesy of Scottish Mining
Museum.

# JOE MALONE

This is a story the brushers love;
　This is a tale they often tell
In the bowels of the earth, when the moon
　　above,
Shines o'er the homes where the miners
　　dwell.

A drunken old brusher was Joe Malone---
　Poor old Joe had many a whim---
He drank all day, but he drank his own;
　He battered his wife and she butchered him.

Work was a pleasure and nothing worse,
　His shovel swung like a sure machine,
To a coaxing lilt or a chiding curse;
　Broad was his back and his tongue obscene.

One pay-night as he rolled from town
　Half seas over---'twas very unwise
God forgive them! They knocked him down,
　Gathered his money, and blacked his eyes.

Oh! what an anger was Dame Malone's,
　Curling her lip at Joe's poor plea,
"Live for a week on sticks and stones."
　And, "May you be carried home dead,"
　　said she.

That same night Joe had for mate
　Simon Levinski, the white faced Pole:
And the drills were hot as a Spaniard's hate,
　For Simon, the willing, bored the hole.

And never a word spoke Joe Malone---
　Joe, the rugged, whose word was law---
Nothing said he as the steel bit stone
　In the level that night in the Pyotshaw.

Tangled forever, the weirds we dree---
　The charge was light and the shot was
　　hung;
On the single head of a faithful tree
Two fathoms of trembling brushing swung.

Beaded and bleached was the young Pole's
    brow,
  "Curse it entirely," said Joe Malone,
"It must be drawn but God knows how—
    And one of us must go in alone."

"Me?" groaned Simon. "I've got a wife,
    And two small boys. Ah, Joe! you swear,
Your talk bites deep like a stabbing knife,
    Yes! –maybe a coward, but—I don't care."

"If ye wont toss fair, then hould the light,
    Ye're foreign spawn an' it's just as well,
I've nothing to live for now but spite,
    An' I'd draw that tree on the hobs of hell."

Boom! Went the sound of the hammer—
    Boom!
    The chuckle and roar of surging rock
Thundered away in the far-flung gloom,
    While girders ground at the coming shock.

"Out,  Joe! Out! Are you turning mad?
  Make for the breakers! Dear God his
    face—
Was ever the face of a man so sad?
    Up to the rise is the safest place."

"Let me abee now! What's the use?
    What does it matter—better be dead!
    It's bad when the tongue of a wife is loose
    And the curse of it screaming above your head."

"Simon, me boy, d'ye wonder at it,
    Why milk turns sour in a dirty dish;
Tell the ould gaffer Joe chanced his mitt,
    But--- tell his ould woman she got her wish."

Tap! Went the hammer, and down it crept—
    Two full fathoms and four feet high—
And Simon thought of his wife, and wept
    For the soul of a brusher passing by.

*"Yost"*
*Circa 1926*

# THE AUCHINRAITH EXPLOSION
# BLANTYRE
# 30.8.1930

Blantyre has gone through many changes over the centuries and the town we see today, looks vastly different from the town as it was seventy years ago, but going even further back in time to the 18<sup>th</sup> Century, it is almost impossible to visualise it as it was then.

The Rev. *Stuart Wright*, Minister of High Blantyre Parish Church, in his Annals of Blantyre, 1885, tells us that a century before, the village consisted of one hundred and thirty families; five hundred and twenty people and that these numbers had remained stable, for as far as could be traced back.
He wrote of the village having been described as *"a sleepy hollow, a quiet and rural retreat and the loveliest village of the plain"* but all this was to change forever when in 1785, Henry Monteith and Company harnessed the power of the Clyde and opened Blantyre Cotton Mills.

Almost overnight, the population increased to 1,751. There then followed a steady increase in the numbers of inhabitants until 1830 when it peaked at a total of 3,000.

The next forty years saw little or no change in these numbers, but in 1867 test bores discovered rich coal fields beneath and surrounding the village, coal mines opened, miner's houses were built and the result was a population explosion.

In just one decade the population increased from 3,000 to 10,000 and Blantyre had gone from a quiet rural retreat, to a noisy industrial town surrounded by tall reeking chimneys that blackened the sky.

The coalfields were to bring great wealth to the Lairds of Blantyre under whose lands the coal lay and to the coal masters who owned the mines, but for the men who tunnelled under the earth to bring the coal out, it brought a poor living, and for many, it brought death or serious injury.

The rush to develop the coal seams resulted in dangerously unsafe pits and as a result, Blantyre's miners paid a heavy price in lost lives and broken bodies.

The first recorded deaths by explosion occurred on 2<sup>nd</sup> March 1874, when two miners *John Kerr* 30, and *Hugh Pollock,* 48, were killed in Priestfield Colliery.

*John Kerr* had been among the great influx of people who settled in Blantyre after the discovery of coal. A Wanlockhead man, he had left the lead mines of his home village to work in Blantyre's coal mines. His body was taken back to Wanlockhead for burial. Hugh Pollock was buried in his home village of Bothwell.

The greatest loss of life occurred on the morning of Monday, 22<sup>nd</sup> October, 1877, when approximately 216 men and boys lost their lives, followed two years later by another 28 men dying, again in Dixon's pits. The tragic toll of deaths by explosion cost the Blantyre mining community dear. Approximately 260 men and boys died. The true number will never be known.

Of all Blantyre's pits, Auchinraith Colliery (or Murray's pit as it was known locally) was an exception, having a very low accident rate and it had the reputation of being one of the safest collieries in Scotland.

However, this changed on the morning of Saturday, 30th August, 1930, when a fire damp explosion ripped through the Black Band seam leaving five men dead, one dying and eight seriously injured.

Despite the violence of the explosion, miners working in other areas of the mine heard nothing. The alarm was raised by *Peter Scullion* one of the uninjured miners, who made his way through the gas filled workings to try to summon assistance.

The first indication to the Blantyre mining community that there had been an accident was when local doctors *Fisher, Stewart* and *La Raine* were seen arriving at the colliery.

Rumours began to spread like wildfire and at 09.10 am the sight of the Coatbridge Mine Rescue Brigade speeding through the town started a stampede of relatives heading towards the pit. Within a short time, large crowds of men, women and children were standing at the pit head. Many of the women, terror etched on their faces, wept openly as they waited for news.

*Women rushing to the pithead*
*Photograph courtesy of Andrew Kalinsky.*

The first injured man was found near the shaft by a miner from another section. *John Copeland* told of how the men had withdrawn from the coal face prior to the firing of a shot when, as he was walking towards his pony and four hutches there was a terrific crash and he was hurled a long distance. He lost consciousness; when he came round he was alone and the pit was in darkness.

Although in great pain, he managed to summon up enough strength to start crawling to safety. Exhausted by the effort he was on the point of giving up when he was found.

The arrival of the Mines Rescue Corps with their breathing apparatus allowed the rescuers to make their way towards the site of the explosion. One of the greatest dangers at this time was the presence of Afterdamp, or carbon monoxide, a highly poisonous gas present after an explosion and a silent killer, so familiar to the Blantyre miners who worked the town's gassy seams and who for three generations, had dug men out, both dead and alive, from previous explosions.

*Waiting for news at Auchinraith Rows*

In the Black Band seam, miners who had survived the explosion relatively unscathed were attending to the injured. With no thought for their own safety they had as their fathers and grandfathers had before them, stood shoulder to shoulder, to ensure the survival of as many miners as possible.

These men were also aware, that if necessary, every miner in the county would step forward to volunteer his services to save them.

Only when the rescue party arrived and took over, did they allow themselves to be taken to the surface. Five men had died instantly and *Richard Dunsmuir* was taken to hospital where he died the following day.

*THE MEN WHO DIED*

*WILLIAM SPROTT* aged 42, (fireman) a married man with a family. When his body was found the battery of his electric cap lamp was attached to his belt and the lamp was still lit. In his left hand was a cartridge of explosive containing a detonator and in his right hand, the key of the shot firing battery or exploder.

*ANDREW KALINSKY* aged 24, a single man and the youngest to die; had been unemployed for some time and had only just started working at the pit that week. On the morning of the explosion he was working an extra shift taking the place of another miner whose sister was critically ill. Andrew was the sole support of his mother; his father had been killed in an explosion in a German coal mine in 1922.

*RICHARD KING* aged 50, left a wife, a young son and two married daughters one of whom was in Canada.

189

JOSEPH REGAN aged 55, a widower for three years left three orphaned children. His eldest child *Margaret* aged 19 had been taking care of the home and her two motherless brothers aged 14 and 3 years.

*Photograph courtesy of Andrew Kalinsky.*

GEORGE SHORTHOUSE aged 63, a single man residing in Burnbank.
Of the nine men who were seriously injured in the blast only two, *Richard Dunsmuir* and *William Stoddart* whose conditions were classed as critical were removed, to Glasgow Royal Infirmary.

RICHARD DUNSMUIR, a single man, lost his battle for life early the next morning.

The other miners, although seriously injured, were taken home, as was the custom at that time, for their womenfolk to nurse them back to health.

Injured miner *Jimmy Russell's* departure from the pit head and arrival home lying on a stretcher on the back of a coal lorry was witnessed by a neighbour and close family friend *Walter Lang. Walter* and two friends ran to the colliery on hearing of the explosion.

He described the huge crowds of men, women and children standing around the engine house waiting on news from underground. Many of the women were carrying babies in shawls and had frightened children hanging on to their skirts.

*Waiting for news from underground. Photograph courtesy of Andrew Kalinsky.*

*Millie Spiers,* 92, recalled how she heard her cousin was among the injured. "There was a loud knock at the door of their home in Earnock Rows and Dr *Neil Douglas*, their family doctor, walked into the house."

Addressing her mother, he said, *"Kate, there has been an explosion at Auchinraith Colliery and Jimmy Russell's been badly burned. We've brought him home but he is going to need a lot of care."* Kate needed no further prompting. Reaching for her coat she followed the Doctor out of the house.

Both *Walter* and *Millie* described Jimmy as being burned black with areas of skin hanging off and not a hair left on his body.
It was to be a year before he was fit to work again.

Years later *Jimmy* was to vividly recall the explosion to his two daughters. There was, he said, a blinding, searing flash, followed almost immediately by a sound like he had never heard before and hoped he would never hear again. Like the rumble of thunder, but ten times more violent. He was aware of his clothes and hair being on fire as he was lifted off his feet by the force of the blast and sent crashing down the roadway, hitting off of unseen obstacles, for some distance.

*Jimmy Russell with Wilma and Eileen*

When he regained consciousness it was darker than the blackest night, he was in great pain and had difficulty breathing.
It was some time before he realised where he was. Dazed and disorientated, he drifted in and out of consciousness, for what he said, felt like two days. It was in fact, only two hours later, when he was found by the Mines Rescue Corps and taken to the surface where he was given morphine to relieve the pain.

Blantyre was a town in mourning on the day five of the victims were buried. In scenes unparalleled since Dixon's explosion, a crowd of fifty thousand people lined the route to High Blantyre Cemetery. The town came to a standstill. Shops were closed and window blinds were drawn in houses all over the town, as a token of respect.

The funeral procession numbering between nine and ten thousand was divided into five sections, each being headed by a local band and followed by the hearse of one of the victims.

*The cortege leaving Auchinraith Colliery Rows with the colliery in the background.*

The hearse containing the coffin of *Andrew Kalinsky,* the youngest victim, led the procession. As it wound its way along Auchinraith Road to the junction of Craig Street the hearse containing the remains of *Richard Dunsmuir* joined the procession. *Auchinraith Road.*

At Auchinraith Terrace, *Richard Sprotts'* hearse followed on and when the procession had passed along High Blantyre's Main Street the hearse containing the coffin of *Richard King* joined on and completed the procession.

At the entrance to the cemetery the mourners passed through the ranks of St Joseph's Silver Band who were playing the Dead March from Saul. The four coffins were placed on crepe covered trestles at the base of the Cenotaph.

The Rev *James Gibb* of Stonefield Church presided over the religious ceremony. There was one joint service before the coffins were taken to their respective graves where individual committal services were held by other members of the local clergy.

After the interments, the procession proceeded to the home of *Joseph Regan* and thereafter, the band and the hearse containing his remains made its way back to the cemetery.

The sight of his fourteen year old son following the coffin accompanied by two boy cousins and a number of friends and relatives was heartbreaking. This small slightly made young boy, desperately tried to stop his tears from flowing, as he walked behind his father's hearse. *Joseph Regan's* interment service was conducted by Rev *Father Fennessy.*

The private funeral of *George Shorthouse* took place at the same time in Hamilton's Bent Cemetery.

*Jane Ferrie*

Among the mourners at the funeral was 74 year old Mrs *Jane Ferrie,* the last surviving widow from the 1877 Dixon's disaster. Her first husband *James Simpson* had been among the dead.

The Mines Department Enquiry into the accident came to the conclusion, that the cause of the explosion was the ignition of Fire Damp by a spark from the exploder cable, at the point where the cable joined on to the detonator wires.

Sir *Henry Walker*, H.M. Chief Inspector of Mines, in his report on the accident wished it to be put on record his admiration of the conduct of the men who were at work in the section and who remained after the explosion to render whatever aid they could, giving special mention to first aid man *John Wailes.*

The men who survived the Auchinraith explosion returned to work after their injuries healed, but for survivor *Jimmy Russell,* there were other unseen injuries which surfaced only with the passage of time. The searing heat of the blast and the effects of toxic gas had damaged his lungs. He spent the last seven years of his life coughing up black coal dust and fighting for every breath he took.

*Jimmy Russell* a coal miner and proud of it, but an old man long before his time because of it, died prematurely in 1960, aged only 52 years.........HE WAS MY FATHER.

## THE INJURED MINERS

*A. Buchanan*, 58 Craig Street, Blantyre, *John Copland*, c/o McKerrell, Radnor Place Blantyre, *William Fox,* 4 Victoria Street, Blantyre, *Kenneth McKerrell* Radnor Place, Blantyre,. *Alex Paterson,* 21 Merry's Rows, Blantyre, *James Russell,* 74 Russell Street, Burnbank, *John Smith,* Merry's Rows, Blantyre, *William Stoddart,* Auchinraith Road, Blantyre, *John Wildman,* Beckford Street, Hamilton.

## THE UNINJURED MINERS

*William Anderson, Robert Inglis, Robert Lowden, George Rhodes, Peter Scullion, John Wildman, John Wailes*.

\*    \*    \*

On the 23rd November, 1931, at Hamilton Sheriff Court, Auchinraith Colliery's manager, undermanager and two of the firemen were tried for a variety of offences relating to the Coal Mines Act, 1911 and the Explosives in Coal Mines Order. All four were found guilty and received fines ranging from £5-£20, with the alternative of imprisonment.

*The funeral service at High Blantyre Cemetery*

# THE PRICE OF COAL

*The funeral of the Auchinraith victims, photograph courtesy of Andrew Kalinsky.*

When the wintry winds are raving
Round the chimney-tops at night,
And you sit at ease and comfort
At the fire so warm and bright,
Does it ever cross your vision
As you heat your slippered sole,
Does it ever seem to strike you
What's the actual cost of coal.

And if your thoughts do tend that way
It's nearly "ten to one."
You calculate your coal bill
At so much for every ton;
But think a bit, and soon you'll see
The sum needs doing twice,
You'll find there's lots of items
Not entered in your price.

There's blinded eyes and broken limbs,
There's doubts and hopes and fears,
There's women's sighs and widow's cries,
There's orphaned children's tears;
There's bitter grief for loved ones lost,
That racks the tortured soul,
There's breaking hearts and mangled men,
There's BLOOD in the price of coal.

*Donald Mathieson.*
*Blantyre. Circa 1924*

# EARNOCK COLLIERY
# HAMILTON

*Courtesy of Scottish Mining Museum*

Situated in the expanse of land lying between Hill Street and Wellhall Road, Earnock Colliery was hailed as a masterpiece of mining engineering technology, when it opened in 1879.

Developed and owned by coalmaster *John Watson,* the colliery, built in the grounds of his Earnock Estate was designed by two men. The surface layout was the work of the first President of the Mining Institute of Scotland, *Gilbert Burns Begg,* a highly acclaimed mining engineer and a grand nephew of poet *Robert Burns.* The design for the underground workings was the brainchild of *James Gilchrist,* Secretary of the Mining Institute of Scotland (founded in Hamilton in 1878) and a colliery manager of exceptional calibre employed by *John Watson* to design and manage Earnock Colliery. *Gilchrist* was only 28 years of age, but he had already worked his way up through the ranks from a boy drawer to hewer, contractor, roadsman, oversman, manager and designer of the most modern colliery in the whole of Scotland.

The colliery was situated only half a mile from Dixon's pit in Blantyre, where, in 1877 and 1879, approximately 244 men and boys had been killed in two separate explosions. In the 1877 disaster, *James Gilchrist,* a former oversman at Dixon's Colliery with extensive and unrivalled knowledge of the underground workings, had been given charge of co-ordinating the rescue teams. *Gilchrist* knew only too well, that the seams to be worked at the new Earnock Colliery were gassy, and, haunted by the spectre of disaster, safety was high on his agenda when drawing up plans for the mine.

The pit head was constructed from steel and wrought iron instead of the usual wood and the headgear of the two shafts stood 50 feet high. Specifically designed to be as safe as possible, the double channelled shafts were mechanically independent from one another and each set of winding gear was fitted with a King's Patent Detaching Hook to prevent an overwinding accident taking place.

The downcast shaft, down which air descended into the mine and up which coal was brought to the surface, had its own independent engine and engine-house. The arrangement was the same for the upcast shaft. This shaft was designed so that in the event of explosion, the gas and transient explosion flames would escape via one of its two channels, leaving the other free and where, if everything went to plan, men might escape. The second channel was used for transporting men to and from the pit bottom and designed to be free from the gas, smoke and filth of the ventilation system which entered the first channel and left via a tall chimney.

Prominently situated at the front gate, was a large notice forbidding smoking and on all the colliery buildings, notices banning the underground use of naked lights were very much in evidence. Miners going underground were searched to make sure that no cigarettes or matches found their way into the workings. No Smoking notices were also on display underground. *John Watson* who must have been greatly influenced by *James Gilchrist* was leaving nothing to chance and with good reason. The incidence of explosion at local collieries was too great to ignore.

 Such were the modern innovations included in the design Earnock soon became a magnet for the mining fraternity. It was a showpiece colliery and *John Watson*, an astute and shrewd businessman, made the most of it. Invitations to tour the colliery went out to all of the prominent men in mining and industry. Frequent large parties of up to a hundred invited guests would be given a tour of the surface buildings and underground workings, followed by lunch at Earnock House.

Ten years after the opening of Earnock Colliery, the danger of explosion was again tragically reinforced when on the morning of 28th May, 1887 less than a mile from Earnock, a catastrophic gas and dust explosion in the Splint seam at Udston Colliery, resulted in the loss of 73 miners, including 6 boys between the ages of 13 and 14 and another 6 aged 15 to 16. Among the first 4 rescuers to be lowered in a kettle (an open metal bucket) 750 feet down into the stricken pit were *James Gilchrist,* Manager of Earnock and *Daniel McPhail* one of his miners.

Earnock Colliery eventually went on to employ approximately 1250 men and produce up to 2000 tons per day of high quality coal. Steam haulage and 140 pit ponies were used underground to transport the coal from the face to the pit bottom, where it could then be taken to the surface via the downcast shaft.

The first principal coal seam to be worked was the Ell coal, found at a depth of 720 feet and almost 7 feet thick. The Pyotshaw and Main coal seams were over 4 ft. thick and worked at a depth of 774 ft. and 786 ft. respectively.

The 7 foot thick Splint and Virgin coal seams were found in the deepest working level at a depth of 854 ft. The Splint coal from Earnock helped to feed the blast furnaces of British industry. Most of the coal was extracted using the stoop and room method, where rooms or chambers 60 to 70 yards square were left after the coal had been extracted. The huge pillars of coal left to support the roof were approximately 60 feet square. Sections of the Pyotshaw and Main seams were worked by the longwall method.

On the 9th August, 1881, Earnock colliery became the first colliery in Scotland to install electricity to illuminate the pit bottom and haulage roadways. Glasgow firm, *Messrs D. & G. Graham* Ltd. Electrical Engineers had been given the contract to install the Swan incandescent lamps, modified for safe use underground. These lamps encased in an outer lantern to prevent breakage cost £1. 25p each to install and 25p each thereafter to replace.

On the surface, a separate building had been erected to house the 12 horse power steam engine and generator built by Earnock engineers in the collieries own workshop. Two cables from the generator were conducted along the roof of the workshops and over telegraph poles for a distance of several hundred metres. Arriving at number two shaft, the cables were led into a galvanised tube which extended down into the workings. Approaching the bottom of the shaft, the cables branched out to supply electricity to the haulage engines and to light the 10 feet wide by 7 feet high main roadways. The cable carried on through the main road ways and into sections of the mine, supplying light for a distance of more than half a mile, from a total of 21 lamps.

Telephones had also been installed, connecting the generator house and the pit bottom. This insured the instant withdrawal of the electric current, should the need arise. The telephone line between the pit bottom and the surface had been installed on the orders of *John Watson*. Ever aware that disaster was only an unguarded moment away, *Watson* felt that in the event of the unthinkable happening, any survivors from an explosion would have a better chance of escaping if they could communicate with the surface via the telephone.

The introduction of electricity underground was highly controversial and again John Watson set in motion his public relations machine. The ceremonial switching on of the underground lights was attended by a large party of distinguished guests, who afterwards, were given a guided tour, to view the wonder of the illuminated workings. Among the party was Lord Provost Ure of Glasgow, who, in an after lunch speech at Earnock House, soundly praised John Watson's achievements to the assembled dignitaries. His speech was received with resounding cheers.

The following Thursday, over one hundred colliery owners and managers, all members of the Mining Institute of Scotland met at Earnock Colliery, where they proceeded to make a minute inspection of the underground electrical system.

After witnessing the wonders of electricity, the visitors met in the colliery workshops to discuss what they had viewed and to hear a description of Swan's System of electric lighting given by Mr *Jamieson*, Principle of Glasgow College of Science and Arts. Afterwards the party adjourned to the colliery office where refreshments were served and photographs taken to commemorate the occasion.

The new underground electric lights would have made a considerable difference to Earnock's coal miners. At the flick of a switch they had gone from working in the very poor light given off by safety lamps, to working in better, but still quite poor visibility. One of the benefits of the lights would have been a reduction in the eye condition Nystagmus, or the "Glenny blink" as it was known as among miners. This condition was caused by working in the poor light given off by the "Clanny" safety lamp. In Scotland the lamp was known as the Glenny lamp, hence the name "Glenny blink."

In 1890, John Watson converted his business into a public company with a capital of £300,000. Watson himself held the position of Managing Director. A third shaft was then added to work the Splint, Blackband and Kiltongue seams. The headgear for this shaft was made from rolled Bessemer steel girders 65 feet high. The colliery was worked at four levels and the labyrinth of underground tunnels and roadways extended for over 800 acres.

*Earnock Recreational Hall prior to demolition, photograph courtesy of Hamilton Town House Reference Library.*

In 1893 John Watson Ltd. used a tiny portion of the profits generated by the mine to build a recreational hall for the use of Earnock's miners, followed some sixteen years later in 1909, by a bowling green. These recreational facilities, erected almost halfway through the working life of the mine, were the forerunners of the many recreational clubs subsequently built under the Miners Welfare Scheme.

# EARNOCK WORKMENS' BOWLING CLUB
# COMMITTEE MEMBERS 1909

*Photograph courtesy of Scottish Mining Museum*

*Top left.*
*James McMillan, (miner) James Gray, (Colliery worker) Matthew Stevenson, (miner) Wm.*
*Bernard, (miner) George McNab, (miner) John Henrietta, (miner)  George Meek, (driver)*
*James Thomson, (brusher) John McDonald,(occupation unknown.)*
*Front left. Angus McKay, (storeman) George Fortune, (foreman) James Hutton, (oversman)*
*Thos. Stevenson, (manager) George Lanyon, (oversman) John Spiers, (oversman)  W.*
*Stewart, (clerk.)*
*With the exception of James McMillan, the above men lived at Earnock.*

Earnock Colliery remained open for 65 years, producing more than 800,000 tons of coal annually and pouring fortunes into the bank accounts of the Watson family and shareholders.  Its productive life came to an end with the exhaustion of the coal seams and the colliery closed on the 18th April 1942.

The site lay derelict for many years, becoming a magnet for local children who spent many happy hours playing on it.  After the pit waste bing had been removed a small industrial estate was developed on the part of the grounds where the colliery had once stood and more recently, private housing estates have used up what was left of the reclaimed land.

Today, all that remains of the colliery buildings are two brick built semi   detached cottages Nos. 92 and 94 Argyll Drive, Earnock.

These cottages were once the homes of the colliery gaffers, the firemen, oversmen and undermanagers.

*92 - 94 Argyle Drive, Earnock*

The pit village built by *John Watson* to house his workforce was known locally as Earnock Rows and consisted of a total of 183 houses. The houses were of a poor quality, built from red brick with outside toilets and wash houses.  There were  36 houses with only one room (single ends,) 138,  2 roomed houses (room and kitchens, ) 7,  3 roomed houses( 2 room and kitchens, ) 1, 4 roomed  cottage and a 9 roomed managers villa.  The village was situated only yards from the colliery gates.

Over the years, the "Rows" were home to thousands of people. Many families could boast of three or four generations of their family having worked and lived at Earnock. The residents of the village were good caring people. If a family fell on hard times neighbours could be relied on to assist in any way they could. No one was allowed to starve.

One story which epitomises this communal caring ethos was recalled by 93 year old *Milly Spiers*, who told of how the neighbours gathered round to help her family when their father John Spiers was in a Glasgow Hospital.  There was no income or cheap coal when a miner was ill and off work and *Millie's* mother *Kate* was having a hard time trying to feed, heat and clothe five children. Down to her last pail of coal, she was at her wit's end worrying how she was going to manage.

Just before the children left to go to school, she sent two of them out to the coal cellar to see if there was any dross left. When they came back into the house, they were staggering under the weight of a full pail of coal. Concerned that they had gone to the wrong coal cellar she ran out to the back court. The first thing she noticed was that there were doormats lying from the front of the close through to the back and when she opened the cellar door, she found to her joy, that it was full and overflowing with coal.

 Later that day, *Kate* found out where the coal and the door mats had come from. During the night, under cover of darkness, some of her husband's workmates had hidden themselves on coal wagons leaving the colliery. Once through the pit gates they started throwing large lumps (rakers) of coal from the wagons and when it was felt that enough coal had been removed, they jumped off returning to collect the coal in pails and sacks.  Not wanting to waken anyone they had borrowed doormats from doorsteps so that their footsteps would be muffled and they would go undetected. For these men to be found stealing coal meant instant dismissal and a heavy fine or jail, but they were willing to take the chance to help another miner's family, knowing that if they were in a similar position, others would do the same for them.

Today the descendants of Earnock's coal miners can be found all over the world. Oversman John Spiers and his wife Margaret, whose home was once one of the surviving brick cottages, have descendants who are citizens of ten countries worldwide.

Included among this international family are great, great grandsons Jameel and Nabil Al Sharif, sons of Nabi and Margaret (Spiers) Al Sharif who still visit their Scottish relatives from their homes in the Arabian Gulf.

*Three generations of John and Margaret Spiers' descendants at home in Bahrain.*
*Jameel Al Sharif (middle, front row) bears an uncanny resemblance to his great-great-grandfather John Spiers, oversman Earnock Colliery, 1900-1926.*
*Photograph courtesy of Anne Winkley (Spiers).*

After the colliery closed, Earnock Rows rapidly fell into disrepair and the village soon became a slum and a health hazard to its inhabitants. By the late 1950's its vibrant close knit community had been broken up and rehoused in council schemes throughout Hamilton.

Earnock Rows, loved by the people who had been born and raised in it, was now inhabited only by the ghosts of the past. When the last of the village was bulldozed to the ground in 1959, many of its former inhabitants watched, with tears streaming down their faces, knowing, that what the community had represented was lost, never to return.

Today people still talk with pride of their childhood in this unique little pit village where poverty was the norm and life was hard, but where the inhabitants not only felt, but in their hearts knew…That they were special.....THEY WERE EARNOCK FOLK

# KNOWN EARNOCK COLLIERY DEATHS

| DATE | NAME | AGE | CAUSE OF DEATH |
|---|---|---|---|
| 06.08.1881 | DANIEL GRAY | 27 | CRUSHED BY HUTCHES |
| 15.02.1882 | JOHN McCLEMENTS | 20 | CRUSHED BY WAGON |
| 16.03.1883 | GEORGE PRITCHARD | 32 | ROOF FALL (Internal injuries) |
| 11.03.1884 | ROBERT LATTA | 45 | KILLED BY EXPLOSIVE |
| 15.04.1885 | JOHN G. McCULLOCH | 21 | RUN OVER BY HUTCH |
| 05.05.1884 | HUGH McCARTNEY | 20 | ROOF FALL (Fractured skull) |
| 17.07.1884 | TERRENCE MURRAY | 36 | ROOF FALL (13 cwts) |
| 18.01.1885 | JOHN ROX | 60 | RUN DOWN BY ENGINE |
| 15.04.1885 | JOHN McCULLOCH | 21 | RUN DOWN BY HUTCHES |
| 20.05.1885 | JOHN FORBES | 17 | RUN DOWN BY WAGONS |
| 05.10.1885 | JAMES DAVIS | 27 | ROOF FALL, (2 tons) |
| 02.03.1887 | ALEX. BROWN | 24 | ROOF FALL (Stone 12ft long) |
| 22.02.1888 | PETER FOX | 22 | ROOF FALL (Compound fracture of skull) |
| 16.09.1889 | JOHN CROZIER | 49 | RUN DOWN BY HUTCH |
| 15.01.1890 | ALEX. McDONALD | 35 | ROOF FALL (15 cwts) |
| 19.12.1890 | JOHN CAMPBELL | 52 | RUN DOWN BY HUTCHES |
| 15.01.1891 | THOMAS MEE | 19 | CRUSHED BY HUTCHES |
| 02.04.1891 | JOHN WATSON | 46 | FELL DOWN SHAFT, (720 ft) |
| 07.07.1891 | NEIL FRASER | 35 | RUN DOWN BY HUTCH |
| 31.08.1891 | ALEX BROWNING Jnr | 15 | ROOF FALL SLAB OF ROCK 6ft X 4ft |
| 27.04.1894 | PETER DIVER | 23 | CRUSHED BY HUTCH |
| 19.05.1895 | ANDREW LEWES | 25 | LEG CRUSHED |
| 22.10.1895 | ABRAHAM McMANUS | 21 | ROOF FALL |
| " | CHARLES RAE | 31 | ROOF FALL |
| 22.01.1896 | WALTER F. JOHNSON | 13 | ROOF FALL (Fractured skull) |
| 03.03.1896 | GABRIEL SEMPLE | 32 | ROOF FALL (2 cwt.) |
| 19.03.1897 | JAMES WYPER | 13 | ROOF FALL (Compound fractures right leg) |
| 26.10.1897 | JOHN MILES | 49 | NO DETAILS (Crushed) |
| 03.01.1898 | GEO. SOMERVILLE | 14 | ROOF FALL |
| 05.01.1898 | JAMES WYPER | 13 | NO DETAILS (Multiple leg fractures) |
| 09.03.1898 | LYLE McKERRELL | 20 | CRUSHED BY WAGON |
| 25.10.1898 | FRANCIS HAILSTONES | 29 | SUFFOCATION- FIRE DAMP |
| 03.04.1899 | THOS. McHAFFIE | 30 | ROOF FALL, ( 3 cwt) |
| 13.07.1899 | JAS. McL. McCAWLEY | 14 | ROOF FALL |
| 05.01.1900 | DONALDSON McF. LEES | 36 | ROOF FALL (Head and chest injuries) |
| 12.03.1900 | HENRY McCARTNEY | 43 | KILLED BY EXPLOSIVES |
| 02.03.1900 | THOMAS PRENTICE | 53 | CRUSHED BY FALLING WALL |
| 18.05,1901 | JOHN RICHMOND | 23 | ROOF FALL (Multiple injuries) |
| 18.07.1902 | KAZAMIERAS SZALCZUIS | 21 | FALL OF COAL |
| 07.11.1902 | JOHN HUNTER | 27 | RUN DOWN BY HUTCHES |

*Earnock Colliery deaths continued.*

| | | | |
|---|---|---|---|
| 14.01.1903 | JAMES WHITE | 32 | FALL OF COAL. (Compound fractures of leg and pelvis.) |
| 10.02.1903 | WM. PATERSON | 38 | ROOF FALL |
| 16.02.1904 | PETRAS USAITIS OR SAVAGE | 22 | NO DETAILS |
| 08.09.1904 | ROBERT BOLTON | 23 | KILLED BY EXPLOSIVES |
| 27.04.1905 | EDWARD C. BAXTER | 40 | FALL OF COAL AT FACE |
| 29.12.1905 | HUGH/EUGINE CARLIN | 34 | ROOF FALL |
| 10.01.1906 | JOHN JOHNSTONE | 27 | ROOF FALL (Trapped 1 hr) |
| 20.03.1906 | WILLIAM CALDER | 31 | CAUGHT BETWEEN BUFFERS AND WAGON (Fractured skull) |
| 03.04.1908 | JOSEPH LASKINS | 35 | FALL OF COAL |
| 20.06.1907 | JOHN COLLIGAN | 42 | LEG INJURY, (Tetanus) |
| 07.11.1907 | JOHN HUNTER | 27 | RUN DOWN BY HUTCHES |
| 27.06.1908 | HENRY McGUIGAN | 37 | ROOF FALL (Multiple injuries) |
| 11.03.1910 | MATTHEW MILLER | 60 | CRUSHED BY HUTCH |
| 10.05.1910 | WM. McKENNA | 54 | HAND INJURED (Cellulites) |
| 11.10.1911 | DAVID ARCHIBALD | 46 | ROOF FALL (2 tons) |
| 14.04.1912 | DONALD McKAY | 33 | CUT TO HEAD (Septicaemia) |
| 14.12.1912 | JAMES CAMPBELL | 26 | CUT FINGER (Septicaemia) |
| 29.01.1913 | WILLIAM FERGUSON | 42 | ROOF FALL (Fractured skull) |
| 15.02.1913 | WILLIAM MILLER | 47 | CRUSHED BY CAGE IN SHAFT (Head injuries) |
| 13.06.1913 | NATHIANAL QUINN | 32 | LOST CONTROL OF HUTCHES (Neck broken.) |
| 13.10.1913 | JAMES LALLY | 40 | CRUSHED BY RUNAWAY HUTCH (Fracture skull) |
| 0.06.1914 | NEIL McKILLOP | 44 | ROOF FALL (Trapped 3 hrs.) |
| 24.11.1915 | JONAS SONAITIS | 36 | ROOF FALL (Fractured skull) |
| 30.05.1918 | ALEXANDER BLACK | 49 | NO DETAILS (Fractured skull) |
| 15.04.1920 | MORRISON DOCHERTY | 18 | HEAD AND NECK INJURIES |
| 22.06.1920 | PETER HANNAH | 24 | MULTIPLE INJURIES |
| 19.04.1922 | ROBERT C. CAMPBELL | 54 | NO DETAILS (Asphyxia) |
| 04.05.1923 | MICHAEL McGHIE | 27 | ROOF FALL (Fractured skull) |
| 07.08.1925 | JAMES McKENNA | 53 | ROOF FALL |
| 14.11.1927 | FRANCIS MARTIN | 20 | NO DETAILS, (Shock following pit accident) |
| 30.03.1932 | JOHN CLARKE | 53 | ROOF FALL (Smashed skull) |
| 05.08.1937 | ARCHD. CAMPBELL | 45 | ROOF FALL (Asphyxia) |
| 27.11.1937 | THOMAS WILSON | 32 | ROOF FALL (Asphyxia) |
| 02.01.1938 | JOHN LOWE | 54 | COLLIERY FIRE (Smoke inhalation) |
| 04.03.1938 | ALEXANDER YOUNG | 56 | COLLIERY FIRE (Pneumonia) |

# EARNOCK FOLK
*
## EARNOCK COLLIERY WORKMENS CLUB
### COMMITTEE MEMBERS
### Circa 1925

*Photograph courtesy of Scottish Mining Museum, names of committee members unknown except for two miners in the top row 1ˢᵗ left John Spiers Jnr, 4ᵗʰ from right his brother-in-law Adam Russell*

## EARNOCK CORINTHIANS FOOTBALL TEAM 1934

*Photograph courtesy of Don Boyle, nephew of Donald Cameron front row second left.*

*Cashier 1912-1942*                    *Cashier's house*

*William Whitehouse*            *71 Earnock Road (site now roundabout at Pollock Ave)*
*Photographs courtesy of Miss Jessie Whitehouse (daughter)*

## THE RUSSELLS

Margaret Russell  (Spiers)

## THE END OF THE AMERICAN DREAM

Top row, left to right; *James,* (7) *Adam,* (father) *Margaret,* (6) middle row, *Gilbert,* (4)
Bottom row left to right; *Willie* (13) *Adam* (14) *and John Russell* (15).
This photograph doesn't look like a happy family group and it wasn't. It was taken in 1916
after the death of Adam Russell's 35 year old wife Margaret Spiers, mother of his six
children. Within months the family were back in Scotland, living in Earnock Rows and
Adam, and his three eldest sons were working underground in Earnock Colliery. The two
youngest boys, James and Gibbie also became Earnock miners. Adam (Yad) Russell could
keep a house as well as any woman. He cooked and baked and made jam from the berries he
grew in his plots at Earnock. He remarried nine years later.

# THE RUSSELL MEN

*Hewer*

*Adam (Yad) Russell, senior*

*HIS FIVE SONS*

*Hewer*

*Willie Russell*

*Hewer*

*Jock Russell*

*Hewer*

*Adam (Yad) Russell Jnr.*
*41 Argyle Buildings*

*Brusher*

*Jimmy Russell*

*Hewer*

*Gibbie Russell*

*Oversman*

*Hewer*     *Pit Joiner*

*John and James Spiers*

*John Spiers with wife Margaret*

*<Three of their sons >*
*      *     ***

*Engineer*

*George Spiers*
*Left pits to become a minister*

*Brusher*

*Thomas M. Wallace*   ·
*Photograph courtesy of son Jim Wallace.*

*Manager, circa 1930's*

*Walter Napier*
*Photograph courtesy of*
*Miss Jessie Whitehouse*

*Winding Engineman No. 1 Pit*

*James (Riddy) Harkness*
*Photograph courtesy of*
*daughter Helen Wallace*

*Fireman*

*Robert Prentice*
*Photograph courtesy of*
*grandson Jim Prentice*

# BLOWING IN THE WIND

*Women at a washhouse in Earnock Rows and Wullie Dale, 62 Albert Buildings on the bike. Wullie was a goalie with Burnbank Swifts.*

# ONE MOMENT IN TIME

*This photograph of Tam Dale on his new bike gives us a view down the back of Earnock's middle row. The remains of the old Wellhall Colliery can be seen at the bottom of the row. The site of the Wellhall Pit is now occupied by the Greenfield Club.  Photographs circa 1930 courtesy of Nancy Bain.*

# THE CAMERONS
## 92 ALBERT BUILDINGS

*Mary and Donald Cameron with daughter Marion*
*Circa 1946-47. Photograph courtesy of Don Boyle (grandson)*

Donald Cameron was born in Skye in 1875, the eldest son of John Cameron of Skye and Marac McKinnon of Coll. At home in Skye, his mother tongue was Gaelic.
Donald left school at the age of 9 years and worked on farms around Stirlingshire and Dumbartonshire.
He returned to Skye when he was 12 and signed on as a cabin boy with his uncle Donald Cameron who was captain of a sailing ship.
On his first voyage the ship was caught in a terrible storm and he was lashed to the mast. He vowed then that if he survived he would never leave dry land again.
He was saved and returned to farming where he became a ploughman.
In his early 20's he was appointed ploughman at the Bowes Lyon estate which belonged to late Queen Mother's family. While he was working there he won the highest award a ploughman could aspire to….. The Highland Award.
In the early 20th century he gave up ploughing to work in Earnock Colliery, so that his wife would be able to devote herself to caring for their children. As a ploughman's wife, she had a lot of duties to attend to, which took her away from her children and this caused her great anxiety, for they had to be left alone.
Donald began work as a brusher, but then was offered the job of Ostler a few years later. This was the kind of life he loved—so much that he won the Professor Blackie award for having the best harnessed horses in Britain.
He worked for 38 years in Earnock Colliery and when it closed in 1942, he went to Dixon's Pit in Blantyre. He continued to work as a boiler fireman at Dixon's until he was 80. He died just a few months after he retired.
He never once, in all his working life, lost a solitary day's work and never once, was he late for his work; a proud record.

# EARNOCK

What was it about Earnock that has had such a lasting and positive affect on so many of us who lived there?

It was certainly not the affluence which pervaded the place—nor was it the architecture or design.

With unlimited funds, we could re-build Earnock Rows—brick for brick and we would be left with 190 houses with outside toilets and no facilities—which no-one would want to live in.

Earnock was of its day—but what a day it was!

Firstly it was a complete enclave and had no adjoining dwelling areas attached. This gave it an identity of its own.

However, the most lasting impression was surely the type of people who lived there. They most certainly identified with each other and they shared a pride in being "Earnock" folk.

Those people, our parents and grandparents, were simple hardworking people who shared life in a society where there was very little opportunity for a person to better themselves.

The most a person could hope for was to be able to work and to have a job of any description that would pay the rent and put some food on the table.

This was a situation that was understood by everyone so there was no room for vanity. They each understood the needs of those around them and cared for each other's well-being. It was a meagre existence for everyone and they didn't wish to see anyone slip further down.

They did enjoy a very great sense of community and prided themselves in it. They socialised with each other and the men enjoyed their football, bools and quoits. Men loved to go walking together and would walk for miles across the country.

We who were born in the 30's had the greatest advantage of living our lives in the company of those who loved us in a very settled and well adjusted society.

For us there was always a feeling of safety about the place. No one I knew ever showed any signs of insecurity. We enjoyed the openness of the area around us. I never heard of any child being ill treated or molested.

Of course, those days were anything but affluent, but there was sameness about us. Our pleasures were very simple.

To go to the Plaza or get a 3d chip was a treat—or to gamble a penny in Bain's "puggy," was a kind of Las Vegas experience.

*A loving family*

There is so much we could write and recall about Earnock, but one thing says it all to me. The late *Eck Shields* told me about a dream he had 20 years ago.

He dreamed he was walking down the middle row and he saw a person on the stairs and he called "Jock-Ah thought ye were deid!"

Jock replied "Ah am deid, Eck. This is Heaven."

Don Boyle. 2005
(Grandson of the
Cameron's of 92 Albert Buildings.)

# THE POETRY OF EARNOCK ROWS

*

# EARNOCK

*Earnock Brig by Don Boyle*

Sae mony places ha'e Ah seen
Sae splendid oan the silver screen
Wi' waving palms and silvery beach
A Paradise beyond oor reach.

But still ma heart wad dance a jig
Tae walk ance maire thro' Earnock brig!
Tae see thae faces that Ah know
Tae hear the weemin, gabbin in the Co!

Tae walk again up a' the ra'
Tae see wee lassies skip and ca'
Tae see the boys play ower the park
Wi' a' their tricks and ilka lark.

Tae hear a voice cry oot ma name
Invitin' me tae jine a gemme
Or meet a dug that wags its tail
A welcome that wad never fail.

A' thae names and faces that Ah ken
Whaure boys are "son" and lassies "hen"
Tae walk thro' closes that Ah knew
And hear each step as Ah gae through.

Tae see a wummin beat a rug
Or watch a man split up a clug
Tae see the boys vault oan a pole
Or fill a pail wi' Earnock coal.

Ah ken that Ah wad never weary
Watchin lassies whup a peerie
Or hear the men laugh an' talk
 As frae the pit they homeward walk.

Wha' could ever ask for more
Than a friendly face at every door
A verse or sae o' an auld Scots sang
Tae ken ye're hame whaure ye belang.

Wi' a' this joy we're rich indeed
Sae mony thochts that fu' ma heid
No' a jot Ah care for fame
The joy for me is bein' hame.

Sae much Ah ken is in the past
And we wha' mind are but the last
 Still one day Ah'm sure we'll find
Earnock is the Heaven God has in mind.

*Don Boyle.*
*(92 Albert Buildings*
*Earnock)*

*Back stairs at Earnock Rows by Don Boyle*

A DYING VILLAGE
*Earnock, back court, front row prior to demolition, circa 1950's. Photograph courtesy of Hamilton Town House Reference Library,*

# CHILDHOOD

In memory let me wander back and tae ye a' reca'
The happy childhood days we spent when oor world
     was truly sma'
Should you wonder who the de'll this is, ye'll realise it a'
When I tell ye I was born and raised in Earnock.

Roon the toll alongside the bank, and past Murin Paul's shoap,
Frae Pollock into Earnock Street, ye don't take time to stoap,
Then tae your richt and thro' the brig ye've nae mair
     need tae mope,
For there jist in front o' ye, is Earnock.

Wi' a motley crown o' people mixed in a' degrees,
English, Irish, Jews and Scots, Protestants and R.C's.,
Although we'd different points of view, we a' felt quite at ease,
For we'd a common bond; we a' belonged tae Earnock.

The year o' 21 an' 26, when the strike was at its hicht,
When as kids we played at fitba', bools and peever, fae
     morn tae nicht,
And the auld folks saw that we got fed and mack everything
     seem a' richt,
We'd nae money, but those were happy days in Earnock.

Wi' soup simmerin' in the wash-hoose an' boolin' on the green
An' the lads aye efter lassies, wi a twinkle in their een'
Playin haun' ba' at the gable-end, and a thing we'd never seen,
Pit pownies trottin' aboot the fields at Earnock.

In summer when wi' gir'n cleek the back roads we could run
Pu'in berries, pitchin' tents, or sliding doon the bing for fun,
Or pinchin' turnips oot the plots, then paiddlin' in the burn,
An' the first hay-cairt comin' thro the brig tae Earnock.

On winter nichts we sat an' sang when gathered roon the fire
An' listened to the harmony at the back-raw crowds' desire
The co-operative Kinderspiels, Tammy Russell's Male Voice
Choir,
We learned tae' 'preciate music back in Earnock.

Time the middle-raw went on fire, and we watched the
          building flare,*
Peepin' Toms, lum-hatted men, that gave us kids a scare,
Coal pails fleein' fae frightened haunds an' clattering
          doon the stair,
These really were excitin' days in Earnock.

Though the place we knew is still on the map, it isn't
quite the same,
And the folks we loved are dead and gone, tho' in mem'ry
          they remain
When the sands of time have trickled out we'll know that
          we've come hame,
When we go to meet the folks that came from Earnock.

*Robert (Boab) Prentice, 6.11.1914---17.11.2003.*

*Boab Prentice was born and raised in Earnock. His father was a fireman in Earnock Colliery but would not allow his son to follow him underground. Boab served his time as an engineering fitter, at Anderson Boyes, Flemington, Motherwell. His job was to make coal cutting machinery. This poem was written in 1958, as a keepsake for his sister Molly.*

\*          \*          \*

*\*In August 1918, 24 houses were seriously damaged or made uninhabitable after a chimney fire set the middle raw ablaze. It was said that the occupier of the house where the fire originated pushed a jumper up the lum and set fire to it to save the cost of a chimney sweep; he burned the building down. He didn't inform the colliery about the jumper.*

# EARNOCK RAW'S

*The middle row was almost derelict by the time this photograph was taken. Photograph courtesy of Hamilton Town House Reference Library.*

The days we spent in Earnock Raw's a place we all love well
And some people known to live there I am about to tell.
The front Raw has a wee co-op shop where everyone bought goods
Porridge, cheese, bread and jam and aw the staple foods.
We start wi' *Peter Mackie* wha kicked a bonny baw,
He could do a lovely dribble, shoot wan in but never fa.

We go then to *Skud Symon* wha liked the countryside,
Wi' a rabbit up his jersey and a snare hidden weel inside.
The *Hawkes* were *Jim and Eddie*; of cricket they were fond,
As off they'd go to *Leslie's* Park, when it wisn'a like a pond.
*McNab* he made his name too, when he signed on for the Hibs
Lang legs he had for jumpin high, hard elbows fur digging ribs.

*Dunsmores, Robsons* and *Rankins* as we get up to the top,
And then of course who could forget *Geordie Meek's* wee sweetie
   shop.
*Tam Falconer* was in the line up, a gaffer at the pit,
To make sure the men were working and aw the lamps were lit.
*McNaughtons, Singers, Straitons, Wull Bernard*, an' doon; the
*Quinns.*
*Rabbie* played for Celtic then, the famous Glesga yins.

*Calderwood* and *Riddy Smith* and doon tae *Johnny Keat,*
He had trouble wi' his saxophone, he had trouble wi' his feet.
Big *Erchie* frae the lamp cabin, was oil from heid tay fit,
But just the same an important man, frae the point aw view o' aw the pit,
The piano Raw they ca-ad it, at least that is what is said,
But we think the pianos were kept below the bed.

The middle Raw was next in line and we find there staunnin' grinning
Another couple o' fitba players *Pud Easton* and *Geordie Winning*
Next to *Paddy Larkins* also *Paddy Maher*
They worked a lot up at the plots and they drank in the Enfield bar.
Big *Shuggie Orr* was also there, so was granny *Broon,*
*Jack* the brickie stayed wi' her, he was aye gaun roon and roon.

The family ca'ad the *Irwins* were an awfy quiet band,
Their faither and mither spoke Irish, because they came from Ireland.
*Through the wa' was Mirrin Easton and Lindsay* next to that,
*Big Jock* could down twelve pint's o' beer, aye at the drop o' a hat.
*Wattie Broon*, his maw and paw, stayed up the very next stair,
And then a singer o' reknown, his name was big *Rag Blair.*

*Geordie McKinley* he was the keeper o' the Earnock Hall,
This was where the miners used to haud their annual ball,
You could play at draughts and dominoes, carpet bools upon the flair.
You could even play at billiards if you went awa up the stairs.
*Turnbull* and *Erchie Adams* are the next yins in the verse,
Wee *Baldy* quite a figure, sitting high up on his hearse.

The *Barratts* and the *Staffords* they selt coal and logs fur splitting,
And when they wurny busy, they would also dae a flitting.
Then doon a wee bit further, ye cam' tae Mrs *Mair,*
The unofficial midwife for aw the women there,
The *Grants* and doon tae *Simpson's* wi' motor bikes and side caurs,
Shiny wheels and polished tanks and great big honelbaurs.

Big *Tam Weir* and *Boab Murray* and doon tae Mrs *Scott*,
Anither place for sweeties, a penny bought a lot,
Then it was *Gillespie* and also *Duggie Young,*
Who talked of submarines and pub shops, and where the kings were hung.
We are back doon at the bottom and a lot o' folks been passed,
But we canna mind the lot o' them, fae beginning tae the last.

The back Raw wis the last yin and there find *Knox* and *Dick.*
A left *hook frae wee Francie could catch you pretty quick.*
*The Doc* steyed next tae *Francie*, he was always pretty cockie,
And by the size o' him, we thochts he'd be a jocky,
*John Stewart* done the paper row, nicknamed big *Tom Toppin,*
His brither when at the school, wi'd say "hey you" nae copying.

*Callaghan* and *Knorker Bell* they helped tae build the bing,
Then there was *Jamie Stuart*, a descendant o' the King,
*Tammy Kelly* we kin mind, he worked at the pithead,
Sortin' oot coal frae stanes, he fairly earned his breid.
*Mick Cuthbertson,* a strong man, wi' muscles bulging oot,
He went in fur health and strength, aye, he was quite a brute.

And further up *Gilroy* and *Weir*, were right up at the top,
Then roon the back tae *Alfie Page,* he had a great big plot.
He kept ducks and geese and hens, he grew vegetables as well,
You could tell the place he kept them, by the rotten stinking smell.
*Jim Kelly* wis a painter, who done a lovely job,
He'd distemper anybody's ceiling; the price was jist a few bob.

*Frank Collins* he went tae the war, wis captured by the Japs,
And by the time he got back, was quite a different chap
Then we had the *Logan's* and also the *Chuckie* Broons,
*Jock Mullen* wis a great big chap who had burst a few balloons.
*Jock Stein* o' Glesga Celtic, quite famous he's became,
But the talent wis that good here, sometimes he could'nae git a
game.

We had Nurkey, Nurkey, fitba, run sheep run,
Hunch Cuddy, Hunch and tossin,
Haun ba' Moshie and bedlum
Some were winning some were losing.
The buskers came to entertain,
They sang and danced even in the rain.

We had donkey's there an aw',
That we could ride right roon the raw.
The I canhopit and Socani wir names o' Wilson's buses,
Oor mothers and faithers used to go, fur a day and never miss us.
*Billy Straiton* and *Joe Beattie*, doon at the bottom stair,
Joe played on his accordion, for the cancan in the open air.

Good luck and joy be wae you, at hame and o'er the sea,
The days o' Earnock Raws are gone, but memories will aye stey
wi' me,
Now this rhyme has got to stop, fur I've came to the end,
But tae the folks o' Earnock Raws,
This message I will send.

*James Irwin,*
*34 Albert Buildings*
*Earnock*

*James Irwin's wonderful poem paints a vivid picture of the residents of Earnock Rows. He is believed to have gone to Australia, the poem was written in 1976.*

# IN MEMORY OF EARNOCK BING
## MY EVEREST
### (The Luge)

*Taken from top of Earnock bing looking towards Burnbank.*
*Photograph courtesy of Hamilton Town House Reference Library.*

Corrugated iron—wae the ends turned up
Blint wi stour and shale
Fifty miles an oor at least
Anither on yer tail.

Earnock bing my Everest
The biggest bing aroon
Ah climbed ye every day in life
The tallest in the toon.

Mony's the time I fell aff the tap
Fae aff yer towr'n heights
Broken taes and fingers
Ah should be deid by rights.

Cadzow bing it wis'nae bad
But wis'nae near sae steep
Naewhere near the broken bones
Aw' right for grazin' sheep.

Dae ye mind wee Wullie doon the road
We put him in a tyre
Ah'm shair it wis aff a Chieftain bus,
An' fae aff yer very spire,

We geid'm sich a hefty shove
He fell oot hauf way doon
He staggert' roon for hauf an oor
An roon n' roon' roon,

As soon as he could staun at peace
He said "Christ that wiz great",
Could we dae it again jist wan mair time"
It wis clear he could'nae wait

So intae the tyre again he went
This time we tied him in
An wi an even harder shove
We sent him for a spin.

Well "Tottie Minto's" pigeon loft.
Ah ken ye've guessed already
It wis quite plain for aw tae see,
Even tae blind Freddy

Unhappy circumstances wid unfold
And mibbie even mair
A heid oan crash, a lot a stour
An feathers everywhere

Deid doos deid as dodos
Died in the loft that day
Like road kill they aw' lay aroon
Ah guess its fair tae say

We thought the wee block doon the road
Wi' the doos had done his dash
Surprise, surprise, would ye believe
Fae in amang the trash

A ghostly figure staggert' oot
An' roon n' roon n' roon
He said "Christ that wis bliddy great"
"ah hope that very soon"

"Will ye dae that again jist wan mair time"
This time ah'll git it right"
At this point ye can guess the rest
It's time to say guidnight

Dear Earnock bing where ur ye noo
Wher'ever did ye go
Scattered to the winds, ah think
Ah' ken ah miss ye so.

Oh Earnock bing my Everest,
It's time to say fareweel
Ah won't forget ye ever
Fareweel! Fareweel!! Fareweel!!!
Thomas Matthew Edgar, Australia. (*Formerly of Hill Street, Udston*)

# CLYDE COLLIERY

## PATRICK McFARLANE
## 1877-1930

*Photograph by kind permission of Patrick Cox, (grandson.)*

*Patrick McFarlane* was one of the last men to be killed at Clyde Colliery. Born in 1877, he was orphaned when very young. Patrick enlisted in the Seaforth Highlanders at Perth in 1908 and remained with the regiment for several years, becoming a reservist on discharge. At the start of the First World War, he was called up and served for the duration of the war. After discharge, he worked as a coal miner.

On the 5th May 1930 a stone weighing more than a ton fell from the roof of the Blackband seam in No. 3 Pit Clyde Colliery crushing Patrick to death. He left a widow and three children, one of whom was Thomas, who, after witnessing his father's death, never went down a pit again.

For sixty two years the Clyde Colliery stood in the area of Hamilton now occupied by Morrison's supermarket. The colliery closed its gates at the end of 1933 after the exhaustion of the coal seams. The following article, written by an unnamed colliery official, was published in the Hamilton Advertiser some months later. It is a wonderful record of the names and characters of many of the men who worked at Clyde Colliery and it is reproduced in this book with kind permission of "The Hamilton Advertiser" and dedicated to the memory of the men who worked and the men who died in the Clyde, Backmuir and Wellhall collieries owned by the Clyde Coal Company.

# CLYDE PIT MEMORIES
# 1933

The old Clyde Pit has gone, but its memories remain. No more will we hear the cheery laughter, or see those well remembered faces, in or about the old Clyde Pit.

For three generations the pithead pulleys have revolved. For Sixty years it has sent forth its quota to keep "the home fires burning" and to help making the homes of the workers free from economic worries.

In a talk some time ago with an old fellow-worker, he said to me, with a wistful look in his face, "There were worse places that the old Clyde Pit." It was a statement with which I heartily concurred.

For the space of twenty-one years the writer worked in and about that old pit. Certainly there were dull days—days which we have no great desire to remember, but on the whole the atmosphere was cheery, and the people with one or two exceptions, kindly, considerate and faithful to a degree.

When we look back there were great moments which we would have liked to have retained just a little longer. There were times when the flush of contentment was on our faces, for something attempted, and something well done. Again, there were periods of disappointments, when we felt as if no matter what we did would meet with a measure of success. Still we must take these things as they come for do they not make up the sum total of life, with its joys and its sorrows, its successes and its disappointments?

One man in our memory stands out, head and shoulders above any other, and that man is the late

## MR ANDREW HEPBURN

For many years *Mr Hepburn* was the manager at the colliery and it is no secret that his heart lay in the work there, and when he left to take up another appointment no one grieved more than he did. He knew his men. And he knew how to get the best out of his men, and did not mince matters when he saw a man who had not the interest in his work, which he should have had. His cheery greeting at the end of the shift we recall with pleasure. After a hard and trying day in which things did not run too smoothly, you had the feeling, that when you were giving your report, that he was putting himself in your place, and therefore, he at once could sense your difficulties. A word here and there was all he needed to show if you had actually tried to do the best you could under the circumstances. And when he saw that you had done everything for the best, then you could expect that little word of encouragement that made us like him, for we saw then that he had thoroughly understood our difficulties and had appreciated how we had acted when things had run against us. When things had gone well his cheery smile in itself was an incentive to carry on the good work.

Andrew was in the habit of calling a spade a spade, and in that he revealed his transparent honesty. I did not always see eye to eye with him, and told him so; often I am afraid with not a little heat. And he retorted often with as much heat, if not a little more! But we knew that deep down in his heart he had admiration for the mind which, free from any taint of snobbery, could think out things, and try to apply the thoughts as occasion demanded. When his untimely death came to the Clyde Pit there were very few of us who realised then what a warm-hearted friend we had lost in *Mr Andrew Hepburn*. *Mr Hepburn* gave to mining several capable officials, *Mr Williamson*, of Cardowan Collieries, is perhaps the best known, though *James Boyd* and *Bob Kirkland* were two efficient and capable officials too.

The gentleman who followed *Mr Hepburn* was one,

## MR WILLIAM BARR

*Mr Barr* was a manager who had wide experience of all classes of mining. He had more of a statistic mind that Mr Hepburn, and spent more time in his office than he did in the mine; the exact opposite in fact of *Mr Hepburn*. He is now, I believe, or was the last I heard of him, a manager in a large group of collieries in England, in the Walsall district. He was a stickler for safety first. To the last a notice posted on No. 3 Pit by his order, stood, before that was razed to the ground. The notice ran; "*Safety First. Best Obtained by Exercising Care Continually.*" It was a notice which might well be posted at every corner of the King's highway!

*Mr Barr,* tall, upright, was the Beau Brummel among colliery managers. This influence spread to his workers. A Saturday night in Cadzow Street, and Quarry Street, was full of Clyde men, with either hard or soft hats! Even the very Poles were stotting about with a soft hat sticking well over one ear! I have remarked since that when *Mr Barr* left there were a lot of hats in Hamilton available for jumble sales! One Pole was said to be economical and took off the light ribbon off his hat and replaced it with a black one. I have often wondered if this was to go funerals with! One of the Clyde's most promising officials and one of the nicest mannered men you could have met with came while *Mr Barr* was there. He was *William King,* and is now I believe, after a time in the Douglas district, a manager near Glasgow. Next we had a manager, a real sport in the person of

## MR JAMES RUSSELL

*Mr Russell* will read this, and he may as well know now that his wee stick was an unfailing source of delight to those on the hill. When things had gone well underground that wee stick used to describe happy little circles in the air, but when things had not pleased him, he used to bring it down smartly; one was glad then that his back was not between it and the ground. Still, even when things were not going too well, he always managed to give us a smile, and he will be always be remembered as a "sport," and when one remembers that for a long time he lived over the wall from Douglas Park, this is no mean tribute to his worth, As to his ability there was never any question. He was recognised as an energetic and capable official, and we feel sure that the Shotts people will find him the same, as we men of the Clyde did. The next manager was one who had been twice stationed at the Clyde Pit, and he was

# MR HUGH PENMAN

The decline of the Clyde pit really commenced during *Mr Penman's* time. His was a hard job; to produce coal from a pit where the seams were nearly exhausted. Many of us thought that the Clyde had but a short time to go when *Mr Penman* first came, but his determination and ability did much to get the maximum amount of coal that could be got from it. You cannot keep a colliery going at maximum speed for sixty years, and it is to *Mr Penman's* credit that he carried it along as he did. Then another manager was twice there: I refer to

# MR GEORGE SYDSERFF

*Mr Sydserff* had also a very hard task. To carry on with the incurable disease of exhausted seams is one of the hardest tasks that a manager can undertake. He had that task, and the sympathy of all decent men goes out to him in his efforts to keep the flag flying.

Of the agents of the old Clyde Pit, there were the *Telfers,* father and two sons. *Andrew* is with the Alloa Coal Coy. and W.H. Telfer is now with the Shotts Iron and Coal Coy. *Mr Willis* was also for a time agent. Then we had *David Black*, who was for a time manager at this pit, and who latterly was appointed agent. *Mr Black* was one of whom I have very kindly thoughts. These reminiscences however, would not be complete without the name of

# MR JOHN SUTTIE

With all the managers named, *Mr Suttie* was undermanager. He too strove hard and well for the welfare of the mine, and while many thought him a trifle brusque at times, one cannot but remember that mining is at all times a trade in which there is very little room for a display of sentiment. Still we all knew *John* Suttie's bark was worse than his bite, and all those under him will wish him well in his appointment in the Fife area. I fancy that John will be wishing he were at Douglas Park these days, where the Accas have lately been giving the fancied teams some severe shocks!

It is only through the lack of space and not through any discourtesy than we can but briefly touch on the names of other officials. *John Potter* is best known; he was the last official left. Then we had *Mr Woods, McNeil* and another whose name I forget at the moment, but who is now in the Shotts area. There were also *Jamie Stoddart, Jock Reid, Jimmy Murray* and the *Blackwoods,* who were at this pit for a long period. Others of whom we remember with pleasure are *Andrew Cosgrave,* the *brothers Jones, Tommy Muir, Willie Paton, Sam Chisholm, John Frew, Tommy Davidson, Kinnie Gibson, Bob Elder, Alex. Trainer, John Greenhorn, Andrew Riddle, Sandy Neil* and big hearted *Tom Wilson, James Moffat,* always a *gentleman was Jimmy, Davie Renwick, Alex. Colquhoun, David Fleming, Tommy Flannagan* and the clerks, *Mr Aitchison, Mr Fraser, Mr Ferguson, Mr Davidson* and the lads *Moyies and Sydserff,* all we remember with pleasure and we hope still to have the pleasure of greeting them on the streets with a smile, *Tommy Davidson* has gone, and so has *Donald Fraser.*

Of our workmates on the surface it is impossible to name them all. As we write, the following come to our memory; *Tommy Brunton, Charlie Durnian, Charlie Moyies, Frank Kane, Guy Cook, Bobbie Gadsden, Jimmy Stewart, Alex. MacCormack, Joe Murray, Bobbie Walton, Bob Turnbull, Willie Neil and Sam Smith* with his outsize in grins! Also *Jimmy Mullholland.*

There have been few changes about the colliery amongst the winding-enginemen the last twenty-one years. I have tried to get some old records, and have failed to trace a fatal accident in the shaft for sixty years. What a wonderful record, and between the two shafts is a large geological fault which tended to throw the "weight" on to No. 3. *John Murphy, John Wardrop* and *Sandy Reid,* together with comparative newcomers, *Willie Baillie and George Anderson,* are no doubt proud of this record, and the pit-headmen, such as *Sandy McGregor, Donald Paterson, Matthew Mitchell, John Caldwell,* etc, can take their share of this credit.

The checkweighmen have been few in number. *Willie Small,* now the secretary of the Miners' Union, was for a time here; *Willie* served a good apprenticeship, matching his wits against *Andrew Hepburn's!* Then for thirty odd years, "wee Dick," as *Mr Sempie* was affectionately known, was in No. 3 box, and lastly *John Heeps.* Jock was a great fitba' fan and managed to tip—not always successfully—the winner of the Scottish Cup before the first round was played! Long may your lum reek, Jock!

The Angel of Death has not a few times hovered over the old pit. To mention names now would but re-open old grief's, and we have too much respect for the bereaved to do so. Suffice it to state that in the case of the younger fellows who went, they will in our memories be always remembered as they were in their youth, and they "shall not grow old."

So good-bye old pit! All that remains now are but memories. We will cherish those memories, and in the coming years, age will but make them more brighter. And who can deny that golden memories crucify despair and transfigure hope?  AN OLD WORKER.

# KNOWN CLYDE COAL COMPANY DEATHS

| DATE | NAME | AGE | CAUSE OF DEATH |
|------|------|-----|----------------|
| 14.01.1877 | DAVID BERRY | 42 | EXPLOSION |
| 12.07.1889 | CONSTANTINE KELLY | 13 | ROOF FALL (Fractures of jaw and skull, multiple lacerations) |
| 02.08.1889 | ANDREW KYLE | 40 | ROOF FALL (Fractured spine) |
| 24.10.1890 | ARCHD FERGUSON | 36 | COMPOUND FRACTURE OF SKULL, FRACTURED CLAVICLE. |
| 25.05.1891 | JOHN McDONALD | 13 | ROOF FALL (Fractured skull) |
| 22.07.1891 | JAMES CULLEN | 35 | HIT BY CAGE (Fractured Spine) |
| 18.01.1892 | ROBERT BOYD | 45 | FELL DOWN SHAFT |
| 25.03.1893 | PETER MCNAUGHTON | 51 | RUN DOWN BY WAGONS |
| 23.04.1893 | DAVID SMITH | 46 | CRUSHED BY HUTCHES |
| 21.08.1893 | JOHN McDOWALL | 20 | ROOF FALL (6-7 tons) |
| 18.05.1895 | PATRICK GANNAN | 26 | FELL DOWN SHAFT |
| 06.06.1895 | THOMAS SIMPSON | 32 | FALL OF COAL AT FACE |
| 12.11.1895 | WILLIAM ALLAN | 15 | KICKED IN FACE BY PONY |
| 02.12.1895 | JOHN W. BEATTIE | 20 | ROOF FALL (30 tons) |
| 04.08.1897 | JOHN ROWAN | 56 | ROOF FALL (Trapped 14 hrs) |
| 11.01.1901 | ISAAC CALLISON | 47 | NECK BROKEN |
| 01.03.1902 | WILLIAM MALEY | 26 | ROOF FALL (Multiple injuries) |
| 09.10.1902 | MUNGO KIRKLAND | 36 | RUN DOWN BY HUTCH |
| 18.02.1904 | DAVID MORRISON | 66 | CRUSHED BETWEEN WAGON AND BUFFERS |
| 19.05.1905 | JAMES McKILLOP | 27 | FELL DOWN SHAFT |
| 10.07.1905 | JOHN PETERSON | 16 | DRAGGED DOWN THE SHAFT HOLDING ON TO CAGE |
| 31.10.1907 | THOMAS SCHOLES | 53 | ROOF FALL (Smashed ribs) |
| 02.07.1908 | WILLIAM NICOL | 49 | EXPLOSION |
| 05.12.1909 | KAZIS WALIULIAUCZIUS | 23 | STRUCK BY HAULAGE PULLEY |
| 14.12.1910 | JAMES CALDER | 29 | ROOF FALL (Suffocation) |
| 12.12.1911 | JAMES MEENAGHAN | 38 | COLLAPSE OF UNDERGROUND WALL |
| 03.12.1912 | THOMAS WATSON | 63 | FALL OF COAL |
| 07.07.1916 | HENRY McK. MURDOCH | 17 | CRUSHED BY HUTCHES |
| 06.06.1917 | ISAAC CALLISON | 16 | RUN DOWN BY HUTCHES |
| 27.09.1917 | JOHN HARVEY | 32 | ROOF FALL (Trapped 2 hrs) |
| 13.02.1918 | THOMAS GIBBONS | 17 | ROOF FALL (Trapped 3 hrs) |
| 21.08.1918 | WILLIAM INGLIS | 15 ½ | NO DETAILS (Fractured ribs) |
| 08.12.1918 | ANDREW HAMILTON | 28 | EXPLOSION |
| 02.05.1922 | SAMUEL GOURLAY | 37 | ROOF FALL |
| 06.12.1924 | PHILIP CUNDELAN | 50 | COLLAPSE OF SURFACE WALL |
| " | ARTHUR ROADNIGHT | 23 | COLLAPSE OF SURFACE WALL |
| 30.04,1929 | JAMES SNEDDON | 51 | EXPLOSION |
| 05.05.1930 | PATRICK McFARLANE | 53 | ROOF FALL (Suffocation) |
| 08.06.1930 | JAMES C. REID | 22 | FRACTURED SKULL |
| 25.03.1932 | DAVID McFALL | 39 | RUN DOWN BY HUTCHES |

# SAME PLACE ~ DIFFERENT TIME

*The Bent Cemetery Hamilton 2005*
*An area of peaceful tranquillity? It has a secret; it was once the site of the*
*Bent colliery*

**1939**

*The same area showing the collapse of Bent Colliery's No. 3 Pit shaft*
*Photograph courtesy of Hamilton Advertiser*

# BENT COLLIERY

*Aerial cable hopper transport Bent Colliery. Photograph courtesy of Hamilton Town House Reference Library.*

*The Bent Colliery photographed from East Glebe Terrace. Photograph courtesy of Hamilton Town House Reference Library.*

# KNOWN BENT COLLIERY DEATHS

| DATE | NAME | AGE | CAUSE OF DEATH |
|------|------|-----|----------------|
| 19.03.1878 | ANDREW RUSSELL | 42 | ROOF FALL |
| 29.12.1881 | ROBERT BROWN | 66 | RUN OVER BY HUTCHES |
| 24.04.1883 | THOMAS STEEL | 16 | CAUGHT BY THE NECK BETWEEN THE BUFFERS OF WAGONS |
| 15.07.1885 | HUGH HASSON | 31 | ROOF FALL (4 - 5 tons) |
| 05.08.1885 | DAVID DUNN | 15 | FALL OF COAL AT FACE (1 ton) |
| 22.08.1889 | JAMES CLELAND | 45 | ROOF FALL |
| 22.09.1891 | OWEN GILLICKS | 18 | ROOF FALL (6-8 cwts) |
| 31.07.1893 | THOMAS BURNS | 55 | ROOF FALL (½ cwt. stone) |
| 13.12.1894 | EDWARD TAYLOR | 24 | FELL INTO SCREE WITH WAGON |
| 25.06.1895 | JOHN CAMPBELL | 57 | ROOF FALL (Buried 3 days) |
| 25.09.1896 | WM. CRAWFORD | 13 | CAUGHT BY THE NECK BETWEEN BUFFERS OF WAGONS |
| 12.12.1896 | EDWARD POTTER | 66 | JAMMED BETWEEN IRON POST AND WAGON |
| 28.06.1899 | EDWARD WILSON | 35 | HEAD INJURIES |
| 19.10.1899 | PETER B. O'BRIEN | 23 | ROOF FALL (1 ton.) |
| 29.12.1900 | JAMES MUIR | 21 | RUN OVER BY WAGONS (Right leg severed at knee) |
| 11.08.1902 | MATTHEW HOSIE | 34 | ROOF FALL |
| 05.03.1903 | ANDREW WEIR | 32 | ROOF FALL (Buried 6 hrs, died 2 days later from shock) |
| 19.03.1904 | WM. NAISMITH. | 62 | NO DETAILS. (Hip dislocated in accident, died under anaesthetic) |
| 05.09.1904 | GEO. B. FLECK | 28 | FALL OF COAL AT FACE (30 cwts. Chest crushed) |
| 20.03.1907 | RBT. GOURLAY | 31 | KILLED BY WAGON |
| 15.02.1910 | PATRICK McCABE | 39 | ROOF FALL |
| 06.10.1911 | JOHN STEVENSON | 35 | KILLED BY EXPLOSIVES |
| 28.12.1912 | GEORGE PATON | 47 | FALL OF ROCK (Buried 4 hrs) |
| 22.05.1914 | JOHN KILDAY | 20 | ARMS AMPUTATED BY THE REVOLVING DISC OF A COAL CUTTING MACHINE. |
| 24.05.1917 | WM. A. MUIR | 54 | TRAPPED IN MACHINERY |
| 19.02.1918 | JOHN TAYLOR | 30 | JAMMED AGAINST COAL FACE BY COAL CUTTING MACHINE. |
| 14.09.1918 | RBT. CAVANAGH | 50 | ROOF FALL (2 tons) |
| 10.01.1924 | RICHARD GLASS | 18 | ROOF FALL |
| 07.08.1927 | THOMAS O'HARE | 60 | BURNING ACCIDENT |
| 31.12.1929 | JAMES QUINN | 57 | BROKEN NECK |
| 28.08.1930 | JAMES REID | 52 | DRAGGED INTO MACHINERY (Arm and leg severed) |

# THE COALMAN

*Photograph courtesy of Willie Devanney, Hamilton.*

The middle man between the Colliery and the customer was the coalman and the familiar sound of his voice could be heard streets away. The customary shout of coal, was repeated three times and it appeared to come from the pit of his stomach, so loud and deep was his cry.

*The coalman cries his merchandise,*
*Coal—coal—coal!*
*His voice so clear, I love to hear,*
*Rising in my ear and soul.*

*Both up and down all o'er the town,*
*You'll hear the same restrain,*
*In street and square you'll find him there,*
*And in the quiet lane.*

*Coal—coal—coal!*
*There's patience in the sound,*
*It sends a call to one and all*
*From the workmen underground.*

*Far down within the deepest gloom*
*Our sons and brothers toil,*
*Far down within a living tomb*
*In danger all the while.*

*Need we grudge them a living wage,*
*Those heroes brave and bold,*
*For from the youngest to old age,*
*They are dear to us as gold.*

*Then let us all stand boldly up*
*For workers down below,*
*And wish them all good work,*
*And wages good also.*

*Unknown.*
*Circa 1913.*

# MY GOD! MA LUM'S ON FIRE

*With the struggle to put food on the table, the chimneysweep was sometimes "forgotten" and the resultant fire meant the occupier had to appear at Hamilton Burgh Court. William Gray failed to appear and sent this poem instead. His pledge of half a crown was forfeited!*

I wis dreaming of some happy days
  When I heard an awfu' roar,
Wi' a sudden leap I sprang richt
  Oot o' bed on tae the floor
Noo, this is true, although
  Ye micht imagine I'm a liar
Fae the bottom o' my he'rt I cried
  My God, ma lum's on fire!

I got up at three the ither morn,
  That's as shair as I'm alive,
Tae sort ma fire and try and hae
  Ma kettle biled by five
I broke the raker up and then
  Slipped back into ma bed
For tae try anither twa oor's sleep
  Tae ease ma aching head.

I had nothing bit ma shirt on,
  And ma he'rt wis achin sore,
And tae mak' ma misery mair complete
  A knock comes tae ma door,
When I opened it I gazed upon
  Two gallant men in blue,
So I whispered tae masel—
  My heavens! "Wull, yer landed noo."

Bit tae gie the men their due
  They hadna very much tae say;
They took doon ma name
  And then they baith slipped away.
I kent they wid report it tae
  Some yin a wee bit higher,
And I'd likely need tae suffer
  For that auld lum gaun on fire.

I have travelled roon the world noo
  For three score years and mair,
And noo this is ma first offence—
  Nae wunner ma hert's sair
But I hope they show me mercy,
  For I'd be far better deid
Than them tae send me for
  A wheen o' year's tae Peterheid.

Noo the nicht before the trial
  I wid like ye a' tae pray,
For the sentence tae be very light
  On your poet Willie Gray,
And I'll tak dasht guid care
  That while I live in Lanarkshire
Nae policeman will ever see--
  Ma lum again on fire.

*William Gray. Circa 1928*

# LOUSIN' TIME

*Photograph courtesy of the Scottish Mining Museum.*

The signal bell rings and we enter the cage,
The toil of the night is o'er;
Retreating again, but tomorrow we'll wage
The battle with Nature once more,
And upwards we speed through the murky gloom,
But never a weary wight,
Casts one backward glance at our ghostly tomb,
When it vomits us into the night.

*T. Carroll*
*Larkhall.*
*Circa 1924.*

# THE MINER'S LAST SHIFT

When the last pit is closed, and to the sun
  The miner turns his face, erect and free,
The last shift worked, and the last black ton won
What do you deem the miner's speech will be?

How will the master-world greet him then?
  I tell you, for I know his mother well,
Stronger than metals she has reared her men,
  I've seen his father carve his bed in hell.

He had no soul to sell; I've heard you say,
  You with your cent percent had naught to buy,
Now he is here, fronting the light of day,
What will you plead the answer to his why?

Far o'er the age-long pits he stood alone,
  A world where none but he might live and rule,
Midst the dead million year's his image shone
One day you called him hero, next, the fool.

Hero or fool he stands before you now,
  That man with whom the sun you would not share,
The dews of stars fall on his rugged brow,
The wandering winds weave music in his hair.

The last pit closed, his last mate starved for bread,
  He stands erect amid the race of men,
The bleached, the broken, and his myriad dead,
The way he came, alone his kingdom then.

I will tell you, for I knew his mother well,
  Stronger than metals him she nursed had soul;
By this sweet light, where God meant men to dwell,
What will ye now do for your bloody coal?

*Edward Hunter, Circa 1936*